# MYSTERIES *in* History

# MYSTERIES *in* History

## A JOURNEY THROUGH THE GREAT UNANSWERED QUESTIONS OF OUR TIME

Bath · New York · Cologne · Melbourne · Delhi
Hong Kong · Shenzhen · Singapore · Amsterdam

This edition published by Parragon Books Ltd in 2015
and distributed by

Parragon Inc.
440 Park Avenue South, 13th Floor
New York, NY 10016
www.parragon.com

ISBN 978-1-4723-4011-5
Printed in China

# Contents

# The Greatest Mysteries of All Time

Atlantis, the Bermuda Triangle, the pyramids, miracles, extraterrestrial visitations... Traditionally described as 'unexplainable phenomena', these and other examples explored in this book have inspired a multitude of paranormal theories and supernatural claims. Science has been entrusted with deciphering many of these questions, dispelling myths and fallacies and, in turn, offering empirical and demonstrable explanations. However, some mysteries still endure. Each time science answers an unknown mystery, new ones appear that lead to new theories and new questions that only time and continual research may eventually resolve.

**The jewels of Giza**
The pyramids of the pharaohs, Khufu (right) and Khafre (left), tower behind the Great Sphinx in Giza.

# CHAPTER 1

# Dinosaurs, Prehistoric Beasts

Since their discovery in the nineteenth century, dinosaurs have become the most intriguing animals from our ancient past. Science has been able to decode some of their mystery, but many unknowns are still to be resolved.

It all began for science almost two centuries ago, in 1824, with the discovery of what appeared to be a giant fossilized tooth in Stonesfield, Oxfordshire, England, and the subsequent studies performed by theologian, naturalist, geologist, and then-President of the Geological Society of London, William Buckland (1784–1856). Buckland gave the animal to whom the tooth had belonged the name *Megalosaurus* ("large lizard"), thus baptizing a dinosaur for the very first time. Shortly afterward, he wrote the first full description of a dinosaur, whose name derives from the Greek *deinos* ("terrible") and *sauros* ("lizard").

However, it was one of Buckland's contemporaries, a French zoologist, who would be named by science as the father of comparative anatomy and paleontology, the science that studies and interprets past life on Earth using fossils. Georges Cuvier (1769–1832) was the first naturalist to classify the animal kingdom based on the "correlation principle." According to his work, *Le Règne Animal Distribué d'après son organisation* (1817), animals should be grouped into four "branches": Vertebrata, Articulata, Mollusca and Radiata, each of which is defined by the unique arrangement of its essential vital systems or cores, that is to say: the brain and the circulatory system.

Thanks to this principle, Cuvier was able to reconstruct entire animal fossils using bone fragments; he was also able to explain the disappearance of species by means of the catastrophism theory. In his opinion, certain catastrophes had the potential to wipe out animal species that had previously been dominant, only to be replaced by others.

**THE FIRST *IGUANODON***
Cuvier was already a famous paleontologist when English doctor Gideon Mantell (1790–1852), a geology fanatic (with his wife, a great collector of fossils), found some large teeth in Cuckfield, Sussex, in 1822, and sent one to the Frenchman in the hope of identifying it. However, Cuvier could not do so. He was only able to establish that the tooth did not belong to a known species and that it was probably from a large reptile.

Finally, Mantell found that the fossilized teeth bore a striking similarity to one belonging to an iguana. He then created a scale drawing of an animal which, in his opinion, would have measured 59 ft/18 m in length, and called it

### *Triceratops*
One of the most easily
recognizable dinosaurs, its shape
is similar to that of a rhinoceros.
It was one of the last dinosaurs to
appear; it lived in North America
and was found for the first time
in 1887.

*Iguanadon* ("iguana tooth"). Later, it would be established that the *Iguanodon* measured just 30 ft/9 m, and the bone drawn by Mantell on the animal's nose, believing it was a horn, was in fact a spur on its paw. To this day, the Natural History Museum in London preserves a model of Mantell's *Iguanodon*, with the size and shape he attributed to it.

English biologist, paleontologist, and anatomist Richard Owen (1804–92), creator of the term "dinosaur," is also linked to Cuvier's theories and his comparative anatomy, which Owen introduced in England. The scientist continued Cuvier's works on vertebrate paleontology and published the first significant general account of the large range of reptiles from the Mesozoic era, a period of Earth's history that began 251 million years ago and ended 65 million years ago. Owen named these animals "Dinosauria," and recognized three types: a carnivore, the *Megalosaurus* discovered by Buckland; an herbivore, the *Iguanodon*; and a third, which he called the *Hylaeosaurus*. From 1870 onward, a large number of huge and surprising fossilized dinosaur bones were discovered. One of the most important discoveries was made in Bernissart, Belgium, in 1878, where a group of miners found an almost entire *Iguanodon* skeleton—the first of 39 in total, which over a number of years were carefully extracted and studied by Louis Dollo (1857–1931). Dollo dedicated 40 years of his life to studying these fossils; he also assisted in the reconstruction of the skeletons, which he stood upright on their hind legs. His work on the *Iguanodon* would be revised almost a century later by English paleontologist David B. Norman, current director of the Sedgwick Museum of Earth Sciences, part of the University of Cambridge, who concluded that Dollo's team had forced the natural direction of the fossilized tail of the *Iguanodon* to give the dinosaur an upright posture. Paleontologists confirmed some years ago that this animal walked on all fours.

### THE BONES WAR

Two distinguished paleontology professors were the protagonists of the so-called "bones war": Edward Drinker Cope (1840–97), from the University of Pennsylvania, and Othniel Charles Marsh (1831–99), from Yale University. They were friends until Cope erected the skeleton of a rare Plesiosaur, in 1870, which he called *Elasmosaurus* ("plated lizard"), inviting Marsh to view the result. The latter informed his friend that he had mounted the head at the end of the animal's tail, which ignited a relxntless rivalry between the two. However, ultimately, science would benefit from this confrontation: between 1870 and 1899, teams managed and financed by both men unearthed tons of fossils, and were able to identify more than 120 new species of dinosaur from the Jurassic and Cretaceous periods.

The nineteenth century ended with the discovery of one of the strangest (and most popular) findings made until then, in Wyoming, by North American paleontologist John Bell Hatcher (1861–1904). Measuring 30 ft/9 m in length, weighing up to 12 tons, it had a short horn on its nose and two longer horns on its forehead. Hatcher sent the fossils to Marsh, who baptized the finding *Triceratops* ("face with three horns").

Science is indebted to U.S. paleontologist Barnum Brown (1873–1963) for the discovery of one of the largest carnivores from the Cretaceous period, which he located at a site in Montana, where he worked between 1902 and 1910. There, he located the incomplete skeletal remains of two huge dinosaurs, one of which was the gigantic *Ankylosaurus* ("fused lizard"). The second, which would be studied and described in 1905 by another North American paleontologist, Henry Fairfield Osborn (1857–1935), was *Tyrannosaurus rex* ("tyrant lizard"), one of the largest, strongest, and fiercest carnivores of all time and, without doubt, one of the best-known dinosaurs. The species lived in North America around 67 million years ago, and has become the epitome of all things monstrous in the world of dinosaurs. It weighed between 6 and 7 tons, it measured up to 43 ft/13 m in length and 13 ft/4 m up to its hips, and was also one of the last dinosaurs to exist prior to the mass extinction experienced toward the end of the Cretaceous period, which has made it a genuine icon in

**↑Founding fossils**
The teeth of the *Iguanodon* discovered by the wife of Gideon Mantell in England. It was the second dinosaur to be described and its teeth are characteristic of an herbivore.

# The path to cloning?

Advances in genetic engineering allow experts to harbor hopes of cloning certain extinct species, provided that soft tissue (i.e. non-bone tissue), such as fat, muscles, fibers, and blood vessels, are preserved. Therein lies the problem, given that the genetic code "lives" in soft tissue. Although at times paleontologists have found protein samples in some dinosaur bones, such as in the discoveries made by Mary Higby Schweitzer in Hell Creek, Montana, published in 1993 and 2005, these samples deteriorated after a short period in the laboratory. The same has happened with organic components and certain genetic structures found in several fossilized Sauropod bones, although it would appear that these DNA sequences have not only suffered considerable deterioration, they are also incomplete. Thus, despite the discovery in the 1990s of a 90-million-year-old bloodsucking tick, pressed in amber, in New Jersey, the possibility of acquiring DNA from species belonging to that period in history has been ruled out.

**←Genetic examination**
*Above*, a tick. *Below*, molecular biologist Chen Zhangliang who claimed, in 1995, to have extracted DNA from a dinosaur egg, although it was impossible to confirm the claim.

today's society. In spite of this, paleontologists are still in disagreement as to whether *Tyrannosaurus rex* was a dominant predator, or simply a scavenger.

### BIRDS AND DINOSAURS

By the 1960s, the fossils of hundreds of dinosaur species had been found worldwide, although it was the idea of another U.S. paleontologist, John H. Ostrom (1928–2005), that would completely revolutionize our way of understanding these animals. Ostrom stated that dinosaurs, in reality, were more similar to birds than lizards, an ideology that had already been put forward in 1860 by British biologist Thomas Henry Huxley (1825–95). Ostrom published his first work to this end in 1976, when studying the osteology and phylogeny of *Archaeopteryx* ("ancient wing"), one of the most primitive birds known to science, which lived during the Jurassic period. Ostrom listed 20 morphological characteristics present in both birds and dinosaurs, which served as the basis to his claim that birds are the direct descendants of carnivorous dinosaurs similar to the *Velociraptor*. His theories appeared to have been backed up by the discovery in China of different dinosaur fossils with feathers, toward the end of the 1990s. However, certain details regarding the relationship between the anatomy of dinosaurs and that of birds are still the subject of debate. Nonetheless, other experts consider that birds and dinosaurs evolved separately from a common ancestor. This is a controversial topic in the anatomy of both animals, which has provided some level of support to the question facing biologists and paleontologists.

### EXTINCTION

At the end of the 1970s, U.S. physicist Luis Walter Alvarez (1911–88), assisted by his son, geologist Walter Alvarez, identified a sudden increase in the level of iridium in the strata of rocks on a global scale, which corresponded to the end of the Cretaceous period. The physicist (awarded the Nobel Prize in 1968) formulated the theory that this high level of iridium was attributable to a huge meteorite impacting the Earth, given that iridium is scarcely found in the Earth's crust while it is common in meteorites. The theory, upheld in 2010 by an international team of scientists, was immediately associated with the mass disappearance of animal species that had until then populated the planet.

The impact of a large-scale meteorite, in addition to generating an enormous amount of energy, would have resulted in global cooling owing to the large level of material released into the atmosphere, preventing sunlight from reaching the Earth's surface. The decrease in sunlight would have hindered the ability of many plants to perform photosynthesis, thus changing the food chain of aquatic and terrestrial ecosystems. Later, in 1990, a number of geologists identified the Chicxulub crater on the north coast of the Yucatán Peninsula, measuring 112 miles in diameter, as the point at which the meteorite impacted Earth some 65.5 million years ago.

Likewise, in 1997, another crater (named Shiva) was discovered on the bed of the Indian Ocean. Some 50 times greater than the Mexican crater, it was also created around the same time as the extinction of the dinosaurs. Discoveries like this one have led to new speculation regarding the size and impact point of the hypothetical asteroid.

## The patterns of birds and lizards

It is accepted that most dinosaurs adopted nesting patterns similar to those used by birds and lizards today. Between 1970 and 2000, a large number of fossilized nests were discovered, which, in addition to suggesting that dinosaurs laid eggs, facilitated the identification of possible parenting behavioral patterns. It is likely that these animals cared for their young for a long time after birth, as the fossilized nests of *Maiasaura* ("caring mother lizard"), found in Montana in 1979, appear to suggest.

This discovery was the first evidence that these dinosaurs tended their young. In 1993, the skeleton of an *Oviraptor* was found in Mongolia in a very similar position to the one adopted by a hen when laying an egg. Initially, it was believed that the *Oviraptor* fed on eggs (its name means "egg thief"). However, today it is believed that it had adopted this position to incubate its eggs. Furthermore, it has been demonstrated that it would have had some type of feathers that would have facilitated this function, just like modern-day birds.

**→First bird**
Copy of the first known fossil of *Archaeopteryx*. It had anatomically mixed characteristics: some typical of a lizard, others of a bird.

# Traces of the past

Although the very first fossil remains of dinosaurs were found in Europe, the main paleontological sites are found in the western part of North America, in eastern Asia, and in the extreme south of South America.

## Main fossil sites

The fossil remains of dinosaurs are spread over all the continents, including the polar regions. Many of these places contain fossils from other geological eras and other types of extinct creatures.

### Lyme Regis, United Kingdom

In 1820, the first fossils were found of animals from the Jurassic age: an *Ichthyosaurus*, a Plesiosaur and the first Pterodactyl.

**Tyrannosaurus rex**
The first one was discovered in the western part of North America.

**Wyoming, USA**
The largest Jurassic deposit was discovered in 1870. Remains of *Apatosaurus* and *Diplodocus* were found.

**NORTH AMERICA**

**SOUTH AMERICA**

## The world at that time

Planet Earth, 250 million years ago, had a single supercontinent called "Pangaea."

### End of the Permian

The fused plates began to separate at the beginning of the Triassic period and produced a massive extinction of life, affecting over 95 percent of marine species and 70 percent of land vertebrates. This prepared the ground for the appearance of the dinosaurs 20 million years later.

North America
Eurasia
Africa
India
South America
Antarctica
Australia

**Patagonia, Argentina**
An area of great discovery: highlighted are *Patagosaurus* and *Carnotaurus* ("carnivorous bull"), the first known carnivores with horns.

**Piatnitzkysaurus**
Jurassic dinosaurs, the first of the Carnosauria, existed in Trelew, Argentina.

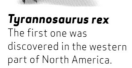

## Are dinosaurs the largest animals that ever lived on Earth?

Some sauropods could have grown longer than 98 ft/30 m, with some enormous creatures like the extraordinary *Argentinosaurus*, which weighed 100 tons. But even these figures are surpassed by those of the blue whale, which can reach 108 ft/33 m long and weigh up to 190 tons.

### Siberia, Russia

The bodies of entire animals, like the mammoth, have been found, with flesh and bones, covered with a thick sheet of permafrost that preserves the remains.

ASIA

EUROPE

### Gobi Desert, Mongolia

Species from the end of the Cretaceous period, including the the *Protoceratops*, the *Oviraptor*, and the *Velociraptor* were found in the Flaming Cliffs in 1920.

AFRICA

AUSTRALIA

### *Hypacrosaurus*

A hadrosaurid that lived in North America at the end of the Cretaceous period.

### Olduvai Gorge, Tanzania

Fossils of the oldest organisms known have been found in this area, including the remains of dinosaurs and the first hominids.

### Ediacara Hills, Australia

Fossils from the oldest multicellular organisms of the Earth, which come from the Precambrian era, about 600 million years ago, have been found here.

# Evolution in the Mesozoic era

Dinosaurs are an example of adaptation to the environment. They dominated Earth for more than 150 million years. These animals appeared in the Triassic era and disappeared at the end of the Cretaceous era, for reasons that are still not clear today.

## The family tree of dinosaurs

Dinosaurs share a common ancestor with pterosaurs and crocodiles, grouped within Archosauria. The specimen of *Eoraptor* found in Argentina, is considered the closest common ancestor of the dinosaurs.

The Saurischians are divided into two groups: sauropodomorphs (large herbivores) and theropods, which moved on their hind limbs and were nearly all carnivores.

These were herbivores, with adaptations in their jaws to process vegetable food. The Ornithischians included some with quadruped gaits, and others that were adapted for bipedal locomotion.

**What is a dinosaur?** It is defined as a type of reptile that stopped existing about 65 million years ago. Other prehistoric animals such as pterosaurs (flying reptiles) and aquatic reptiles are excluded from this definition.

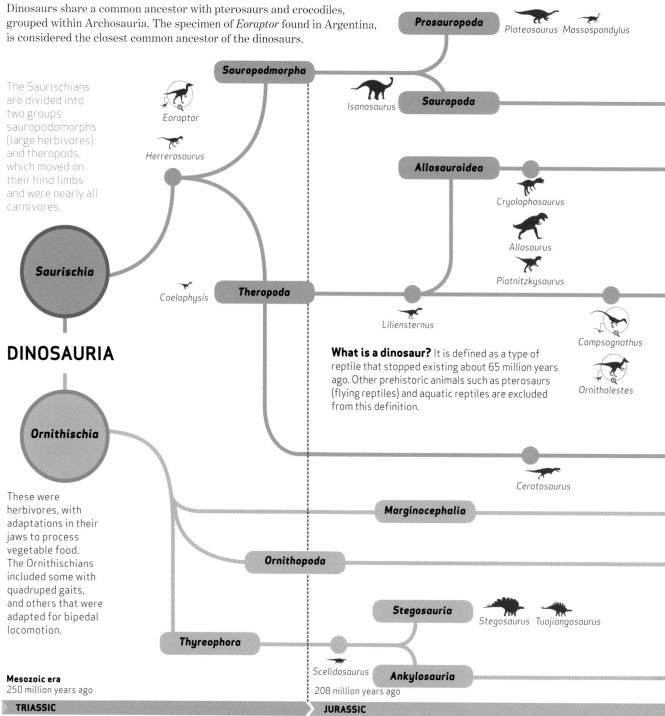

**Prosauropoda** — Plateosaurus Massospondylus

**Sauropodmorpha**

*Eoraptor*

*Isanosaurus* **Sauropoda**

*Herrerasaurus*

**Allosauroidea**

Cryolophosaurus

Allosaurus

Piatnitzkysaurus

**Saurischia**

*Coelophysis* **Theropoda**

*Liliensternus*

Compsognathus

Ornitholestes

**DINOSAURIA**

Ceratosaurus

**Ornithischia**

**Marginocephalia**

**Ornithopoda**

**Stegosauria** — Stegosaurus Tuojiangosaurus

**Thyreophora**

*Scelidosaurus* **Ankylosauria**

**Mesozoic era**
250 million years ago

208 million years ago

**TRIASSIC**

**JURASSIC**

## How did large herbivorous dinosaurs manage to transport blood to the brain?

The large sauropods had very long necks, and it has been suggested that the heart would need to pump blood with great force to be able to reach the brain. Some paleontologists have suggested that because of this, many sauropods could not raise their necks too high, and that they shared characteristics of their circulatory system with warm-blooded animals.

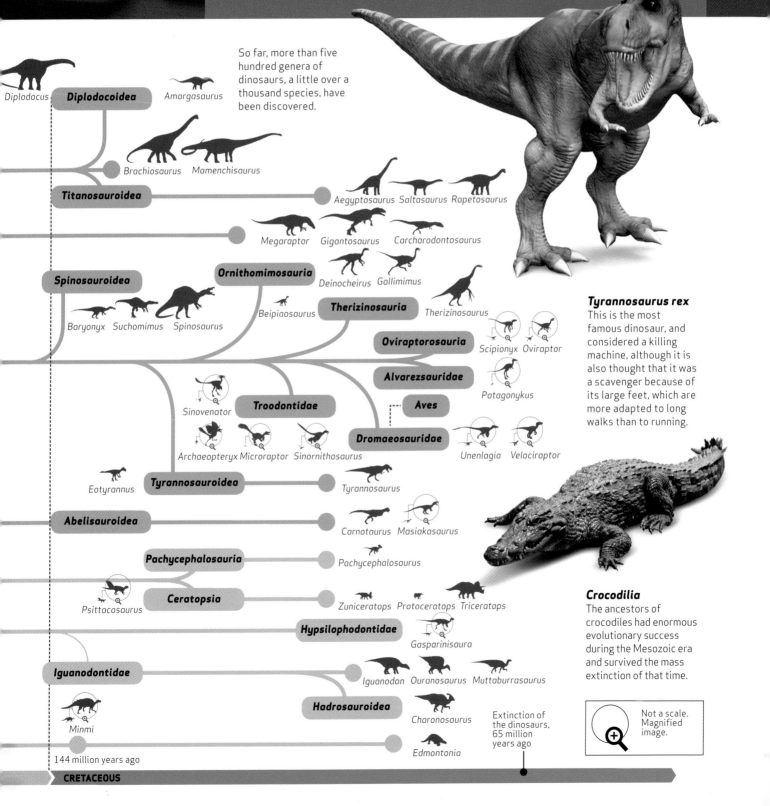

So far, more than five hundred genera of dinosaurs, a little over a thousand species, have been discovered.

Diplodocus
**Diplodocoidea**
Amargasaurus

Brachiosaurus   Mamenchisaurus

**Titanosauroidea**
Aegyptosaurus  Saltasaurus  Rapetosaurus

Megaraptor  Gigantosaurus  Carcharodontosaurus

**Spinosauroidea**    **Ornithomimosauria**

Deinocheirus  Gallimimus

Baryonyx  Suchomimus  Spinosaurus

Beipiaosaurus    **Therizinosauria**    Therizinosaurus

**Oviraptorosauria**
Scipionyx  Oviraptor

**Alvarezsauridae**
Patagonykus

Sinovenator    **Troodontidae**    **Aves**

**Dromaeosauridae**

Archaeopteryx Microraptor Sinornithosaurus    Unenlagia  Velociraptor

Eotyrannus    **Tyrannosauroidea**    Tyrannosaurus

**Abelisauroidea**
Carnotaurus  Masiakasaurus

**Pachycephalosauria**    Pachycephalosaurus

Psittacosaurus    **Ceratopsia**    Zuniceratops  Protoceratops  Triceratops

**Hypsilophodontidae**
Gasparinisaura

**Iguanodontidae**    Iguanodon  Ouranosaurus  Muttaburrasaurus

Minmi    **Hadrosauroidea**    Charonosaurus

Edmontonia

144 million years ago

Extinction of the dinosaurs, 65 million years ago

**CRETACEOUS**

**Tyrannosaurus rex**
This is the most famous dinosaur, and considered a killing machine, although it is also thought that it was a scavenger because of its large feet, which are more adapted to long walks than to running.

**Crocodilia**
The ancestors of crocodiles had enormous evolutionary success during the Mesozoic era and survived the mass extinction of that time.

Not a scale. Magnified image.

# The tragic end of an era

The catastrophe that put an end to the dinosaur era must have left a devastating panorama in its wake. The phenomenon that resulted in their death made no distinction between large and small, with no continent escaping the consequences.

## Cataclysm

Whether it was an earthly or a heavenly phenomenon, a series of volcanic eruptions or a meteorite shower (or a mixture of both), it is irrefutable that the catastrophe that put an end to the Mesozoic era represents one of the largest examples of mass extinction in the history of planet Earth. Around 70 percent of all animal species disappeared.

### Fatalities
The giant *Triceratops* of North America was one of the victims of this natural phenomenon. North American paleontologists have discovered sites with hundreds of such fossils.

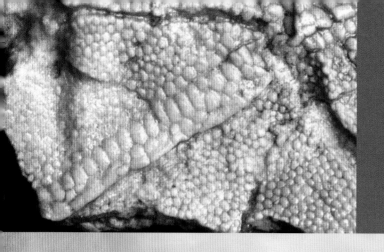

## Skin color

Despite the efforts of science to pinpoint the appearance of dinosaurs, it is possible that the skin texture and color of many of these animals will forever remain unknown. In a number of exceptional cases (such as the example in the photo to the left), the imprint left by the dinosaur's skin has been enshrined in fossils. In 2010, for the first time, pigmentation organelles were found in the fossilized feathers of a dinosaur.

**Cloudy sky**

It is believed that the impact of the meteorite may have resulted in a thick cloud of dust permanently covering the sky, making photosynthesis difficult and interrupting the food chain from the very bottom. Furthermore, the atmosphere would have been filled with toxic gases.

**Great cemetery**

With the passing of the millennia, the surface of the Earth became a huge cemetery, which, in certain parts of the planet, preserved the remains of the dinosaurs in the form of fossils.

# Dinosaur gallery

The most well-known of the species are the giant carnivores and herbivores, such as *Tyrannosaurus rex* or *Apatosaurus*. However, there were dinosaurs of all shapes and sizes. A few examples are presented here.

## Archaeopteryx

Considered the oldest known bird, this species represents a vital link in the evolution of dinosaurs to birds. It lived 150 million years ago and had wings on its back legs. Given its morphological composition, whether it could fly or simply glide is subject to debate. A dozen fossil examples have been found, all in southern Germany.

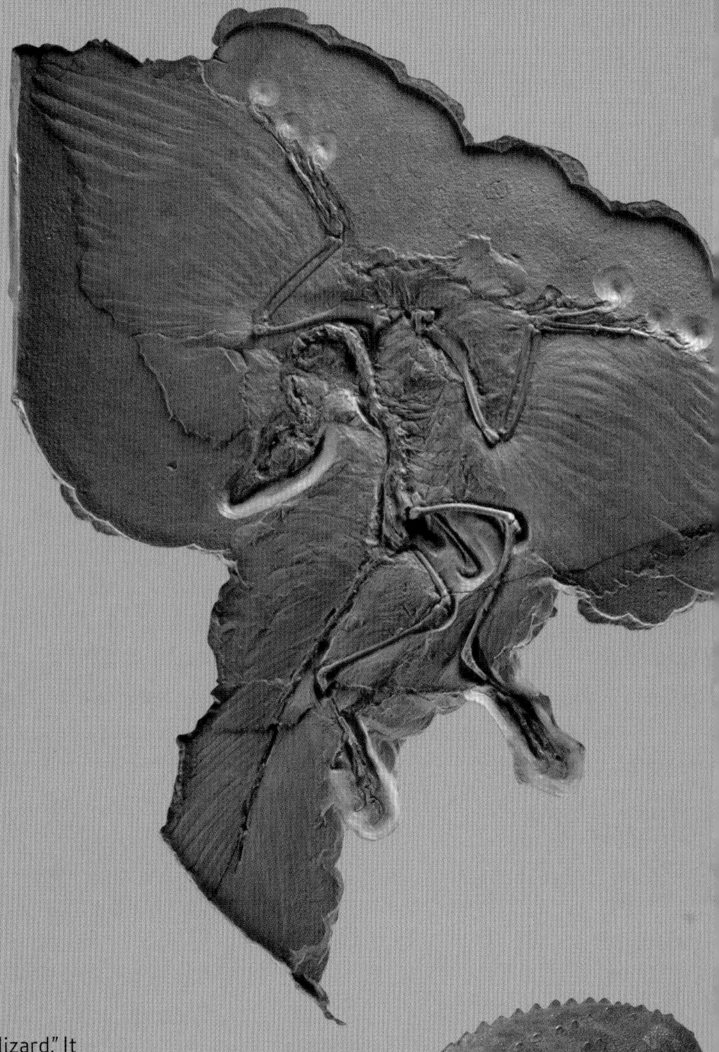

## Velociraptor

A carnivorous dinosaur with feathers that lived around 75 million years ago in present-day Mongolia. It measured around 6 ft 6 in/2 m in height.

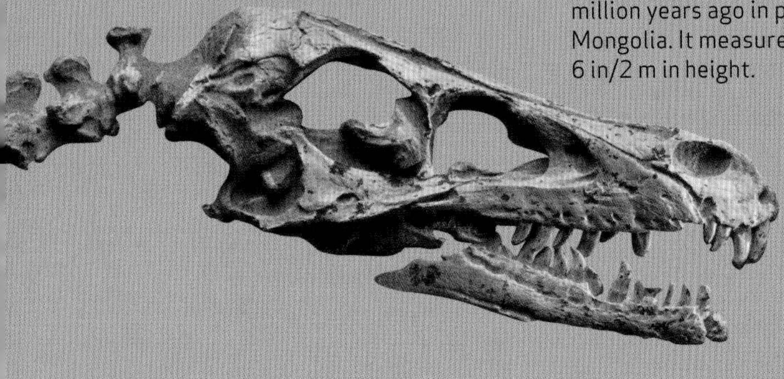

## Ankylosaurus

Its name means "fused lizard." It measured 30 ft/9 m long and its tail was armed with a heavy mallet.

## Triceratops

One of the last dinosaurs, it measured up to 33 ft/10 m long and weighed up to 10 tons.

## Diplodocus

One of the most recognizable dinosaurs, given its thick, stumpy feet and its long neck and tail. This is the longest dinosaur known based on its skeleton. Its neck contained fifteen vertebrae (compared to seven in mammals), and it is believed that it was unable to lift its head much higher than its shoulders. It lived at the end of the Jurassic era, around 150 million years ago.

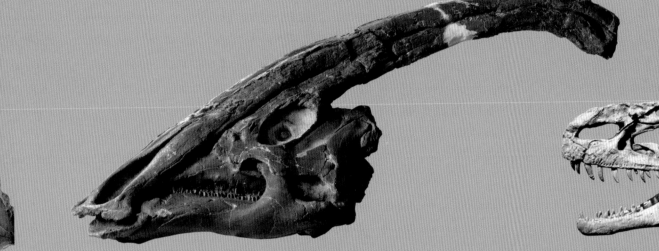

## Parasaurolophus

This dinosaur belonged to a type of herbivore species known as "duck-billed" dinosaurs or "hadrosaurids," and was characterized by its long bony crest. This unusual structure, measuring up to 6 ft 6 in/2 m long, was hollow and its function is unknown. In total, the animal was around 33 ft/10 m long.

### Monolophosaurus

One of the fiercest carnivores, it lived toward the end of the Jurassic era, 150 million years ago. It was similar to the *Allosaurus* in appearance, although it was not closely related to the species.

### Stegosaurus

A North American herbivore recognizable thanks to the characteristic plates along its back.

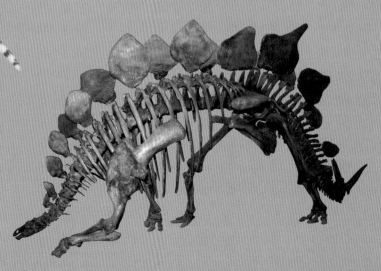

### Eoraptor

A small two-legged hunter just 1 ft 8 in/50 cm in height, it is believed to have been one of the first dinosaurs. It lived 230 million years ago, and was discovered in Argentina.

# CHAPTER 2

# The Long Journey to Humans

Where are we from? Who are our ancestors? For how long have we been humans? Although there is no doubt about our species' animal origins, science and religion have reached an agreement: we are descendants of Adam and Eve.

The most recent biological and genetic research on human evolution proposes a conclusion that, interestingly, concurs with the essential ideas proposed by the three main monotheistic religions. For more than half of the seven million years that human beings have populated the Earth, the contents of the sacred books of Christianity, Judaism, and Islam have always presented an unquestionable truth. They affirm that God created man in His own image and likeness, called him Adam, and decided to place him, along with Eve, the first woman, in a paradise from which both were expelled for eating the forbidden fruit from the tree of the knowledge of good and evil. They also state that all

humans are descendants of the first couple. Recently, science has dared to confirm that, in essence, this ancient story about the origins of man is true: each and every person who inhabits the Earth is a descendant of a common female ancestor, an Eve known by science as the Mitochondrial Eve, and a male ancestor known as the Scientific Adam.

The Bible, through the Gospel according to Luke, details the full ancestral lineage from Adam to Jesus Christ, covering a period of just over 4,000 years. However, although science has been unable to establish our family tree with the same precision as the New Testament, it places our common ancestor much farther back in the history of man. That Scientific Adam, the father of all mankind (in Hebrew, Adam means

"man" in addition to "all" and "flock"), would have lived, according to Spencer Wells, U.S. anthropologist, geneticist, and explorer at the National Geographic Society, around 60,000 years ago (some 2,000 human generations).

However, a study completed in 2011 by Italian researchers Fulvio Cruciani, Beniamino Trombetta, and Andrea Massaia, from the Department of Biology and Biotechnology at the University of Rome, places man's origins at around 140,000 years ago, more than 4,000 generations ago. How has science reached these conclusions?

**A GENETIC JOURNEY INTO THE PAST**
Today, genetics has become a kind of time machine that allows us to travel into our distant past. Biology and biotechnology, capable of an

**Use of fire**
*Homo erectus* harden the tips of spears in the fire, discovered around 500,000 years ago.

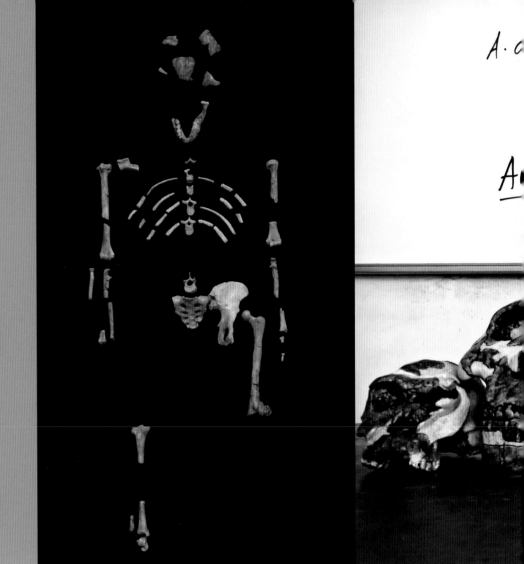

**→ "Lucy"**
Discovered in 1974 in Afar (Ethiopia), the bones of little Lucy, who was just 3 ft 7 in/ 1.1 m tall, suggested that *Australopithecus*, unlike apes, walked upright three million years ago.

**→ → The evolutionary puzzle**
Several cranium models from different species underpin a kind of human evolution in which the unanswered questions remind us of the many mysteries that are still to be solved.

addition to the DNA of our forefathers (provided that residual organic matter is found), have found a series of mutations in the "Y" chromosome found in men in our shared genetics that links all men to just a single ancestor from a distant past.

That patrilineal descent, which has been traced by analyzing hundreds of thousands of samples of genetic material taken from men from practically all corners of the Earth and comparing them, has allowed scientists to identify the chromosomal and Scientific Adam, who is known to have lived in West-Central Africa.

### MITOCHONDRIAL EVE

As regards the Mitochondrial Eve, the situation is similar. Just as "Y" chromosomes are exclusively inherited through paternal lineage, only women inherit, through maternal lineage, a characteristic DNA feature: the mitochondrial genome. Thanks to this, it has also been possible to trace a matrilineal descent. The most recent calculations position the Mitochondrial Eve around 200,000 years ago, also in Africa, although to the east of the continent.

Naturally, neither Scientific Adam nor Mitochondrial Eve were the only human beings on Earth at the time, and it would appear they were not even alive during the same period. Science has established only that they are our ancestors and that we inherited the DNA we all carry with us today from

them. However, the conclusions reached by geneticists and paleontologists may change as new fossils are uncovered, or new evidence is found in the "Y" chromosome or in the mitochondrial genome.

When handling data that covers so many thousands of years, the slightest variation in calculations or the emergence of an unexpected factor can result in changes to dates and unravel a theory as if it were a loose thread of yarn. In fact, the estimate made by the professors in Rome quoted in relation to the age of Scientific Adam (which more than doubles the estimate made by Spencer Wells in his Genographic Project), is based on the discovery of two small mutations that, currently, have positioned us 80,000 years closer to our common male and female ancestors, making them "almost" contemporary (140,000 and 200,000 years).

### AFRICAN ORIGIN

Today, anthropologists support the hypothesis that modern man is of African origin. However, others also maintain that the polygenism theory is correct. This theory proposes that *Homo sapiens* evolved as a species connected to *Homo erectus*. Furthermore, its supporters propose that the great genetic similarities between all humans do not prove we have a shared ancestry, but that they serve to reflect the interconnected nature of human communities worldwide.

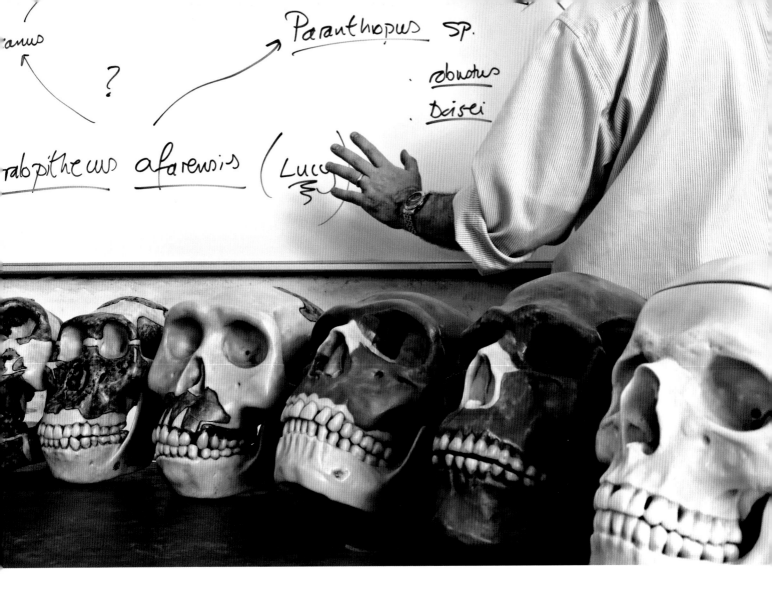

In addition to basing itself on paleoanthropological records and archaeological remains, the theory that defends the African origin of modern humans is supported by fossil and microbiological evidence. Its main argument is based, however, on the genetic differences observed in modern-day humans and the traces left in our DNA.

Although British ethnologist James Cowles Prichard had defended the African origin of modern man in the nineteenth century, the existence of a single shared ancestor of all mankind was not proposed until 1980, as a result of mitochondrial DNA testing. In 1987, researchers Rebecca Cann, Mark Stoneking, and Allan Wilson demonstrated that *Homo sapiens* originated in Africa between 200,000 and 140,000 years ago, suggesting that the species emigrated from there to the other continents.

This mitochondrial DNA, the comparison of which between different ethnicities in different regions suggests that all its sequences have a common molecular coating, evidences the matrilineal ancestry, an evolutionary path that begins with the Mitochondrial Eve.

Science has established that we have been "humans" for 2.5 million years, since at some stage during the Paleolithic period, in a chain of hominids that dates back to seven million years ago, a type of scavenger species capable of fashioning tools from stone was born. He has been identified as belonging to the genus *Homo*, and he is credited with having a significantly larger brain than his ancestors, in addition to a highly developed capacity for phonation (the ability to produce sounds). At some time, a primitive form of language arose that made this species progressively more sociable, sensitive, and intelligent.

Scientists agree that using language, a process of meta-observation, of "conceptualizing oneself" began; codes and formulas developed that served to encode and decode, construct and deconstruct messages. This factor clearly distinguishes communication between humans from communication established between certain animals, which is transmitted genetically and not through learning.

### THE "SKILLFUL" MAN

The protagonist of this key phase in the ancient history of humankind (a "moment" that lasted around 500,000 years) is *Homo habilis*, discovered between 1961 and 1964 in the Olduvai Gorge in Tanzania. The species was awarded the qualifier of *habilis*, meaning "skilled," because, next to the fossil of a skull, stone instruments that he himself probably created were found. However, some authors do not agree with assigning him to the genus *Homo*, but place him on the boundary between that genus and *Australopithecus* (bipedal hominids that lived around four million years ago).

**←Depiction of a Neanderthal**
Recreation of the profile of a Neanderthal man, which allows us to see the morphological features of his skull.

## How did the Neanderthals become extinct?

Neanderthals were robust, fair or red-haired, had a wide chest, thick bones and short limbs, a low and slanting forehead, a jaw with no chin, and a significant cranial capacity. They lived in groups of 20 or 30 members, organized in a hierarchy, performed funeral rituals, and were perfectly adapted to extreme cold. They used rudimentary language, made tools from stone and bone, were excellent hunters and gatherers, and they populated Europe and Central Asia for 200,000 years. However, they became extinct around 20,000 years ago, after co-existing with *Homo sapiens sapiens* for 5,000 years. Why did they disappear? The reasons for their disappearance are still cause for debate.

Some scientists maintain that their rapid extinction was related to the arrival of *Homo sapiens sapiens* in Europe; others suggest that a form of hybridization took place between both species and that the Neanderthal was absorbed by the *sapiens*, a species ten times greater in number. It is also possible that they became extinct as they were unable to compete for food with the new arrivals, or that they were susceptible to new illnesses, or they were simply wiped out. Their last strongholds were found in the south of the Iberian Peninsula, and are dated as being 28,000 years old.

Before them, in the evolutionary path plotted by science, came *Homo ergaster*, the first hunter, who inhabited our planet two million years ago. It is believed that this *Homo* was the first to leave Africa, 1.7 million years ago, during the migration known as "Out of Africa 1." From this continent, they arrived in Asia, where between 1920 and 1940 fossil remains of a new *Homo* were found, belonging to a group considered by some to be the closest to humans: *Homo erectus*. This species used stone tools, in addition to others made from bones, and cooked with fire.

### THE FINAL LINKS

Around one million years ago, a new link in the chain of human evolution emerged: *Homo heidelbergensis*. It is known that the species used wood and stone to make primitive dwellings. Next came *Homo neanderthalensis*, also known as Neanderthals, around 200,000 years ago. The Neanderthals, who lived during the second half of the Middle Pleistocene, were the first to live in complex societies. They were also capable of ritualizing certain behavior, and it is believed that they started the practice of burying their dead. Science has confirmed that they became extinct around 20,000 years ago on the Iberian Peninsula. However, the discovery of a possible new species on European soil at the end of the twentieth century could challenge the validity of the previously accepted evolutionary tree. Known as *Homo antecessor*—found in the Atapuerca Mountains in Burgos in the north of Spain—this would be the oldest species of hominid to have inhabited Europe, approximately one million years ago.

*Homo antecessor* was tall and strong, with a smaller brain than modern-day man, and his identification is attributable to the remains found in 1994 in the Atapuerca Mountains and the discovery in Ceprano, Italy, during the same year, of the upper part of a *Homo* skull with very similar characteristics. A direct descendant of *Homo ergaster*, several possibilities are debated about its position in the evolutionary jigsaw puzzle: whether solely an ancestor of *Homo heidelbergensis*; whether solely an ancestor of *Homo sapiens*; that it had its own evolutionary path with no descendants; that it is simply a variation of *Homo ergaster* or *Homo heidelbergensis*.

### ANATOMICALLY MODERN MAN

A descendant of either *Homo antecessor* or *Homo heidelbergensis*, *Homo sapiens*, contemporary with the Neanderthals, finally came into existence around 200,000 years ago. *Homo sapiens* is considered the first anatomically modern human being. It is suspected that he may have bred with the Neanderthals, but to date no DNA evidence has been found to support this possibility. He evolved into *Homo sapiens sapiens*, a socially aware human being, conscious of his own existence, who created what we today know as "culture." He was able to paint pictures on the walls of caves and carve images and icons in stone, such as the famous Venus of Willendorf. Everything would seem to suggest that our first ancestors, the Mitochondrial Eve and the Scientific Adam, lived during this period. Their descendants then arrived in Europe from Africa around 60,000 years ago, in a migratory wave known as "Out of Africa 2."

# When did we start speaking?

Most experts in historic linguistics believe that it would be impossible to reconstruct languages that may have existed over 5,000 years ago. However, defenders of the common origin of humanity theory sustain that there must have also been a language shared by all mankind, a proto-language from which all the world's different languages have derived. This original language would have split during the "Out of Africa 2" migration, around 60,000 years ago, when the African ancestors of *Homo sapiens sapiens* abandoned the continent to populate the rest of the world.

There may have been a link between the genetic classification of human populations and the phylogenetic classification of languages spoken by different groups of humans.

A study on phonemic diversity carried out by Quentin Atkinson in 2011 has established that the languages containing the most sounds are spoken in Africa, and those with the least sounds are spoken in South America and Oceania, which demonstrates that languages originated in the south of Africa, strengthening the *proto-sapiens* language hypothesis.

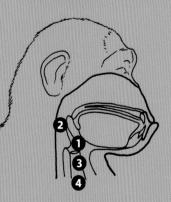
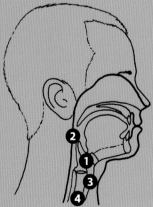

1. Larynx
2. Epiglottis
3. Vocal chords
4. Windpipe

# The Origin of Humankind

*Homo sapiens sapiens*, the scientific name for modern human beings, is the result of a long evolutionary process that began in Africa about seven million years ago.

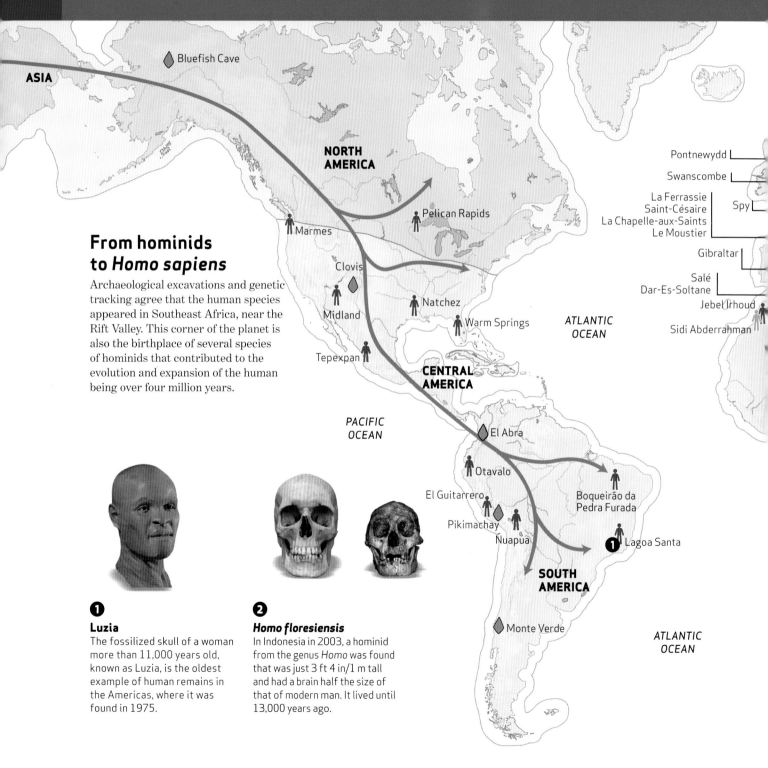

ASIA

Bluefish Cave

NORTH
AMERICA

Pelican Rapids

Marmes

## From hominids to *Homo sapiens*

Archaeological excavations and genetic tracking agree that the human species appeared in Southeast Africa, near the Rift Valley. This corner of the planet is also the birthplace of several species of hominids that contributed to the evolution and expansion of the human being over four million years.

Clovis

Midland

Natchez

Warm Springs

Tepexpan

CENTRAL
AMERICA

ATLANTIC
OCEAN

Pontnewydd

Swanscombe

La Ferrassie
Saint-Césaire
La Chapelle-aux-Saints
Le Moustier

Spy

Gibraltar

Salé
Dar-Es-Soltane

Jebel Irhoud

Sidi Abderrahman

PACIFIC
OCEAN

El Abra

Otavalo

El Guitarrero

Boqueirão da
Pedra Furada

Pikimachay

Nuapua

Lagoa Santa

SOUTH
AMERICA

Monte Verde

ATLANTIC
OCEAN

**❶**
**Luzia**
The fossilized skull of a woman more than 11,000 years old, known as Luzia, is the oldest example of human remains in the Americas, where it was found in 1975.

**❷**
*Homo floresiensis*
In Indonesia in 2003, a hominid from the genus *Homo* was found that was just 3 ft 4 in/1 m tall and had a brain half the size of that of modern man. It lived until 13,000 years ago.

# Why did one African ape species set out on a different evolutionary path?

The sinking of the Rift Valley caused the separation of the human lineage from the rest of the apes. Thirty million years ago, East Africa began to sink. Separated from the mainland by lakes and rivers, the area underwent a climate change. The forest gave way to savannah and the primates were forced down to the ground and began the evolution to bipedalism.

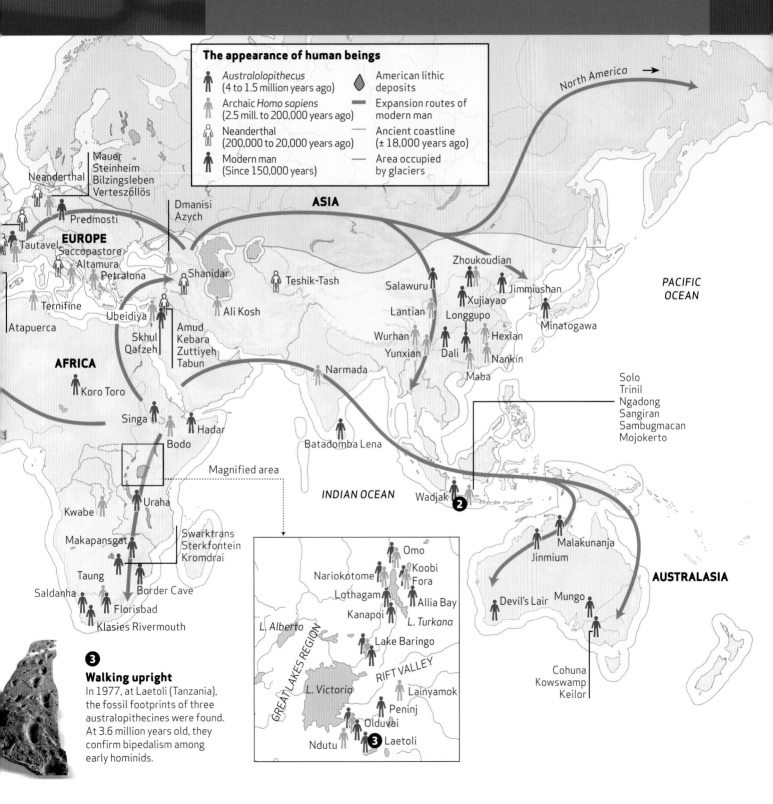

### The appearance of human beings

- *Australolopithecus* (4 to 1.5 million years ago)
- Archaic *Homo sapiens* (2.5 mill. to 200,000 years ago)
- Neanderthal (200,000 to 20,000 years ago)
- Modern man (Since 150,000 years)
- American lithic deposits
- Expansion routes of modern man
- Ancient coastline (± 18,000 years ago)
- Area occupied by glaciers

North America →

ASIA

EUROPE

AFRICA

PACIFIC OCEAN

AUSTRALASIA

INDIAN OCEAN

Magnified area

**Place names (Europe/Africa region):** Neanderthal, Mauer, Steinheim, Bilzingsleben, Verteszöllös, Predmosti, Tautavel, Saccopastore, Altamura, Petralona, Ternifine, Atapuerca, Ubeidiya, Koro Toro, Singa, Hadar, Bodo, Uraha, Kwabe, Makapansgat, Taung, Swarktrans, Sterkfontein, Kromdrai, Saldanha, Florisbad, Border Cave, Klasies Rivermouth, Skhul, Qafzeh, Amud, Kebara, Zuttiyeh, Tabun

**Place names (Asia region):** Dmanisi, Azych, Shanidar, Teshik-Tash, Ali Kosh, Salawuru, Lantian, Longgupo, Wurhan, Yunxian, Dali, Zhoukoudian, Xujiayao, Jimmiushan, Hexian, Nankin, Maba, Minatogawa, Narmada, Batadomba Lena, Wadjak ❷

**Place names (Australasia/Solo region):** Solo, Trinil, Ngadong, Sangiran, Sambugmacan, Mojokerto, Jinmium, Malakunanja, Devil's Lair, Mungo, Cohuna, Kowswamp, Keilor

**Magnified area (Great Lakes Region / Rift Valley):** Omo, Koobi Fora, Nariokotome, Lothagam, Allia Bay, Kanapoi, L. Turkana, L. Alberto, Lake Baringo, L. Victoria, RIFT VALLEY, Lainyamok, Peninj, Olduvai, Ndutu, Laetoli ❸, GREAT LAKES REGION

❸

### Walking upright

In 1977, at Laetoli (Tanzania), the fossil footprints of three australopithecines were found. At 3.6 million years old, they confirm bipedalism among early hominids.

# The evolution of human beings

**Bipedalism was the first milestone in a process of humanization that took millions of years to reach the present stage of evolution. During that time, between 25 and 30 human species appeared and disappeared.**

## A long road

The path of evolution is marked by archaeological discoveries that shed some light on the changes and adaptations in the species in question. Many findings have forced us to revise the schemes used to explain the past of mankind.

### Australopithecus
Considered one of the first links in the chain of human evolution, this bipedal ape became extinct 1.5 million years ago.

### On two legs
Walking upright led to physical changes such as stretching of the neck.

### Hands free
This was an advantageous consequence of bipedalism.

### Walking upright
Requires less energy to move and increases the field of vision, although speed is lost.

### Homo habilis
The first link of the genus *Homo*, it underwent significant physiological changes from its predecessor.

### Brain
The brain size increased by 44 percent compared to its predecessor (much more than the rest of the body).

### Opposable thumbs
These were used to make the first stone tools.

### Homo erectus
The first human species was a migratory hunter who left Africa and spread to Europe and Asia.

### Language
The finding of a bone from the larynx allowed experts to infer that this hominid could speak.

### Fire and axes
Believed to have been the first species to use fire. It also developed a lithic industry of stone axes.

## Evolution

The scientific consensus has established that walking upright was the first stage on the path of human evolution that began at least four million years ago.

4 million years ago

| ARDIPITHECUS | | AUSTRALOPITHECUS | | PARANTHROPUS |
|---|---|---|---|---|
| | | | | *P. aethiopicus* |
| A. ramidus | A. anamensis | A. afarensis | | A. africanus |
| | | | | ??? |
| | | | | A. garhi |

# When did mankind reach its modern body proportions?

Homo ergaster was the first species with a modern-looking body. The finding of the Child of Lake Turkana, the fossil skeleton of an Ergaster of between 12 and 15 years of age and 1.6 metres (5 ft 3 in) in height confirmed this. Anatomists calculated that in adulthood she could have reached 1.80 metres (5 ft 11 in) tall. Her pelvis was narrower than that of Homo sapiens, suggesting that she was also a swift biped.

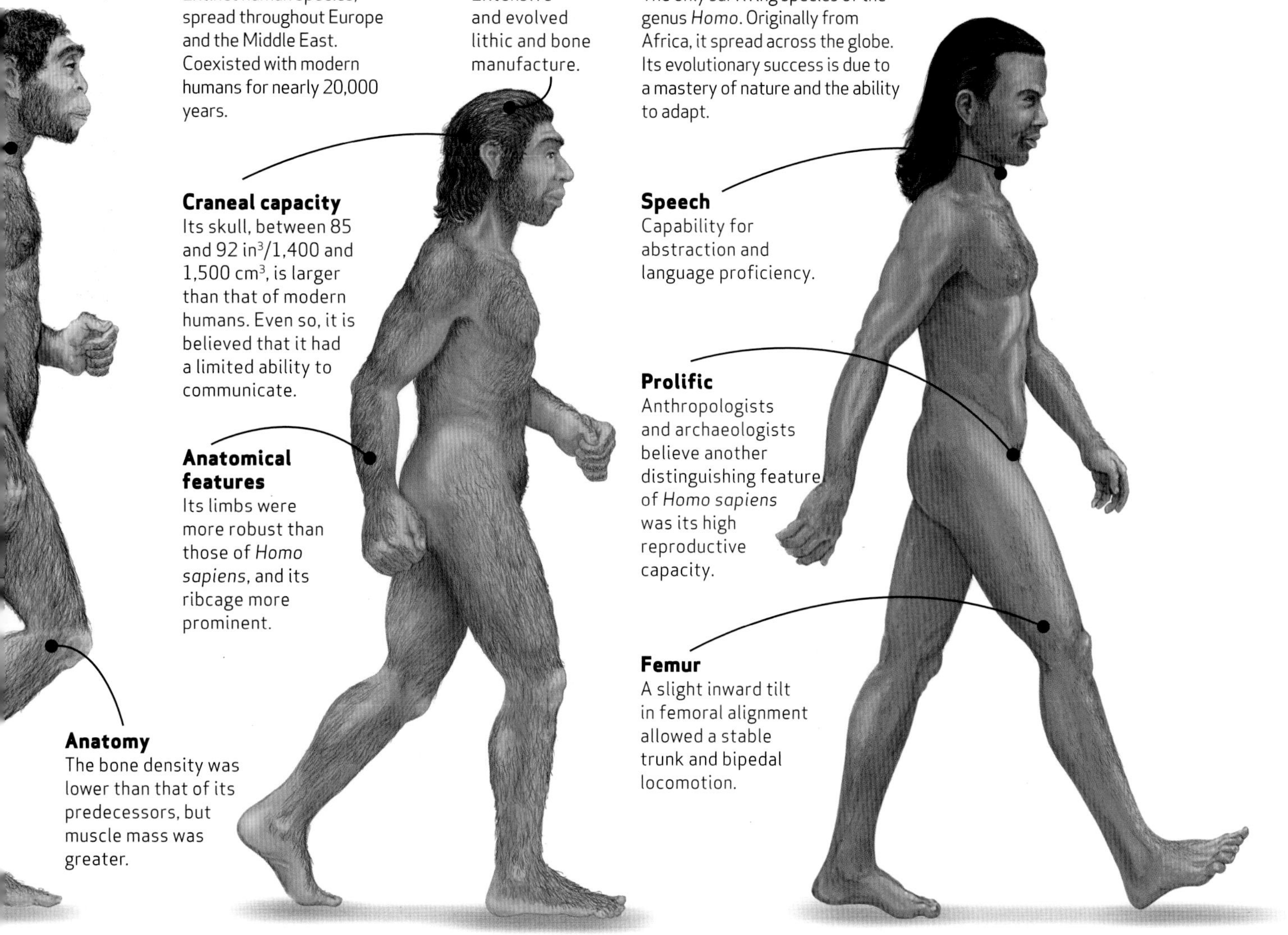

### *Homo neanderthalensis*
Extinct human species, spread throughout Europe and the Middle East. Coexisted with modern humans for nearly 20,000 years.

### Culture
Extensive and evolved lithic and bone manufacture.

### *Homo sapiens*
The only surviving species of the genus *Homo*. Originally from Africa, it spread across the globe. Its evolutionary success is due to a mastery of nature and the ability to adapt.

### Craneal capacity
Its skull, between 85 and 92 in³/1,400 and 1,500 cm³, is larger than that of modern humans. Even so, it is believed that it had a limited ability to communicate.

### Speech
Capability for abstraction and language proficiency.

### Anatomical features
Its limbs were more robust than those of *Homo sapiens*, and its ribcage more prominent.

### Prolific
Anthropologists and archaeologists believe another distinguishing feature of *Homo sapiens* was its high reproductive capacity.

### Anatomy
The bone density was lower than that of its predecessors, but muscle mass was greater.

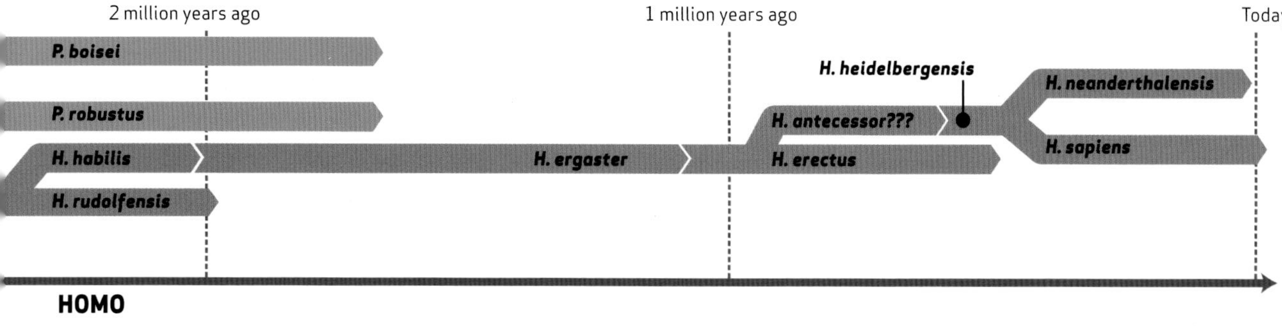

### Femur
A slight inward tilt in femoral alignment allowed a stable trunk and bipedal locomotion.

| 2 million years ago | 1 million years ago | Today |
|---|---|---|

P. boisei

P. robustus

H. habilis

H. rudolfensis

H. ergaster

H. erectus

H. heidelbergensis

H. antecessor???

H. neanderthalensis

H. sapiens

**HOMO**

# Stone and bone

Because of their durability, only stone and bone have survived the passage of the centuries to show us what type of material humans initially employed to survive, fight, and represent their beliefs through art.

## The tools

Stones have been the basic tool used by humans for millions of years. Stone carving, started incipiently by *Homo habilis*, was converted into a flourishing industry by *Homo ergaster*; it would take over 1.5 million years for *Homo sapiens* to become a predator and perfect the art of stone carving.

### The first stone-carving technique
This chopping tool, a pebble sharpened on one side, illustrates the Oldowan technique, the oldest known to man, employed by *Homo habilis* 2.5 million years ago.

### Progress of the double-edged cleaver
Double-edged stone cleavers were first produced 1.6 million years ago. Originating in Africa, *Homo ergaster* took them to the Middle East, Europe, and South Asia.

### Double-edged cleaver
Highly versatile, the double-edged cleaver was the longest-lasting stone instrument in the history of mankind, lasting until the Neolithic period.

### Flint knives
Lithic reduction (the extraction of fragments of stone from a larger core) dates back to the Mid and Late Paleolithic period. It was employed by Neanderthals and *Homo sapiens*.

### Arrowheads
The technique that facilitated the carving of stone arrowheads is attributable to *Homo sapiens* and lasted throughout the 22,000 years of the Upper Paleolithic period.

### Spear thrower
This spear thrower is decorated with the image of a horse. The decoration of these weapons during the artistic Magdalenian period suggests roles were split into a hierarchy.

## Prehistoric music

The discovery of flutes carved from bones at sites across Europe dating back to the Aurignacian period (the image represents one found in the French Dordogne) demonstrates that *Homo sapiens* developed their sense of music. However, the 1995 discovery of a flute dating back 45,000 years attributed to the Neanderthals, in Divje Babe (Slovenia) reopened the debate on the evolutionary level of this species.

### Needles and projectile points

Made from bone, sewing needles **1** are a product of the Solutrean culture from the Magdalenian period; the projectile points **2**, made from sharpened bone flints, date back to the earlier Aurignacian culture (38,000–30,000 BCE).

## Art

Around 30,000 years ago, the concept of using stone and bone solely as raw material to fashion tools was replaced, and the material became a way of expressing the symbolic thought processes of human beings. The figures known as Paleolithic Venus figurines date from this period: the sexual attributes on these small sculptures of women were exaggerated as a kind of fertility worship. Most date back to the Gravettian culture (30,000–22,000 BCE).

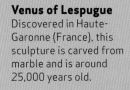

### Venus of Lespugue

Discovered in Haute-Garonne (France), this sculpture is carved from marble and is around 25,000 years old.

### Venus of Laussel

Found in the Dordogne, France, this Venus, carved in relief, represents the transitional phase between the Gravettian and Solutrean cultures.

### Venus of Savignano

Carved in steatite, this figurine was found in an alluvial deposit close to Modena (Italy). Measuring 9 in/22.5 cm in height, it is one of the largest ever found.

### Spears

The tips of these fishing spears are similar to modern fishing instruments. According to archaeological records, they are around 14,000 years old.

### Venus of Willendorf

The most famous Palaeolithic Venus was found in Austria and carved from sandstone. It is around 22,000 years old.

# CHAPTER 3

# The Pyramids, Symbol of Eternal Life

More than 4,500 years after their construction, the pyramids of Egypt continue to defy imagination. How were they built? Who built them?

A sacred river divides the land into two. It runs south to north before it opens up into the Mediterranean Sea like a lotus flower. Every day, on its eastern shore, the Sun God Ra, whom the ancient Egyptians associated with Atum, the primordial god, and also with Horus, comes to be in the Land of the Living. On its western shore, when the day is spent, the sun is swallowed by Nut (the Sky Goddess) and goes to the Land of the Dead, the resting place of the deceased.

The ancient Egyptians believed that the sun's journey across the sky represented Ra crossing the ocean on his barge. He was conceived anew during the night, to be reborn in the early hours of the morning. From the dawn of history they attributed a divine origin and nature to their kings. To the Egyptians, the pharaoh was the personification on Earth of Horus, the god-king. And as god, the pharaoh had a more sublime destiny than other mortals. After his death on Earth, he had the right to a "heavenly" existence. Purified by the waters of a mythical lake, the pharaoh occupied a place on the solar barge, at Ra's side, every day crossing the ocean of the sky.

Despite knowing quite a lot about the origins of the Egyptian civilization, even experts disagree about when to define the different epochs and periods of its history, as they are dealing with margins of time with differences spanning 50 to 200 years between them. However, there is information about the development of Egyptian daily life, such as their social structure, customs, and beliefs, from the murals and the texts rescued by the scholars and researchers of the Old Kingdom (2686–2134 BCE). This period covered more than half a millennium and saw the rise and fall of the Third to the Sixth dynasties. It was a time in which the Old Kingdom reached its greatest period of splendor with the construction of the pyramids.

It was at this point when the Great Pyramid of Giza was built on the outskirts of Cairo (the pyramid of Khufu), the only one of the seven wonders of the world still standing. It was also when the idea began to emerge that a god was intimately bound to funerary rites, and therefore, with the pyramids: Osiris, believed to be the archetypal image of the dead kings.

**Pyramid of Khafre**
Forms part of the Giza necropolis. This picture was taken from the summit of the pyramid of Khufu, which is very close to the pyramid of Khafre.

←**Necropolis**
The pyramids of Giza and the Great Sphinx are the most visible monuments of a necropolis that also includes other cemeteries, houses, and workshops for the workers who built them.

→**Hieroglyphics**
The Egyptian writing system was based on a combination of phonetic and ideographic principles. After years of research, Frenchman Jean-François Champollion deciphered it in 1822.

Elevated to the status of sovereign over the land of the blessed, Osiris represents royalty, explains the continuity of the monarchy, and is identified with the legend of the dead king who dies and is resurrected in beautified form, transferring his status to his son Horus.

It is not known with any certainty whether the pyramids were solely royal tombs or places for the sojourn and the resting place of the pharaoh's soul ("ka"), but all kings who succeeded to the throne of Egypt passed through these two states: they were endowed with the title of Horus during their reign, and at the end of it they transformed into Osiris and were honored as such by their sons and successors.

There is no doubt that the pyramids formed part of the complex and divine ritual universe of the pharaohs and their journey to the afterlife. However, there are many questions that still remain concerning these marvelous constructions, both a scientific challenge and an enormous arena for the most fantastic speculations. To date, the existence of at least 120 of these spectacular works of art are known, all of them located on the western side of the Nile Valley, in the Land of the Dead, and although they are identified with the entire Egyptian civilization, they are characteristic of just one single period: the Old Kingdom.

In subsequent reigns, during the so-called Middle Kingdom (between approximately 2030 BCE and 1640 BCE) there was a reduction in size and quality of the pyramids. And in the New Kingdom, they only appear as external decoration on the tombs of some craftsmen. But it is the three pyramids located on the Giza plateau—the pyramids of Khufu, Khafre, and Menkaure (in Greek: Cheops, Chephren, and Mycerinus, respectively)—that have become the symbol of ancient Egypt. Products of a culture as sophisticated as it is enigmatic, they are still objects of fascination, particularly the first and largest of them, the construction of which was ordered by Pharaoh Khufu around the year 2580 BCE, and designed by architect Hemiunu.

### THE CONSTRUCTION

The first known description of the methods employed in the building of the pyramid of Khufu is from the Greek historian Herodotus in his second book, *Euterpe*. "This pyramid," he wrote, "was built on a hill in a succession of steps which some call shelves or crossai and others, shrines or bomides (...). The first part to be finished was the upper region of the pyramid, then they finished the lower sections." Herodotus' description was thought to be reliable until the nineteenth century when, after more was known about the interiors of the pyramids, uncertainty increased. Today, the majority of Egyptologists agree that the construction process took the following steps:

1. Leveling out. Between 1880 and 1882, English archaeologist Sir William Matthew Flinders Petrie (1853–1942) carried out one of the first scientific studies on the Giza plateau. He suggested that the Fourth Dynasty Egyptians had stabilized and leveled out the area on which they built the Great Pyramid, excavating the rock into which they dug a network of shallow channels that were filled with water. Next, the depth excavated was reduced or increased until the land on which this great stone structure was to be built was perfectly leveled out. One century later, Egyptologist Mark Lehner, author of *The Complete Pyramids of Egypt* and of the detailed map of the Giza plateau, argued that, in reality, the Egyptians did not work on the entire area occupied by the pyramid, but simply, by digging narrow ditches under its edges, the level of water would have ensured the support base was flat.

2. Alignment. It is evident that the ancient Egyptians used their knowledge of astronomy to map out the lines and angles of their buildings and to orient the slopes and corners of their structures to line up with the heavenly bodies. To achieve this, they used instruments and tools such as the "merjet" (an instrument used by the Egyptians to measure time, similar to an astrolabe): a horizontal bar, made from bone, with a weight hanging from a hole located at the end, which was controlled by a wooden handle; and the bay, made

with a palm leaf cut into the shape of a V. Both instruments, whose margin of error was around 0.5 degrees, could be used to locate the cardinal points very accurately by observing the stars, and could also be used in the *pedj shes* ("tug-of-war") ceremonies that took place prior to beginning the construction, based on the observation of the Great Bear and the circumpolar stars.

3. Underground chamber. Once the land had been leveled out and the alignment of the future pyramid established, construction began on the so-called Underground Chamber, excavated in the rocky subsoil. The Great Pyramid has a rectangular floor and contains two living spaces: a shaft and a small gallery that is accessed through a descending passageway, which is actually an extension of the pyramid entrance. The chamber is linked to the Grand Gallery by an almost vertical tunnel. A hoist would have been installed at the end of this enclosure to raise the blocks of stone through this tunnel.

4. Ramps. Despite the fact that there are no remains of ramps around the Great Pyramid, the majority of archaeologists agree that they would have been used to transfer the millions of blocks of stone used in constructing the pyramids, because their remains have been discovered in other similar constructions. It is thought that different systems were used: a smooth ramp inclined (probably used in the step

# Metropolis and good food

The work of Egyptologist Mark Lehner has brought to light what appears to be the houses and workshops of the workers who built the pyramids. The investigations of this Egyptologist into the builders of the Giza necropolis prove that a suburb must have existed close by, where those who built the pyramids went about their daily lives. In fact, it is estimated that between 20,000 and 30,000 workers were needed to build the pyramids. A city has been found and is thought to be a center for storage and production, with three paved streets and large buildings. In addition, they have also found remains that confirm that the workers of the pyramids were very well fed. Recently, a high number of cow and fish bones have been found, enough to feed thousands of men for several years. According to calculations by experts, Egyptian families donated 21 head of cattle and 23 sheep every day to feed the workers who built the pyramids.

The entire pyramid project allowed workers, in the best cases, to prosper, and in the worst, to be buried in the vicinity of the tombs of the kings. For the ancient Egyptians, this meant there was a chance that the pharaoh would intercede for the salvation of their souls, which almost guaranteed access to the afterlife.

**↓City**
There must have been a city in which the workers lived while the pyramids of Giza were being built.

---

Pyramid of Djoser at Saqqara); or several ramps, in a staircase or zigzag layout, which supported each of the pyramid's faces, connected to each other and the row of stones. One of the latest theories in this respect was devised by French architect Jean-Pierre Houdin in 2007, after a microgravity test carried out in 1986 at the Great Pyramid, which detected a less dense structure in the shape of a spiral in the interior of the building. According to this researcher, the Egyptians produced an external ramp measuring some 130 ft/40 m and from there they built another internal one in the shape of a spiral with an inclination of seven degrees and gaps for the corners through which they inserted the stone blocks.

### WORKERS AND FREE MEN

Some 20 years ago, a tourist's horse stumbled over a piece of wall buried in the Giza terrace to the southeast of the Pyramid of Menkaure, which turned out to be what was later called "the cemetery of the builders." The discovery contradicted the old theory that the pyramids were the work of slaves, because the discovered burials were found in the sacred and ceremonial area of the Giza enclosure, to the south of the pyramids and the Sphinx: that is, too close to the pharaohs to imagine that the occupants were treated as slaves. Until quite recently, the tombs of 32 foremen and 600 workers had been found, but now new burials have been discovered that confirm that the construction of the pyramids was completed by free men, who worked on a large community project, which, it is discovered, implies that the whole society of the period was involved.

According to the renowned Egyptologist Zahi Hawass, the number of workers would have been around 10,000. They fulfilled their duties over a three-month period and were then replaced by others when they had finished. Those who died during construction were buried in the same place, and medical assistance was given to the sick and injured. From the human remains discovered, it has been deduced that emergency treatments such as resetting bones were carried out. There is some evidence of amputations and evidence of degenerative arthritis in the lumbar region and knees of some workers, probably due to the enormous efforts required to move large weights. There is also evidence that doctors applied splints and bandages to treat fractures and used various techniques to suture wounds or stop hemorrhages.

Among the more recently discovered tombs there is one rectangular structure that stands out. It has an external covering of bricks whitened with plaster, with numerous shafts and funerary niches that belonged to a person called Idu. The tomb had a domed exterior, symbolizing the primitive hill where, for the ancient Egyptians, creation began. For specialists, this indicates that it was built during the Fourth Dynasty, during the same period that the Great Pyramid was built.

Today, it is estimated that only 5 percent of the total area of this huge workers' cemetery has been excavated. In some tombs, the title of the person buried there is written. In others, titles such as "bricklayer supervisor," or "director of craftsmen," or "director of workers' bakery" have been found, confirming the existence of a complex and detailed organization of the tasks.

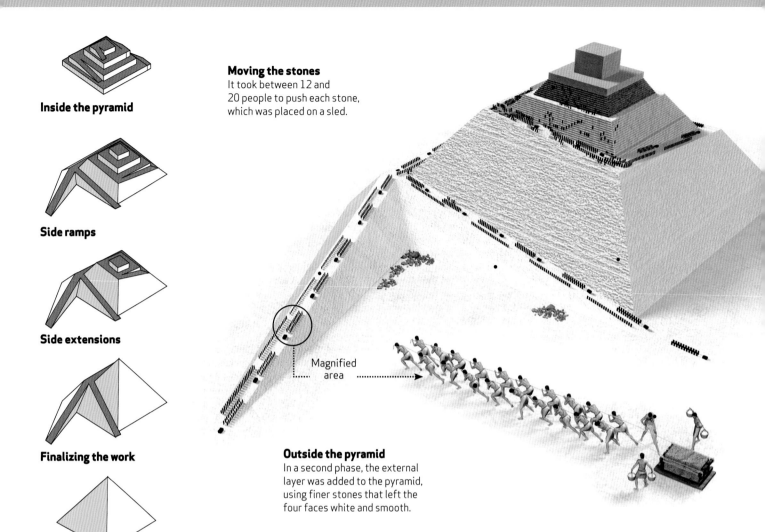

**Inside the pyramid**

**Side ramps**

**Side extensions**

**Finalizing the work**

**Removing the ramps**

**Moving the stones**
It took between 12 and 20 people to push each stone, which was placed on a sled.

Magnified area

**Outside the pyramid**
In a second phase, the external layer was added to the pyramid, using finer stones that left the four faces white and smooth.

## Stone or concrete?

It has been calculated that 89,029,115 ft³/2,521,000 m³ of rectangular and square blocks of stones, each weighing at least 2 tons, were used for the construction of the Great Pyramid of the Pharaoh Khufu. Today, there are still doubts about the technology applied to maneuver the stones that were used to build the pyramids. Professor Michel Barsoum published an article in the National Science Foundation in which he proposed that these stones were not cut or carved, but made using an Old Kingdom cement technology. Thus, the stones of the pyramids were made using a type of concrete made from limestone, clay, lime, and water.

However other researchers continue to believe that the stones were carved from natural blocks of limestone. The King's Chamber of the Great Pyramid, for example, was originally covered by some 27,000 pieces of white polished limestone. It appears that the majority of these blocks were cut in quarries close to the place where the pyramid was built, although others were transported in boats along the Nile. To achieve this, it is possible that they used copper saws with grains of quartz moistened with water. This system helped prevent the metal from wearing away and utilized the abrasive properties of quartz.

**↑Ramps**
Ramps and embankments had to be built to transport the stones, and were later removed at the end of construction.

# Separated pyramids

These are the highest expression of the architecture of the Old Kingdom and the most important part of the architectural complex for the worship of the pharaoh. Many were never used as tombs.

## The plain of Giza

Although Egypt has at least 120 pyramids, those at Giza are undoubtedly the most famous of all.

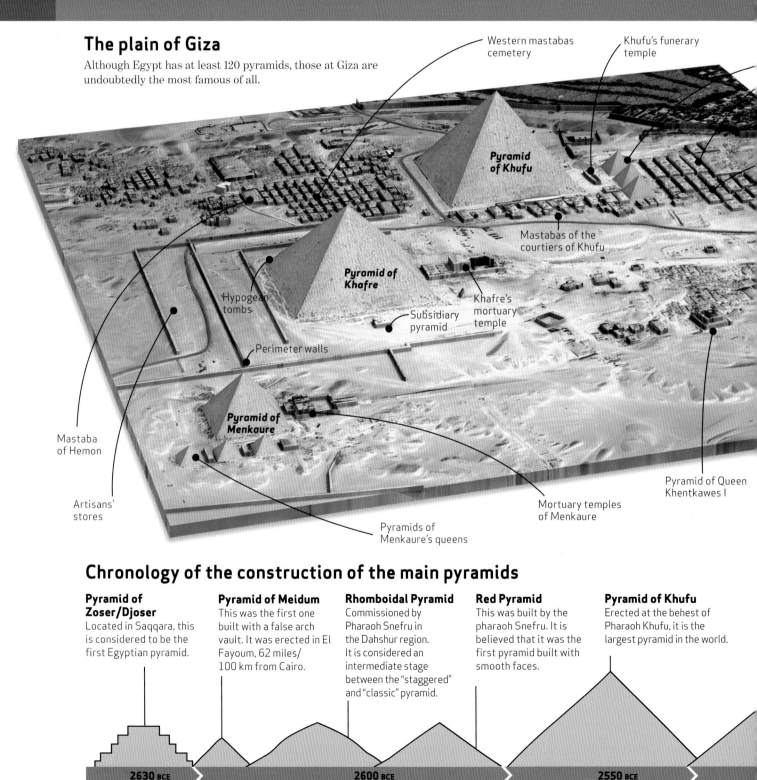

Western mastabas cemetery

Khufu's funerary temple

Pyramid of Khufu

Mastabas of the courtiers of Khufu

Pyramid of Khafre

Khafre's mortuary temple

Subsidiary pyramid

Hypogean tombs

Perimeter walls

Pyramid of Menkaure

Mastaba of Hemon

Artisans' stores

Pyramids of Menkaure's queens

Mortuary temples of Menkaure

Pyramid of Queen Khentkawes I

## Chronology of the construction of the main pyramids

**Pyramid of Zoser/Djoser**
Located in Saqqara, this is considered to be the first Egyptian pyramid.

**Pyramid of Meidum**
This was the first one built with a false arch vault. It was erected in El Fayoum, 62 miles/ 100 km from Cairo.

**Rhomboidal Pyramid**
Commissioned by Pharaoh Snefru in the Dahshur region. It is considered an intermediate stage between the "staggered" and "classic" pyramid.

**Red Pyramid**
This was built by the pharaoh Snefru. It is believed that it was the first pyramid built with smooth faces.

**Pyramid of Khufu**
Erected at the behest of Pharaoh Khufu, it is the largest pyramid in the world.

2630 BCE          2600 BCE          2550 BCE

## How long did it take to build a pyramid?

Hemiunu, the architect who led the work at Giza, spent a lot of time planning the work and set a timeline according to religious tradition. According to that plan, during the first thousand days of work the first course of masonry was laid, the next thousand was spent to reach the King's Chamber, and after a thousand more, the pyramid was completed.

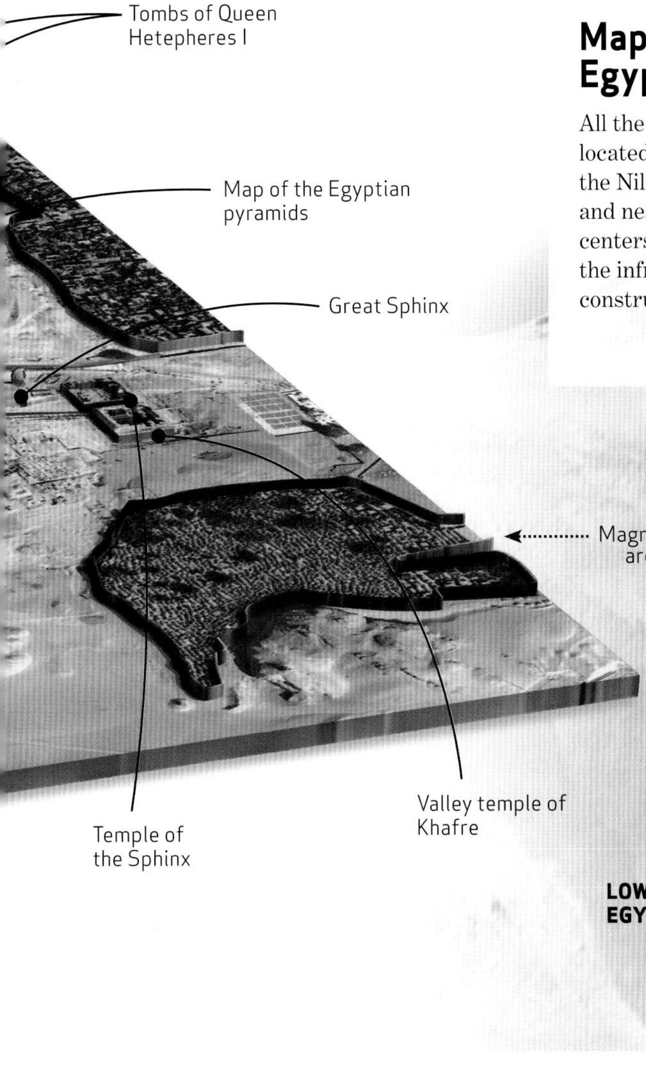

Tombs of Queen
Hetepheres I

## Map of the Egyptian pyramids

All the Egyptian pyramids are located on the west bank of the Nile, the place of the dead, and near certain population centers, perhaps to provide the infrastructure needed for construction.

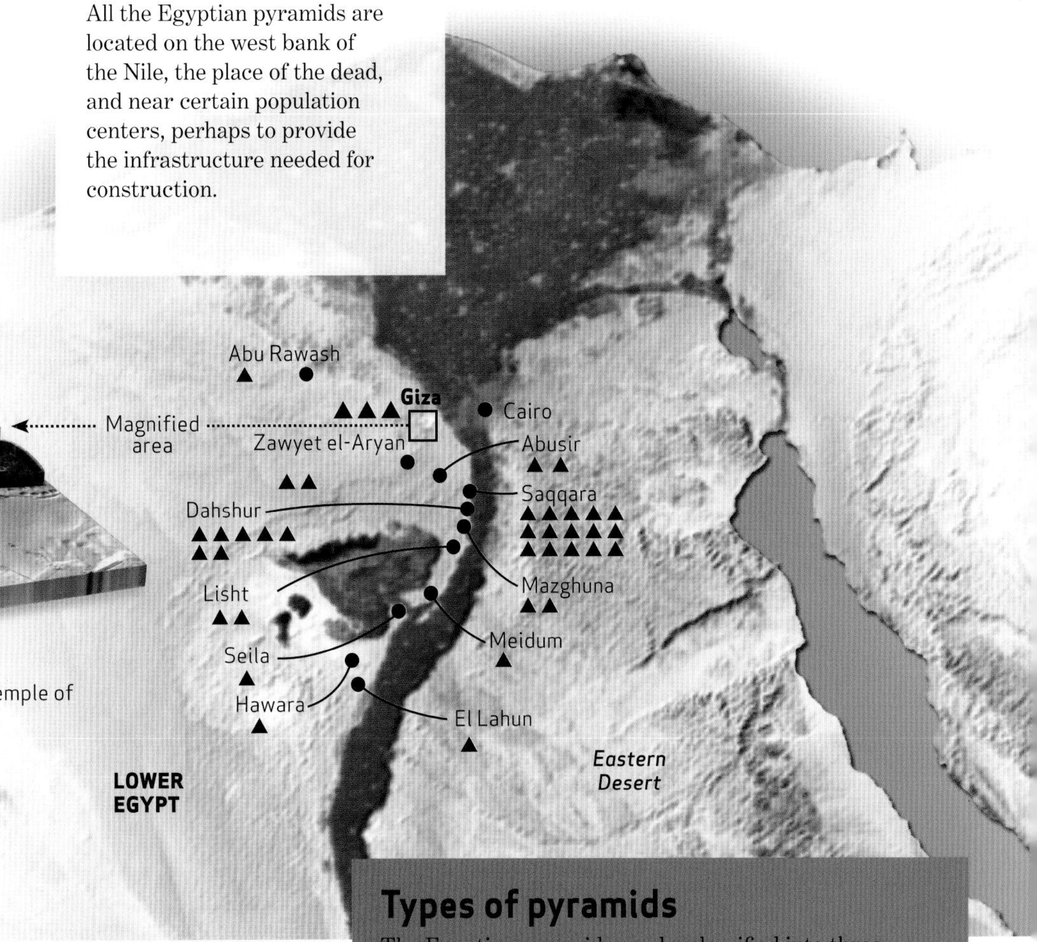

Map of the Egyptian
pyramids

Great Sphinx

Temple of
the Sphinx

Valley temple of
Khafre

Abu Rawash

Magnified
area

**Giza**

Zawyet el-Aryan

Cairo

Abusir

Saqqara

Dahshur

Mazghuna

Lisht

Meidum

Seila

El Lahun

Hawara

**LOWER
EGYPT**

*Eastern
Desert*

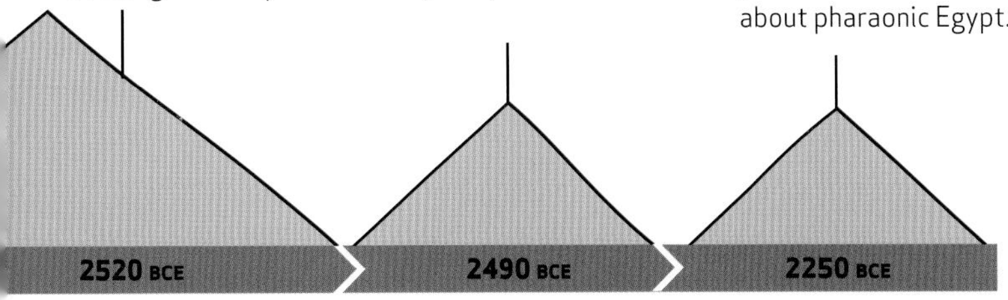

## Types of pyramids

The Egyptian pyramids can be classified into three types according to their morphology:

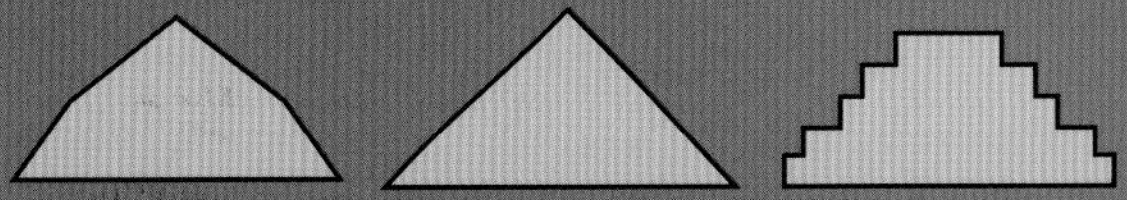

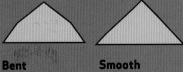

**Bent**
Its dual slope is due to a calculation error: a correction to prevent its collapse.

**Smooth**
On a square base, it becomes progressively smaller toward the top.

**Step**
Consists of six truncated pyramids on a rectangular base, narrowing toward the tip.

**Pyramid of Khafre**
Located next to Khufu's Pyramid, it was built by the Pharaoh Khafre, who also ordered the building of the Sphinx.

**Pyramid of Menkaure**
The smallest of the three most famous pyramids. It was built by Menkaure, pharaoh of the Fourth Dynasty.

**Pyramid of Pepi II**
Erected at Saqqara by the last pharaoh of the Sixth Dynasty. It preserved texts that provide information about pharaonic Egypt.

2520 BCE

2490 BCE

2250 BCE

# The Great Pyramid of Giza

The Pharaoh Khufu commissioned the construction of the Great Pyramid in the year 2550 BCE. It was located in the center of a complex of religious buildings, some of which have disappeared. Though its entrance was hidden, it was looted in 2150 BCE.

## A monumental work

Some 4,000 men, including quarry workers, porters, and builders, worked for nearly 30 years on the construction of this pyramid, which, when completed, weighed about six million tons.

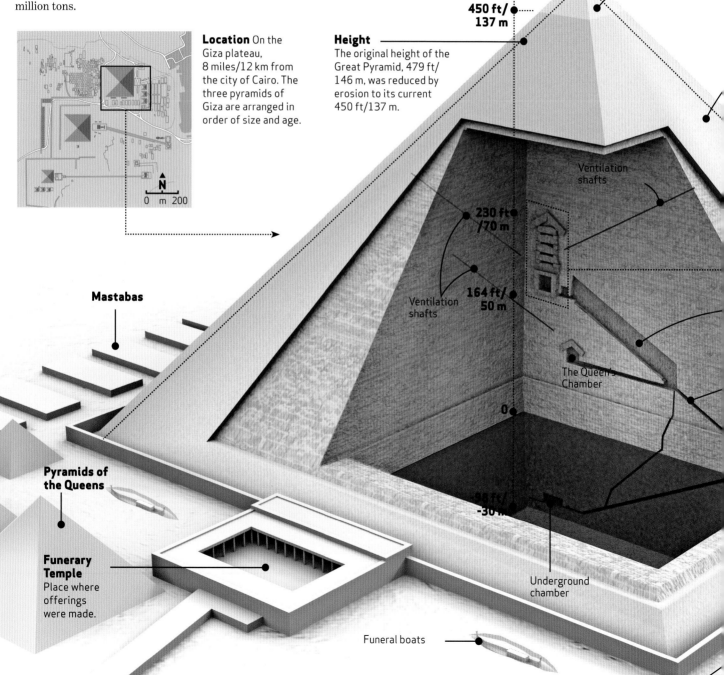

**Location** On the Giza plateau, 8 miles/12 km from the city of Cairo. The three pyramids of Giza are arranged in order of size and age.

0   m   200

**Height**
The original height of the Great Pyramid, 479 ft/146 m, was reduced by erosion to its current 450 ft/137 m.

479 ft/146 m

450 ft/137 m

230 ft/70 m

164 ft/50 m

Ventilation shafts

Ventilation shafts

The Queen's Chamber

0

-98 ft/-30 m

Underground chamber

**Mastabas**

**Pyramids of the Queens**

**Funerary Temple**
Place where offerings were made.

Funeral boats

## Where is the mummy of Pharaoh Khufu?

The official theory says that Khufu's tomb was looted at the beginning of the reign of his grandson Menkaure. Other hypotheses suggest that, anticipating it would be pillaged on his death, those faithful to Khufu hid the pharaoh's body in a secret place in the Great Pyramid. One theory speaks of the existence of a fourth secret space under the Queen's Chamber, where the pharaoh still rests.

**Pyramidion**
This stone pyramid symbolizes the resting place of the god Ra.

The original cover was of fine white limestone, which shone in the sunlight.

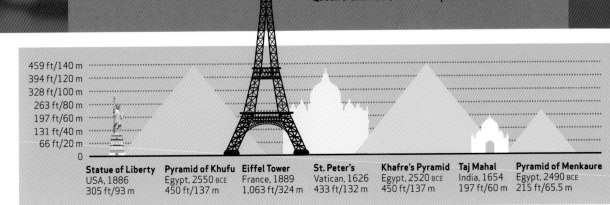

| | 459 ft/140 m |
| | 394 ft/120 m |
| | 328 ft/100 m |
| | 263 ft/80 m |
| | 197 ft/60 m |
| | 131 ft/40 m |
| | 66 ft/20 m |
| | 0 |

| Statue of Liberty | Pyramid of Khufu | Eiffel Tower | St. Peter's | Khafre's Pyramid | Taj Mahal | Pyramid of Menkaure |
|---|---|---|---|---|---|---|
| USA, 1886 | Egypt, 2550 BCE | France, 1889 | Vatican, 1626 | Egypt, 2520 BCE | India, 1654 | Egypt, 2490 BCE |
| 305 ft/93 m | 450 ft/137 m | 1,063 ft/324 m | 433 ft/132 m | 450 ft/137 m | 197 ft/60 m | 215 ft/65.5 m |

The Great Pyramid consists of 2,300,000 blocks of stone, each with an average weight of 2.5 tons, although there were also some larger blocks.

## The King's Chamber

The final resting place of Pharaoh Khufu is made of granite. The roof has stones of about 50 tons each. It also has five drainage compartments.

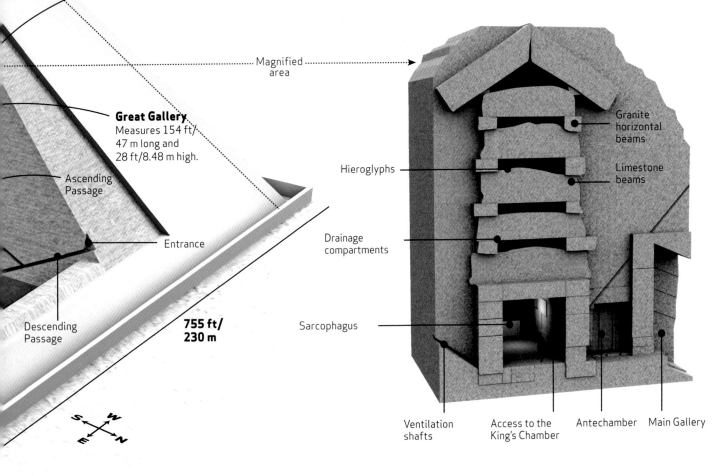

Magnified area

**Great Gallery**
Measures 154 ft/ 47 m long and 28 ft/8.48 m high.

Ascending Passage

Entrance

Descending Passage

**755 ft/ 230 m**

Hieroglyphs

Drainage compartments

Sarcophagus

Granite horizontal beams

Limestone beams

Ventilation shafts

Access to the King's Chamber

Antechamber

Main Gallery

# Symbols of power

The continuity of the symbols of power during 3,000 years of monarchy highlights the stability and conservatism of ancient Egyptian society. Objects symbolizing power were repeated, dynasty after dynasty.

## Crowns

In ancient Egypt, the crown fulfilled a dual political and religious function and, from the New Kingdom, it served to distinguish the dynastic origin of the sovereign. In addition to the royal crown, other crowns strictly for ceremonial and religious purposes were used.

**Hedjet**
An oblong-shaped miter representing the monarchs of Upper Egypt. It was the crown of the Theban dynasties.

**Deshret**
Red in color, with a raised arm and a curled protuberance at the front, linked to the bee, the symbol of the dynasties. It was the crown of Lower Egypt.

**Khepresh**
This blue crown had a liturgical function. The pharaohs wore it during offerings to the gods.

**Shuty**
Formed of two large plumes, it was the crown of the god Amun. In the New Kingdom, the women of the royal house and some priests wore it.

**Atef**
The crown of Osiris, deity of the Underworld, combined the ostrich feathers of his cult with the Hedjet crown of Upper Egypt.

## Crown and materials

No mummy was ever found in the pyramids, and similarly the crowns of the different Egyptian dynasties did not withstand the passage of time, perhaps because of the materials from which they were made: wood, cloth, or papyrus. Before the discovery of Tutankhamun's tomb, the only royal adornment discovered was the Uraeus of Senusert II (see below), found in his pyramid in 1919.

## Emblems of authority

The authority of the supreme monarch was not only identified by the crown. Insignias, scepters, tiaras, headdresses, and other splendid adornments were part of an extensive collection that helped the pharaoh and his family to maintain a reverential distance from their subjects.

**Ritual beard**
This false beard was used by the pharaoh on grand occasions. It was identified with Osiris.

**Lavishness**
Lavishness, as exemplified by these sandals that belonged to Tutankamun, was the common denominator of royal attire.

**Sejem scepter**
Symbol of the force and magic energy of the king, his family, and the nobility. This image shows Queen Nefertari with the *sejem*.

**Nemes**
The *nemes* was a cloth headdress that was used in place of the crown during the pharaoh's daily activity. It was held on his head with a tiara.

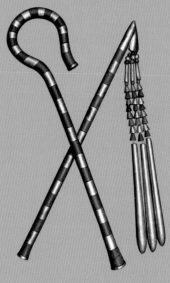

**Crook and flail**
The *heka* crook and the *nekhakha* flail were royal emblems. These pastoral implements signified that the pharaoh was the leader of his people.

**Uraeus**
A representation of the cobra goddess Wadjet, protector of the pharaohs, who were the only people permitted to wear it on their clothing.

**Diadems**
They served to display royal dignity with or without the *nemes*. They were used by the pharaoh's children.

# The construction work

The colossal effort that went into building the pyramids of Egypt is a clear reflection of the wealth and centralization of power that fell into the hands of the pharaohs in the Old Kingdom, as well as the organization in this society.

## The workforce

According to information from experts, the construction of the Pyramid of Khufu involved 4,000 stonecutters, stonemasons, stone transporters, smelters, brick manufacturers, and tool sharpeners.

## Organizational capability

The Egyptians must have had accurate planning and administration methods to manage the tasks—even more so, taking the precarious methods they used into consideration.

## The ramps

Each ramp used during the building process had to be equivalent to two-thirds the volume of the pyramid. It is thought they were made of adobe bricks filled with sand.

**Weight of the blocks**
It is estimated that the blocks of stone weighed between 2 and 15 tons.

# CHAPTER 4

# The Mystery Child who became Pharaoh

Tutankhamun lived 23 centuries ago, and died just 19 years old. The "resurrection" of the Egyptian pharaoh began in 1922 under the direction of English Egyptologist Howard Carter. Finding Tutankhamun's tomb was one of the greatest discoveries in archaeology.

The pharaohs of the Egyptian dynasty prepared, in life, for their journey to the afterlife. From the reign in approximately 3000 BCE of the first king Narmer (or Menes), who unified Upper and Lower Egypt, to the reign of the last, Ramesses XI, around 1078 BCE, all the kings sailed in the same eternal direction on board the solar barge. In the protective shadow of related gods, converted into terrestrial objects of incalculable value, the divine dead believed they would find safe harbor within the darkness of the necropolis built by teams of laborers, craftsmen, and scribes. But in the light of day, the tomb raiders never missed them. Only the niche of Tutankhamun, one of the last kings of the Eighteenth Dynasty from the New Kingdom, appeared to have saved him from destructive plunder. It was the greatest discovery in Egyptian archaeology.

### THE CONQUEST OF EGYPT

Along the River Nile a constellation of dynasties grew, leaving permanent footprints on the two riverbanks.

However, that magnificent fluvial valley gave life to a civilization that would never die in peace. A series of Berber, Nubian, Hellenic, Roman, Arabic, Umayyad, Abassid, Fatimid, Ayyubid, and Mamluk conquerors are added to the history of Egypt before the signal to disembark was given to the French republican army under the command of Napoleon Bonaparte, in July 1798. This military expedition included a group of scholars who contributed to the birth of Egyptology. The French philologist Jean-François Champollion (1790–1832) gave the coup de grâce to the active afterlife of the pharaohs by deciphering hieroglyphic writing in 1822. This came after centuries of a great lack of understanding about the monumental civilization buried under the sand, destroyed by invaders, buried and forgotten. Only the tomb raiders took advantage of the situation, dazzled by the golden journey of the royal mummies.

For the western world, the doors of perception to ancient Egypt were opened between 1707 and 1712 thanks to a French Jesuit priest, Claude Sicard (1677–1726), who discovered the ruins of Thebes and the necropolis of the Valley of the Kings.

The landing of Italian explorer Giovanni Battista Belzoni (1778–1823) in the Egyptian port of Alexandria

**The treasure**
The funerary mask of
Tutankhamun is the most
famous item from the tomb.

in June 1815, paved the way for pillage, in the service of the British consul to Egypt. Among the items that Belzoni transported to London were the bust of Ramesses II, weighing 7 tons, and the obelisk of Ptolemy IX, 23 ft/7 m tall. He also worked on opening the entrance to the Pyramid of Khafre and cleared the temple at Abu Simbel, which was covered in sand. In the Valley of the Kings, he penetrated the labyrinth of tombs. Very few of them contained mummies, but tombs such as that of Seti I were filled with enigmatic symbols and drawings.

### CHAMPOLLION: A VISIONARY
After Belzoni left Egypt and returned to Europe in 1819, convinced that nothing more remained to be discovered in the Valley of the Kings, Englishman John Gardner Wilkinson, following Champollion's method, was the first to read the pharaoh's name in 1827, and allocate a number to each of the known tombs. When Champollion journeyed to Egypt one year later, from August 1828 to December 1829, he deciphered the significance of the royal valley. "I am a man who has just been resurrected," he said, with an air of going beyond what was already known. He even established that the Valley of the Kings was the necropolis of the pharaohs of Thebes. And he moved time forward by saying that they would find tombs of the Eighteenth Dynasty there.

When Champollion died, only a handful of occasional explorers took his place in the role of shedding light on the marvels of ancient Egypt.

### THE LETTERS OF AMARNA
Meanwhile, in Amarna, 250 miles/400 km from the Valley of the Kings, other sensational discoveries were being made. Akhetaten (modern-day Amarna) became the new capital of the Egyptian Empire when it was founded by Akhenaten, who is believed to have been Tutankhamun's father, in order to deify the new cult of Aten (the "solar disc"). In 1887, some Egyptian farmers were looking for mud to make adobe bricks when, instead, they found hundreds of clay tablets bearing correspondence between pharaohs and kings of other regions. Over time, these archaeological treasures were slowly looted and distributed on the antiquities black market, but then science took over. The first archaeologist to visit the region to recover the tablets was legendary English Egyptologist William Matthew Flinders Petrie, in 1891. The tablets, which today number around 400 (half of which are in the Berlin Museum), provide valuable information about the period in which Tutankhamun, as well as his ancestors and predecessors on the throne, Pharaohs Akhenaten and Amenhotep III, lived. These writings in Akkadian cuneiform, the lingua franca of the time, add up to around 300 letters.

**← Wife and sister**
Ankhesenamun, Tutankhamun's wife, anoints the pharaoh with oil. This relief was discovered at the back of the king's golden throne. As the daughter of Akhenaten and Nefertiti, she was Tutankhamun's half-sister.

**→ The Discovery**
Howard Carter (kneeling) sees for the first time the sarcophagus of the pharaoh covered by four sepulchers, in the early part of 1924. Lord Carnarvon had died eight months earlier and never saw the mummy.

Known as "The Armana Letters," their discovery raises a range of questions: many of the messages are addressed to "the pharaoh," without further information, which makes it difficult to place them chronologically.

## RESURGENCE IN THE VALLEY

The Valley of the Kings rose from the ashes to enter the twentieth century. In 1891, Englishman Howard Carter, just 17 years old, arrived in Egypt. Son and grandson of artists, he soon earned a place in the world of archaeologists, drawing sketches of the tombs and familiarizing himself with the environment of the pharaohs. This was a time of extraordinary discoveries: those of Amenhotep II and Amenhotep III, among other kings, gave rise to the tourist invasion. From the city of Luxor (ancient Thebes) on the other bank of the Nile, some 3 miles/5 km to the west, endless excursions to the valley necropolis were organized. In 1900, Gaston Maspero, a self-taught and renowned archaeologist, named Carter general inspector of Upper Egypt. In 1902, a wealthy American called Theodore M. Davis (1837–1915), a retired lawyer and collector of *objets d'art*, decided to take part in the exploration of the pharaohs in Egypt. Gaston Maspero was glad to accept the money needed to invest in the badly worn treasures of the Antiquities Service in exchange for an excavation permit, which ran until 1915.

## ARCHAEOLOGY FEVER

The valley that "loved the silence" of another time, protected by a mountainous summit in the form of a pyramid, saw a team of people arrive, turning over all parts of the land in search of tombs. Howard Carter, as general inspector of the region, was responsible for archaeological management. His magnificent work in the Theban necropolis led Maspero, in 1904, to put him in charge of the jewel of Lower Egypt, the location of Memphis and Giza. It was indeed a prize, but he accepted with sadness, having to say goodbye to his beloved valley. The following year he stood up to a group of drunken French tourists, who were also very influential in diplomatic circles, and Carter was obliged to resign his post. However Maspero, with a guilty conscience for having dispensed with his services, put him in contact with English aristocrat George Herbert, fifth Earl of Carnarvon (1866–1923), who was looking for a chief of excavations. And so in 1907 began the story of a partnership that would end in glory.

At the beginning, they obtained permission to work in a little favored region of Thebes. But Carter never took his eye off the Theban necropolis. The undiscovered pharaoh Tutankhamun had been in the sights of the English Egyptologist ever since the discovery, by the Davis team in 1905, of an alabaster jar with Tutankhamun's name on it. While Carter and his team continued to reap the rewards of small successes

## Did the boy-king really govern?

In the eighth year of the reign of Akhenaten, the "living image of Aten" was born—Tutankaton, later Tutankhamun.

These were times of reform in the Eighteenth Dynasty of the New Kingdom. During the fifth year of governance, the son of Amenhotep III (1390–1353 BCE) and his first wife Tiye changed his name from Amenhotep IV to Akhenaten. With the new cult of Aten, the pharaoh removed power from other divinities, and especially from the clergy.

Akhenaten had six daughters with his first wife Nefertiti, but it was from a relationship with one of her sisters that Tutankhamun was born around 1341 BCE. In 1332, the son of Akhenaten was named pharaoh with the name of Tutankaton. A child of eight or nine years, he was influenced by two of the most powerful men of the time: Vizier Ay and General Horemheb. He married the third daughter of Akhenaten and Nefertiti, Ankhesenamun, eight years older than him. This marriage between half-brother and sister left two aborted foetuses of girls in the tomb of the pharaoh, who died in 1323.

The young pharaoh was forced to restore the cult of Amun and other gods from the fourth year of his reign and began to call himself Tutankhamun. Memphis returned to being the political capital and the religious center. Internal religious peace and external diplomatic equilibrium must have been significant factors in his government.

→**Ay, successor**
In Tutankhamun's tomb, Ay, his successor, can be seen before the mummy of the pharaoh.

(tombs of nobles, remains of temples, and objects of notable interest), Davis's excavation ambitions were waning. After 12 consecutive winters, with more than 30 tombs and the possible mummy of the controversial reformer Akhenaten in his possession, the old American came to the conclusion that both he and the valley were exhausted.

### CARTER'S HOUR

Carter obtained permission to excavate in the Valley of the Kings from 1914. World War I brought a halt to the beginning of his new adventure, but at the end of 1917 he got down to work. First, he had to clear away the huge mountain of rubbish that had accumulated in the region and take it out of the valley. Carter dreamed day and night about Tutankhamun. After five years of fruitless searching, Lord Carnarvon's patience and money were almost exhausted. The obstinacy of the Egyptologist, willing to bear all costs and ruin himself in the process, led the aristocrat to give him one more chance.

The final campaign began on November 1, 1922. Carter stopped paying attention to tip-offs from American Egyptologist Herbert Winlock, who believed he had seen the residual elements of embalming for Tutankhamun's funeral in the contents of a small tomb discovered by Davis in 1907. With the dynamism of a visionary, Carter began the desperate operation, searching just below the entrance to the tomb of Ramesses VI. On the third day of excavation the first step of a staircase covered in rubble appeared. Once it was cleared, Carter descended 16 stairs until he arrived at a sealed door. Through a hole he realized he could see a passageway filled with stones. Without losing his composure, he ordered the entrance to the tomb to be closed and sent a telegram to Lord Carnarvon to inform him of the discovery.

On November 26, Carter and Lord Carnarvon stood opposite the second sealed door at the end of the passageway. The name Tutankhamun left them in no doubt. Carter was able to put his head through a hole and see through to the other side, illuminating it with a lamp. Silence reigned. Lord Carnarvon broke it, asking Carter: "Can you see anything?" Dazzled by the glare of the gold, he responded, "Yes, wonderful things."

That antechamber led into an annex, open and filled with extraordinary objects in a disorganized state that made them think of a disturbed or small-scale robbery. It took years of work to organize all the material, but at two o'clock on the afternoon of February 17, 1923, Carter entered the funerary chamber. A grandiose chapel occupied almost all the space of the intact chamber, with walls and roof painted like an open book. Just to the side, another magnificent surprise: the treasure chamber. On February 3, 1924, he could see Tutankhamun's sarcophagus with three caskets inside. Inside these, the mask of gold covered the face and shoulders of the mummy wrapped in linen bandages. Lord Carnarvon had died on April 5 the year before and never got to see the most famous object of his final Egyptian adventure. The story of the supposed curse of Tutankhamun served to feed popular morbid curiosity. Carter had more luck. He died aged 64, perhaps frustrated at not having fulfilled his promise of discovering the tomb of Alexander the Great, and was buried quietly in a London cemetery.

## ↓Mosquito and a razor

A mosquito bit Lord Carnarvon at some point during the time he was in the tomb. A little while later, while shaving, he opened the wound, which became infected. He died within six weeks.

## Is there a pharaoh's curse?

The discovery of the tomb unleashed a storm of bad press. The explorers, they said, would be punished for their sacrilege. A series of deaths in later years, exaggerated by the press, fed the story of the curse. The mosquito bite on the face, the accidental nicking of the small bite with a straight razor, and the subsequent serious infection led to the death of Lord Carnarvon on April 5, 1923. The press did not waste any time printing the news with a headline that caused quite a stir: "Revenge of the pharaoh."

In 1892, German lexicographer Adolf Erman had translated a text found in the tomb of a noble from the Sixth Dynasty that read: "If you enter this tomb to take possession of death, I will capture you as if you were a wild bird and the great God will judge you for it." The deaths attributed to the curse were increasing and, judging by the sensational newspaper articles, this made them the "accursed." However, it did not stop Howard Carter from standing up against what he called "ridiculous stories."

## The death of Tutankhamun

On January 5, 2005, a national team from Egypt under the command of archaeologist Zahi Hawass, a director of the Supreme Board of Antiquities of Cairo, scanned the mummy for 15 minutes. After viewing the 1,700 images taken, the hypothesis of the pharaoh's assassination was unanimously discarded. The tomography made it possible to see that Tutankhamun had a fracture on the lower part of the left femur, and some scientists believe it to have caused the death of the pharaoh as it had left an open wound, which healed badly, became infected, and led to his early death. Later, DNA studies, published in 2010, showed that Tutankhamun had a bone disease and that he also suffered from malaria (plants used for alleviating the fever were found in the tomb), a combination that proved fatal for the pharaoh.

→**Zahi Hawass**
The Egyptologist directed the 2005 tomography.

# The Valley of the Kings

From the sixteenth to the eleventh century BCE, the Valley of the Kings was the preferred site for the pharaohs to be buried. Since then, 63 tombs and chambers have been explored. The largest, KV5, belonged to the sons of Ramesses II.

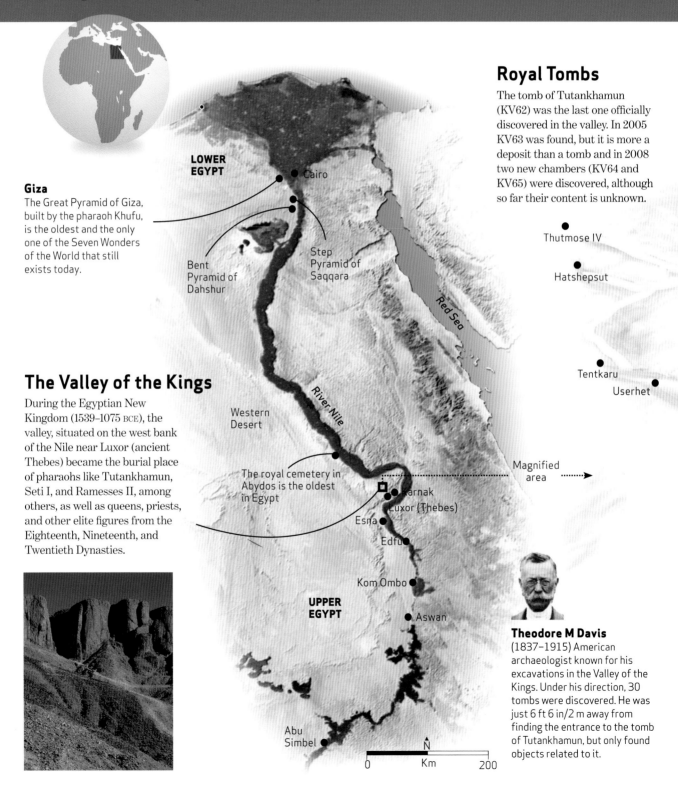

## Royal Tombs

The tomb of Tutankhamun (KV62) was the last one officially discovered in the valley. In 2005 KV63 was found, but it is more a deposit than a tomb and in 2008 two new chambers (KV64 and KV65) were discovered, although so far their content is unknown.

Thutmose IV

Hatshepsut

Tentkaru

Userhet

## Giza

The Great Pyramid of Giza, built by the pharaoh Khufu, is the oldest and the only one of the Seven Wonders of the World that still exists today.

LOWER EGYPT

Cairo

Bent Pyramid of Dahshur

Step Pyramid of Saqqara

Red Sea

## The Valley of the Kings

During the Egyptian New Kingdom (1539–1075 BCE), the valley, situated on the west bank of the Nile near Luxor (ancient Thebes) became the burial place of pharaohs like Tutankhamun, Seti I, and Ramesses II, among others, as well as queens, priests, and other elite figures from the Eighteenth, Nineteenth, and Twentieth Dynasties.

Western Desert

River Nile

The royal cemetery in Abydos is the oldest in Egypt

Magnified area

Karnak

Luxor (Thebes)

Esna

Edfu

Kom Ombo

UPPER EGYPT

Aswan

Abu Simbel

N

0    Km    200

## Theodore M Davis

(1837–1915) American archaeologist known for his excavations in the Valley of the Kings. Under his direction, 30 tombs were discovered. He was just 6 ft 6 in/2 m away from finding the entrance to the tomb of Tutankhamun, but only found objects related to it.

**What is the identity of the "young lady" of tomb KV35—could it be Tutankhamun's mother?**

Today, we know that the pharaoh's mother is the "young lady" from tomb KV35. Her identity, however, is still a mystery. We know she was the sister—both by father and mother—of Akhenaten, and she could have been one of his two younger sisters.

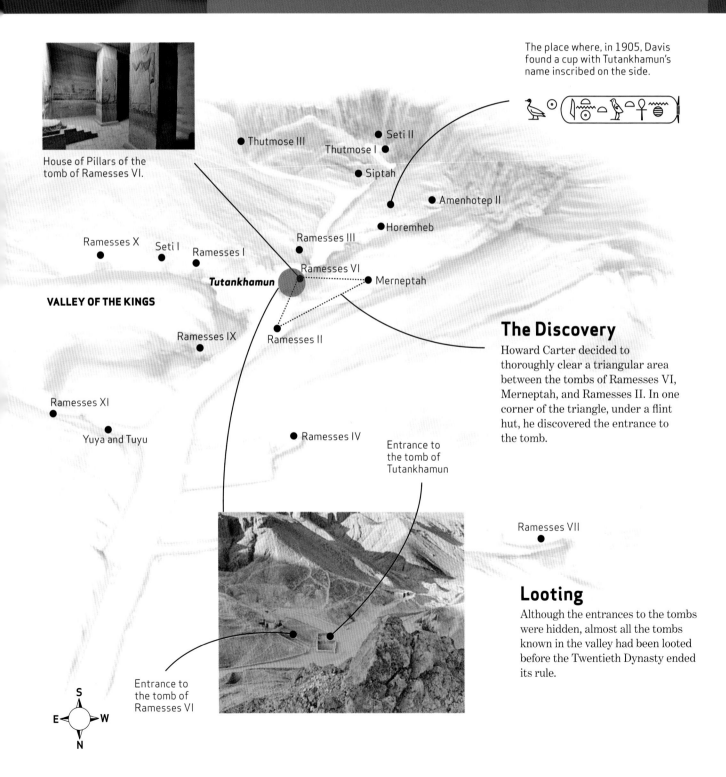

House of Pillars of the tomb of Ramesses VI.

The place where, in 1905, Davis found a cup with Tutankhamun's name inscribed on the side.

Thutmose III

Seti II

Thutmose I

Siptah

Amenhotep II

Horemheb

Ramesses X   Seti I   Ramesses I

Ramesses III

Ramesses VI

*Tutankhamun*   Merneptah

**VALLEY OF THE KINGS**

Ramesses IX   Ramesses II

Ramesses XI

Yuya and Tuyu

Ramesses IV

Entrance to the tomb of Tutankhamun

## The Discovery

Howard Carter decided to thoroughly clear a triangular area between the tombs of Ramesses VI, Merneptah, and Ramesses II. In one corner of the triangle, under a flint hut, he discovered the entrance to the tomb.

Ramesses VII

## Looting

Although the entrances to the tombs were hidden, almost all the tombs known in the valley had been looted before the Twentieth Dynasty ended its rule.

Entrance to the tomb of Ramesses VI

# The Tomb of Tutankhamun

It is small for the final resting-place of a pharaoh—a sign that it was not originally built for the young king. It follows the structure of the other tombs in the valley: a passageway leads to an antechamber, which in turn leads to the burial chamber.

## The lost tomb

Only luck kept the tomb of Tutankhamun intact. The young king's burial chamber was built in the Valley of the Kings, and 200 years later the Egyptians dug out the tomb of the pharaoh Ramesses VI above it. That work left the tomb of Tutankhamen covered with stones.

**Annex**
Behind the furniture another entrance was hidden, leading to an adjacent room. It was the last to be examined, as there were a variety of pieces crammed together.

**Entrance**
Hidden in the rocky soil of the Valley of the Kings, on November 24, 1922, the archaeologist Howard Carter, after five years of searching, discovered the entrance to the tomb of Tutankhamun.

**Antechamber**
The entire room was sealed by walls. When Carter broke through the first door, he found a room full of objects of the pharaoh, many of them made of gold or gilded carved wood.

5 ft 6 in/1.7 m

6 ft 6 in/2 m

**The Treasury**
Through the burial chamber, behind an open door, is the Treasury. A statue of Anubis guards the entrance and the Canonic Chapel is protected by four goddesses.

**The Canonic Chapel**
Contains the organs of the pharaoh. The liver, lungs, stomach, and intestines were removed from the body to keep them from degrading inside the mummy.

**The Canonic Chapel**

**Egyptian Goddess**

**Golden Vault**
It held four chests, or "jars"

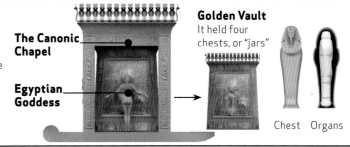

Chest    Organs

## Why were the objects in the various rooms of the tomb so disordered?

Even before entering the tomb, the archaeologist Carter realized that it had been desecrated, and his suspicions were confirmed when he found missing valuables. What was more difficult to understand was why the officials who returned to bring order to the grave did it so carelessly.

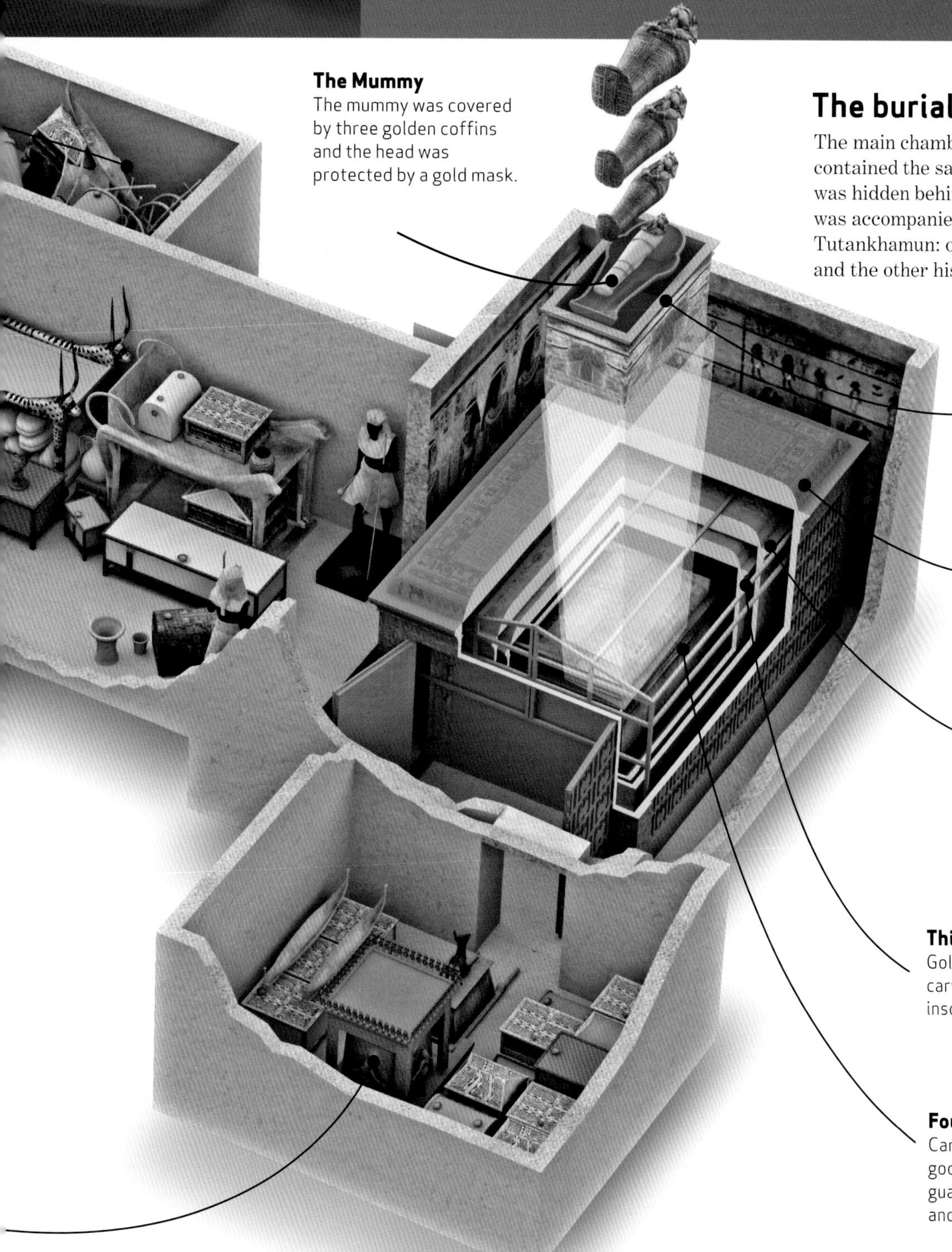

**The Mummy**
The mummy was covered by three golden coffins and the head was protected by a gold mask.

## The burial chamber

The main chamber of the tomb, which contained the sarcophagus of the pharaoh, was hidden behind a sealed wall. The entrance was accompanied by two life-size statues of Tutankhamun: one represented the young king and the other his *ka*, or "spirit."

**The sarcophagus**

**First Sanctuary**
The first tomb was made of carved cedar with blue earthenware fragments.

**Second Sanctuary**
The second was covered by a wooden frame draped with a cloth of fine linen.

**Third Sanctuary**
Gold, and, like the others, carved with religious inscriptions.

**Fourth Sanctuary**
Carved with images of gods—Isis and Nephthys guard the doors, and Nut and Horus, the roof.

# This was Tutankhamun

Led by Egyptologist Zahi Hawass, a team of archaeologists examined the mummy by tomography and provided further insights into the features of the pharaoh, also dispelling doubts about his mysterious death and delving into the details of his life.

## Advanced Technology

Tomography, used since the 1930s, is a diagnostic system that, instead of taking a single X-ray image (like conventional X-rays), takes several, and as a result provides a cross section of a body part. A scanner was invented in 1972 to do the job and process it digitally with a computer. In 1996, a technique to record volume was invented, making it possible to obtain 3-D images. This is the technology that was used in early 2005 to examine the tomb of the unfortunate Tutankhamun.

### The skull in detail

The king's head was scanned in slices just 0.62 mm thick, to show as much detail of its complex structure as possible.

## The color of his skin

The skin color of the pharaoh will probably be forever unknown to us. Restorers base their reconstructions on paintings and busts of Tutankhamun (left) and his close relatives. The color variations of the current Egyptian population were also used as a reference, and a medium shade was selected.

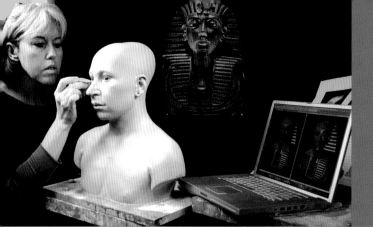

## Art and Science

Elisabeth Daynes, an artist specializing in reconstructing animals and people from ancient times, was commissioned to give the pharaoh the most accurate reconstruction of his face ever made, based on the tomography data.

## How the reconstruction was made

### Scanning
The scanner took about 1,700 digital X-ray images of the mummy, which were fed into a computer.

### 3-D Model
The software performs a volumetric projection, to make a three-dimensional picture.

### Reconstruction
From the 3-D image, forensic anthropologists work on an actual mold from the skull and reconstruct the pharaoh's face.

### The king's face
Supported by sculptures of the pharaoh and his family, a model was developed that resulted in a corrected reconstruction of Tutankhamun's appearance at the time of his death.

# Tutankhamun's funeral

The sudden death of the young sovereign forced the priests to prepare an "emergency" funeral, and many of the ornaments that were part of the funerary complex were not originally intended for Tutankhamun.

**Ankhesenamun**
The queen and widow was one of the leading figures in the funeral procession. She laid flowers on the mummy that could still be admired when Carter opened the sarcophagus.

**Canopic Shrine**
This is where the internal organs were stored. The brain was removed through the nose and discarded.

**Ay**
The counselor and successor of Tutankhamun, who married his widow, officiated as high priest and led the procession.

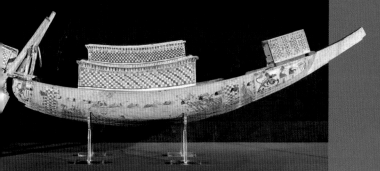

## Traveling to the afterlife

To the Egyptians, boats were the means of transport of the gods of heaven. The pharaohs were carried in funerary boats (pictured, a model found in the tomb of Tutankhamun) to their final resting-place in the Valley of the Kings, across the Nile from Thebes. It was believed that they would reach the afterlife in a boat.

## The funeral cortege

The procession was headed by the successor to the pharaoh, Ay, followed by members of the royal family, army generals, and officers of the court. The procession started from the temple city of Thebes (capital of the empire) finishing in the Valley of the Kings, across the Nile. Despite the large procession, the specific location of the tomb was maintained in utmost secrecy.

**The mourners**
A group of women brought up the rear in the main group, weeping and mourning the death of the pharaoh.

**The sarcophagus**
The mummy was brought to the tomb in its sarcophagus, then taken out for the final rituals to be performed before being deposited in the mortuary.

**Servants and slaves**
They were loaded with supplies for the tomb and hauled the sarcophagus and canopic shrine.

# CHAPTER 5

# A Continent Submerged in Time

Atlantis is one of history's greatest mysteries, starting with the fact that nobody knows whether or not it actually ever existed. The first mention of its appearance as a city dates back to the fifth century BCE.

The very existence of Atlantis is the subject of a centuries-old debate, with scholars and skeptics taking up opposing arguments. Whereas for some, there is no doubt about the historic relevance of this ancient civilization, for others (mostly celebrated historians) it is pure fiction idealized by Plato. Greek historian Pierre Vidal-Naquet states that Plato conceived his *Timaeus* (and subsequently *Critias*) as a radical criticism of Athens' maritime expansionism. To Vidal-Naquet, Plato did not speak of a war between Athens and Atlantis, but of an imaginary war between two Athens separated by a thousand years of history.

The Greek philosopher dedicated a large part of his dialogues to discussing Atlantis. Given the scarce number of ancient texts preserved, two texts from the same author quoting the same place, which is described in detail, proves that this was a topic to which his contemporaries must have given some kind of attention. It at least demonstrates the importance that Plato bestowed on the example given by this ancient civilization.

## THE VISION OF THE PHILOSOPHERS

There was no mention whatsoever of Atlantis until Plutarch, in his *Parallel Lives*, highlighted the formidable figure of Athenian lawmaker and traveler, Solon. He mentioned Sonchis of Sais and Psenophis of Heliopolis as Egyptian priests who taught Solon about the history of Atlantis. It would not be until the fifth century that Byzantine philosopher Proclus rescued the figure of Crantor of Cilicia who, at the start of the third century, wrote an exegesis on *Timaeus*, in which not only did he support the accuracy of Plato's account, but he even referred to one of his own visits to Egypt, where he consulted a number of stelae that confirmed Plato's account.

Furthermore, during the second century BCE, Posidonius, and a century later Strabo, discussed the account, believing it could be true. Their contemporary, Pliny the Elder, stated in his *Natural History* that, if what Plato had said was true, the Atlantic Ocean would have previously grown, submerging these vast lands.

In the Platonic dialogue, it is Critias to whom the account is attributed. He insisted a number of times on highlighting the historic nature of tales recounted and the society mentioned. Along these lines, he worked in detail on an in-depth and realistic description of his subject. The reference to Solon, who is

**Greek Foundations**
One of many legends placed the city beyond the Pillars of Hercules.

→**Crete**
The island of Crete is considered by some to represent the greatest splendor of the Minoan culture. There, the Palace of Minos was built, which houses artistic objects and constructions that are compatible with the legendary descriptions of Atlantis.

→→**Fresco**
The Minotaur is one of the oldest Greek legends and was much feared by Minoan culture, which flourished throughout the Aegean Sea well before Athens became the most famous city in Classical Greece.

claimed to have learned the tale from Egyptian priests in the city of Sais, gives the actual existence of the subject of his discussion even greater credibility.

It is strange that the story invoked by Plato mentions that the first contact between Athens and Atlantis was the result of a warlike conflict in which the two united against a region, which must have been Attica given the period in which he sets the story, 9,000 years before Solon (around 638–558 BCE). Let's do the sums: around six or seven hundred years before, the Mycenaean culture was extinguished as a result of the Dorian invasion. Today, almost nothing remains of Agamemnon's Mycenaean walls. Nonetheless, they were in no doubt about the feats of Achilles and Odysseus during the Trojan War.

Some time before this period (around 3,500 years ago), the only activities recorded in the region with similar characteristics to those described in the case of Atlantis are the Cretan raids. They were launched from a large island, although on a different scale to the amazing size Critias attributed to Atlantis, which is claimed to have been organized into a highly developed "thalassocracy" (a political system based on domination of the seas). The travels of the Minoan people throughout the blue backdrop of the Aegean Sea during the second millennium BCE have given rise to countless tales, which have come to represent the body of ancient Greek tradition. From a strictly chronological perspective, this saga is light years away from the period mentioned in the Platonic dialogue. It

cannot be denied that notions of chronology overwhelmed ancient populations. Without claiming originality, it is worth mentioning that the first Western text that we consider as historiographical, or at least the mythical founder of such studies, belongs to the generation preceding Plato: it is attributed to Herodotus of Halicarnassus, author of *The Histories*.

## AN OBLONG-SHAPED ISLAND

Critias describes an oblong-shaped island measuring 3,000 by 2,000 stations, approximately 325 x 217 miles/523 x 349 km. The island of Crete is around 186 miles/300 km in length by around 37 miles/60 km at its widest point. The Minoan civilization left records of its existence dating back 6,000 years BCE. Furthermore, there are numerous remains of its splendor that date back to midway through the third millennium BCE. Archaeology has established that this civilization suffered two catastrophes: midway through the fifteenth century and toward the end of the eleventh century BCE. The latter could be linked to the invasion of the Dorians in the eastern Mediterranean, or perhaps with a conquest of the seas: in any case, there is evidence of a tsunami, perhaps caused by a volcanic eruption on a nearby island.

Could Critias be making reference to the Cretans in the dialogue documented by Plato? There is a considerable amount of time between the two events. Some researchers have put forward alternative theories: if Solon received this information

from Egyptian priests, this would contaminate the data available given that the calendar in question was Egyptian, the accuracy of which has been challenged. However, this objection is hardly convincing. Perhaps instead, it would be worth considering the maritime battles in an area that had only recently experienced the Neolithic revolution.

To this day, the precision of the sentence uttered by Critias still confuses: "Let me begin by observing first of all, that nine thousand was the sum of years that had elapsed..." Nine thousand: this hardly provides us with an exact date. It would appear more a product of speculation than a result of consulting the "manuscripts given to his great-grandfather Dropides by Solon," which Critias claimed to have in his possession.

It is irrefutable that there is more than just one chronological issue. In the dialogue, it is asserted that the huge island of Atlantis was to be found beyond the Pillars of Hercules. And these pillars, according to all classical sources, are located between Gibraltar and the northern tip of Morocco. By the power of deduction, Atlantis would therefore have been located in the Atlantic. The similarity of the names is not to be taken as evidence of a link, given that the ocean was so named owing to the supposed existence of the island. Perhaps close to the African coast, like the Canary Islands: could this volcanic archipelago represent the remains of the island, claimed to be the same size as Libya in ancient times? Could the Azores and Madeira be the remnants of the island that sank into the sea?

On the other hand, it is true that there is no way to prove the vast majority of mythical Greek references to the island; for centuries, it was believed that the narrative set out by Homer in the *Iliad* was mythical, until amateur archaeologist Heinrich Schliemann discovered the city of Troy in Turkey in 1870, at the site of modern-day Hisarlik. And what's more, until archaeologist Arthur Evans unearthed the city of Knossos, in Crete, in the twentieth century, Daedalus, the Minotaur, and King Minos himself were believed to be nothing but legend. Today, they are parts of a substantial culture about which scholars hope to expand their understanding. Does this represent irrefutable proof of the historic nature of the Atlantis myth? No, but it does pose a serious challenge to any claim that Atlantis is purely make-believe.

### THE ATLANTIS MYTH

The story of Atlantis is short. It is merely made up of the dialogues transcribed by Plato and the comments of his contemporaries and immediate successors. However, there is considerably more to the myth than meets the eye. It is difficult to establish exactly when it first came to light, although it is irrefutable that the discovery of America by the Spanish awoke a whole range of speculation to this end. Since then, the attributing of Atlantic origins to the Aztecs, Mayas, and Incas has become commonplace in literary speculation. The most extraordinary part of this case is that speculation

**↑Guimar crater**
On Tenerife, evidence of old maritime cultures has been found; some have linked the evidence to Atlantis.

## Evidence of its existence?

During the Middle Ages, a theory that identified the Canary Islands, Madeira, and the Azores as the corners of a triangular island, located to the east of the Strait of Gibraltar, gained popular support. The island of Tenerife is an almost perfect cone, the center of which is dominated by the Teide, and the entire island occupies the slopes of the volcano that, for many geologists and volcanologists, bears all the hallmarks of having experienced a tremendous volcanic eruption accompanied by an enormous earthquake. Clay residues, extracted from a depth of 4.5 miles/7.2 km, gave strength to the hypothesis that part of the mainland sank.

A series of artifacts found on the Canary Islands date back to the fifth century BCE and link its past occupants with solar cultures that were typical of Cretans and Phoenicians. Spiral carvings, dating much farther back in time than those of the Canaanites, were associated with the design that represented the city of Atlantis in the Platonic Dialogue.

In the mid-nineteenth century, the legend of Atlantis fascinated contemporaries, leading to debate about exactly where it had been located. United States congressman Ignatius Donnelly wrote *The Antediluvian World* in 1883, a text that suggested that Atlantis had once stood at the heart of the Atlantic Ocean.

is still rife today. Whereas the first historical mention of the island seeks to disparage it as perverse and degenerate, new versions coined by German Romantics, as modernity progressed, have presented it as a lost paradise. Much of this can be attributed to the belated awakening of many European nationalities toward the end of the eighteenth century. This was so in the case of the great German Romantic poets, such as Novalis (1772–1801), and Italian poets such as Count Gian Rinaldo Carli (1720–95). With the strengthening of the Christian faith after the downfall of the Roman Empire, the Bible became almost the only viewpoint from which the dawn of European humanity could be regarded. It is believed that Italian and German nationalities sought Atlantic origins to escape what they viewed as the constraints of Jewish ancestry. During the nineteenth century, Jules Verne and Pierre Benoit bestowed a new character upon Atlantis, converting it into a utopia, a vision that was required for a society that was experiencing the brutality of early capitalism.

What's missing is contemporary history. The last 50 years have been witness to the spread and proliferation of science fiction. The powerful Soviet production of the 1970s was met with an equally significant response from Western Europe and the United States. As part of this strong movement, the myth of Atlantis returned to the spotlight, on library bookshelves and, moreover, TV screens in the form of documentaries and feature films. Recent years have also seen archaeological, terrestrial, and submarine expeditions, with new technologies applied to analyzing the seabed in addition to both aerial and satellite photography. In all, significant investment has been made to resolve the mystery.

Did Atlantis ever exist? In search of this utopia, more and more other previously unknown lost cities, which were not part of the original investment, have been found. For centuries, Atlantis has existed beyond its tangible existence. Philosophers, scientists, archaeologists, historians, and a whole host of storytellers and opportunists have recreated a wide range of different theories. The Platonic Dialogues created an enigma that has fascinated the world to this very day. The countless astonishing treasures found under water at all latitudes have served to reinforce the search that has seen a coming together of historic and cultural patrimony with adventure. However, the continuing mystery that enshrines the lost city can also be attributed to moral lessons set out in the Platonic discourse.

A number of authors have agreed that the descriptions that appear in *Timaeus* and *Critias* do not address a real civilization, but, on the contrary, they represent an ideal that humans could reach by correctly adhering to the processes of good governance, mutual respect, and good neighborliness. Thus, to Plato, the richness and excellence of Atlantis are born of the harmonious relationship between the Gods, nature, and humans, resulting in a triumphant and progressive social state. However, Plato created this exceptional achievement of Atlantean society to raise awareness of the terrible consequences of breaching the basic principles from which it was born. Thus, when its kings became ambitious and in war sought a way to satisfy their greed for material and possessions, the great island succumbed, destroyed by volcanoes, earthquakes, and huge waves. Although the Greek philosopher described the destruction of Atlantis as a punishment handed down by angry Gods, the moral can still be applied to this day.

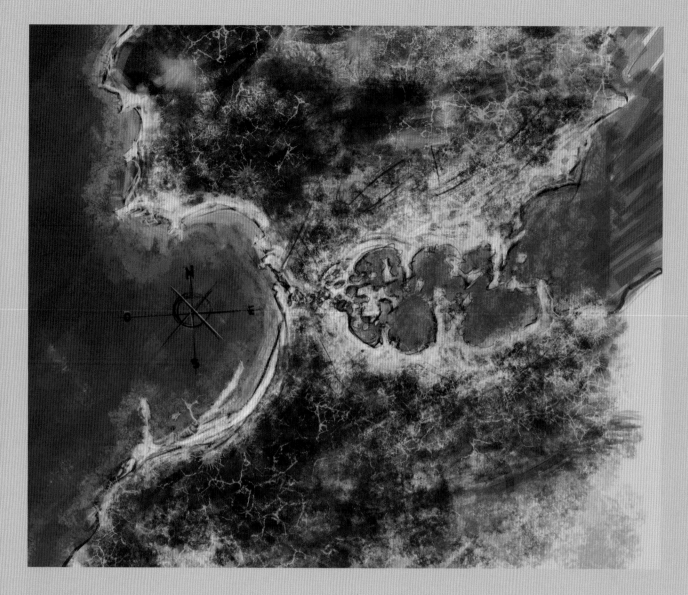

## Tartessos: the lost Atlantis?

Those who support a link between Atlantis and the Kingdom of Tartessos, a millennia-old culture to the south of the Iberian Peninsula, believe that the region's geography was completely different 11,500 years ago. At the time, the Atlantic and the Mediterranean were 330 ft/100 m deep and it was possible to walk from Africa to Spain, with Spain and Libya connected by an archipelago that extended almost 373,000 square miles/600,000 km². The end of the Ice Age resulted in a significant increase in the total surface area occupied by the sea and a decrease in the amount of emerging land. Around 9,000 years BCE, the sea grew suddenly and Atlantis disappeared underwater forever. Close to Cap Spartel in Morocco, a submerged island was found 150 ft/46 m below the surface, which French investigator Jacques Collina-Girard claims belonged to Atlantis.

Professor Paulino Zamarro claims that he can prove how the Strait of Gibraltar was created around 7,500 years BCE, when the waters of the Atlantic violently flowed into the Mediterranean. To the far east, it breached the Dardanelles, flooding the Black Sea. Zamarro believes, just like Greek investigators, that the island of Atlantis was in fact in the Aegean, close to the Cyclades, and a violent eruption could be linked to a tidal wave that battered the islands and coastline of the Aegean Sea.

Notwithstanding, Tartessos has philosophy on its side. The word "Atlas" means "intermediate space" in Iberian, Greek, and Berber languages. Atlantis would therefore mean "city in the intermediate space."

**↑United**
A re-creation that shows Africa and Europe united by the Strait of Gibraltar, where many place the "Pillars of Hercules."

# Atlantis according to Plato

The Greek philosopher wrote about a circular-shaped marine city inhabited 9,000 years ago. Its canals, palaces, fountains, and gardens became a myth that continues to intrigue explorers throughout the world to this day.

## The city of canals

The main features of the city are the concentric circles of land, separated by lanes of water. The central island was occupied by the Acropolis, a racetrack, and houses in which the loyalist troops lived.

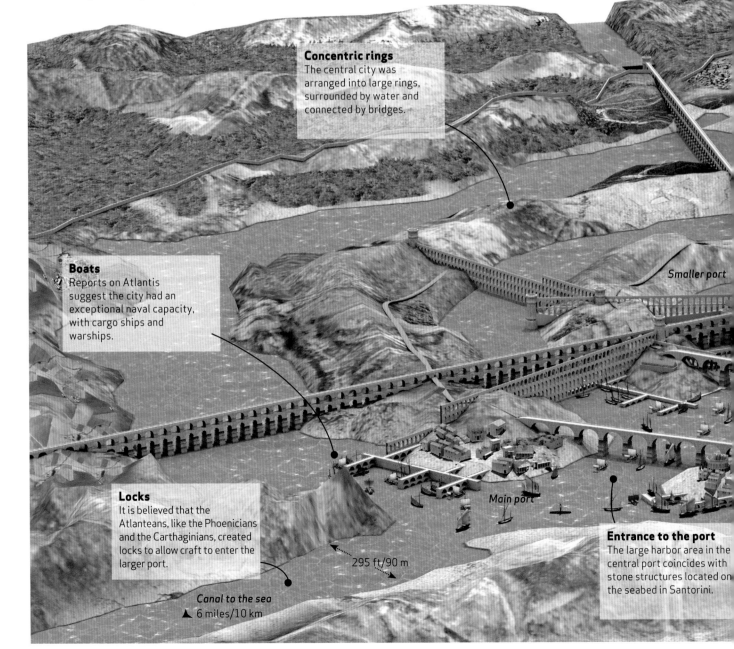

**Concentric rings**
The central city was arranged into large rings, surrounded by water and connected by bridges.

**Boats**
Reports on Atlantis suggest the city had an exceptional naval capacity, with cargo ships and warships.

*Smaller port*

**Locks**
It is believed that the Atlanteans, like the Phoenicians and the Carthaginians, created locks to allow craft to enter the larger port.

*Main port*

**Entrance to the port**
The large harbor area in the central port coincides with stone structures located on the seabed in Santorini.

295 ft/90 m

*Canal to the sea*
▲ 6 miles/10 km

# Did this mythical circular city really exist in southern Spain?

Scientists from different specialist areas have discovered evidence of a circular formation beneath the Doñana wetlands, in Cadiz, Spain. Satellite images published by National Geographic suggest that Atlantis could have sunk there.

## The government of Atlantis
The island was governed by ten kings, originally five sets of twins, who met every five or six years, alternately. They passed judgment on those who had breached the laws posted on a column in front of the Temple of Poseidon, who was the most powerful deity there. In fact, according to Plato, all the twins were sons of Poseidon that he had with Cleito.

## Royal palace
Plato states that two temples were to be found inside the Acropolis, encompassed by a kind of fence of pure gold.

## Infrastructure
Walls, columns, and floors were covered in orichalcum, a metal precious to Atlanteans. Statues and fountains completed the decorations.

Aerial view of the city

**CITADEL**

**SMALLER LAND MASS**

*Second Port*

**LARGER LAND MASS**

## Communication
A complex infrastructure of walkways and aqueducts connected the entire city.

## Plato
In his two most renowned works, *Timaeus* and *Critias*, this Greek philosopher (428–347 BCE) proposed that Atlantis existed, though no further records about the city have been found. Plato died having completed work on the latter dialogue.

# The location of Atlantis

There are three main theories about the location of the lost city: the first claims that it was on the Iberian Peninsula, the second puts it somewhere in the Atlantic Ocean, and the third in the Mediterranean or Aegean Sea.

## Those supporting the Iberian theory

**1** **1592**
Priest Juan de Mariana was the first to link Plato's Atlantis to Spain.

**2** **1673**
José Pellicer de Ossau Salas y Tovar linked Tartessos with Atlantis. He maintained that the island on which the Cleito temple stood was at the mouth of the Guadalquivir River.

**3** **1801**
Writer Fabre d'Olivet stated that Atlantis was located in the Western Mediterranean, between Spain and Morocco.

**4** **1803**
Naturalist Bory de Saint-Vincent claimed that the Canary Islands are part of the missing island.

**5** **1874**
Geographer and archaeologist E.F. Berlioux linked the mythical island with the Atlas Mountains in Morocco, and Gibraltar.

**6** **1911**
Juan Fernández Amador de los Ríos affirmed that Atlantis is Tartessos and the Iberian Peninsula.

**7** **1920**
Geologist A.L. Rutot mantained that Atlantis was located in Morocco.

**8** **1922**
Archaeologist Adolf Schülten believed that Atlantis was Andalusia and the kingdom of the Tartessos.

**9** **1928**
Elena Wishaw, Director of the Ancient Mediterranean Research Association, claimed to have located the submerged ruins of the capital of Atlantis on the coast of Cadiz.

**10** **1984**
Philologist Jorge María Ribero-Meneses highlighted the link between Tartessos, the Tartars, and the Titans, and that the Egyptians and Phoenicians originally came from Cantabria.

**11** **1994**
Jorge Díaz-Montexano stated that the center of Atlantis was the south of Spain (Tartessos) and Morocco.

**12** **2001**
Jacques Collina-Girard mantained that Atlantis was to be found in the mouth of the Strait of Gibraltar, on Spartel Island.

ATLANTIC OCEAN

Yucatán Coast (Mexico)

Bimini Islands (Bahamas)

Lake Titicaca (Bolivia)

## Was the island of Thera the center of Atlantis?

Several pieces of evidence can be used to back up this theory: a) Plato described palaces spread over several levels, like the palaces of Thera; b) the blocks of gypsum must have shone in the sun "like silver," a link to Timaeus; c) Santorini is at the center of a volcano that exploded during the sixteenth century BCE and caused a tsunami that affected the entire region; and d) walls and canals such as the ones described by Solon appear in frescoes at Akrotiri (Santorini).

Dogger Bank

North Sea

South Brittany

Mediterranean Sea (around Marseille, France)

The Azores

Doñana National Park, Cadiz (Spain)

Mediterranean Sea

Morocco

Canary Islands

Strait of Gibraltar

Atlas Mountains

Sahara Desert

Troy (Turkey)

Santorini (Greece)

Crete (Greece)

Aegean Sea

Cape Verde Islands

## Those in favor of the Mediterranean and Aegean Sea theory

**13 1907**
British scholar K.T. Frost highlighted the possibility that Minoan Crete could have been the true Atlantis.

**14 1965**
Spyridon Marinatos, head of the Greek Archaeological Service, connected the eruption at Thera, modern-day Santorini, with the demise of Atlantis.

**15 2000**
Axel Hausmann, a physicist at Aachen University, mantained that Atlantis was located on the seabed, between Sicily and Malta, at a depth of 328 ft/100 m.

**16 2004**
Paulino Zamarro suggested that the mythical civilization was located on the modern-day Cyclades Islands and Crete.

## Those supporting the Atlantic theory

**17 1644**
John Swan held that Atlantis was to be found in the Atlantic.

**18 1655**
German Jesuit Athanasius Kircher suggested that Atlantis was located between Europe and America.

**19 1912**
Heinrich Schliemann placed Atlantis close to the Azores and Madeira.

**20 1960**
Ignatius Donnelly, a U.S. congressman, undertook research that placed Atlantis in the Azores.

**21 1980**
The theory linking Atlantis to the Bahamas (Bimini) is supported by several writers: Dr. J. Manson, Dr. Valentine, Charles Berlitz and P. Carnac.

**22 1982**
Helmut Tributsch, a professor at the University of Berlin, supported a theory that the island was located in southern Brittany, on the island of Gavrinis.

**23 1990**
Jean Deruelle proposed that Atlantis was in the North Sea, at Dogger Bank.

# Cultural heritage

The discovery of the ruins of the Palace of Minos, in Crete, facilitated the reconstruction of Minoan culture, which preceded the Mycenaean culture and is associated by many researchers with Atlantean origins.

## Sculptures

Minoan art did not leave large-scale artifacts, although numerous statuettes measuring between 3/4–8 in/ 2 –20 cm have been found. Motifs tend to express a certain level of naturalism in civilization, with animals and people of both genders dressed in gold, ivory, and bronze, although various other pieces in nacre, ceramic, and marble have also been found. Animal figures are linked to religion, and the figure of the bull stands out in particular, revered as the incarnation of male fertility.

**Offering table**
Found at Knossos, made from black ceramic, its Linear A inscriptions are of particular interest; this was a Cretan writing particularly used in official religious or palatial ceremonies.

## Paintings

The numerous frescoes were the decoration of choice at the Palace of Minos. Their lively colors were found spread across the main walls and columns of the complex. The notable similarity in lines, color nuances, and motifs with those found during the 1960s in Akrotiri (Santorini) reinforces the concept of a close link between the two cultures, identified as descendants of the Atlanteans.

# The great Cretan discovery

In 1900, British archaeologist Arthur Evans discovered the ruins of the palace in Crete, which he identified with the legendary labyrinth of the bull at Minos and King Knossos. The characteristics of the building itself and the objects found in it unveiled the development of a pre-Hellenic culture between 3000 and 1400 BCE.

## Phaistos Disk

Minoan jewelers produced works in gold that contained inscriptions. In particular, this disk shows a form of linear writing, that has yet to be deciphered, read in a spiral format.

## Jewelry

Necklaces, earrings, and bracelets were made, especially in gold. It is believed that some pieces were inscribed with the name of their owner.

## Jars

The sizes and shapes of the jars, made using clay and ceramic, were dependent on their purpose—from collecting and preserving water and oil, to storing seeds and grain.

## Shapes and motifs

The vases were long, with a wide mouth, a small base, and wider in the middle. Decorations range from rectilinear to curved, with images of elongated leaves and stylized waves.

## Snake queen

Made from glazed ceramic, this feminine figure was depicted wearing a dress and jewelry; she represents a god or priestess, and it is believed she represented female fertility.

# CHAPTER 6

# An Epic of the Bronze Age

The basis of a Greco-Roman epic, the Trojan War was narrated in a series of poems of which only two have survived intact: Homer's *Iliad* and *Odyssey*. But did Troy really exist? Was there really a war?

An eighth-century BCE Greek poet called Homer gave wings to an epic oral poem about the legend of the Trojan War, which has become a masterpiece of Western literature. Although legends are not history, Troy has become part of a past worthy of recollection where few can distinguish the line between fact and fiction. In the hexameter verses of the *Iliad*, a tale unfolds that is told through 24 epic songs with tragic overtones, where the divine and the human merge with the war horse and death, both in anger and in pity. The stories of this universe, inhabited by gods and heroes, spread by word of mouth between singers until they took a more fixed form in Homer's poems in the *Iliad* and the *Odyssey*.

In the *Iliad*, the singer begins the tale in the tenth and final year of the Trojan War, in the middle of a plague sent by the god Apollo to the camp of the Achaeans, who were the second invaders from the North (before the Dorians and after the Ionians) and spoke an Indo-European tongue from ancient Greece. Mindful of their Greek identity in a period of Mycenaean civilization (1600–1200 BCE), in Peloponnese, they put an end to the brilliant Minoan seafaring civilization that spanned eleven centuries (2600–1500 BCE), and whose developments in the Middle and Late periods (from 2000 to 1570 BCE and from 1570 to 1400 BCE) are represented in the Minos Palace, on the island of Crete.

Bleaker still seemed the future for the Achaean military expedition that set off to punish the Trojans because of the alleged abduction of Helen, wife of Menelaus, King of Sparta, by Paris, son of Priam, the King of Troy: it was a conflict that mobilized immortals, albeit with human emotions, and divine heroes, the puppets of Olympus.

### SETTING THE SCENE FOR WAR

In the poem, the war is situated in Asia Minor, next to the western entrance of the Hellespont, the modern-day Dardanelles Strait, which connects the Aegean Sea to the Sea of Marmara and the Black Sea. The Homeric poems narrate an apparently ancient story, but in reality they describe the eighth-century BCE society in which the author lived at the end of the Dark Ages and the beginning of the Archaic period. One thousand ships set sail from the Boeotian port of Aulis for Troy, under the command of Menelaus' brother, the king of kings, Agamemnon, King

**Key dates**
Ancient works of art that illustrate details of the Trojan War, such as this frieze discovered in Turkey, are enormously valuable for researchers.

of Mycenae, an area of such great importance that this period and civilization is known as Mycenaean. The ships came from Athens, Salamina, Argos, Arcadia, Lacedemonia, Mirmidonia, and Crete, united to avenge the kidnapping of Helen. Opposed were the Trojans, with their Dardanian Pelasgian, Thracian, and Phrygian allies. The gods pulled on the strings of tragedy, deceiving the humans, making alliances with different groups, meting out death and fighting in Olympus. But was there really a Trojan War, or is it just a fantasy in verse?

### REASONS FOR THE OUTBREAK OF WAR

The gods of Olympus never stopped playing dice. During the wedding between the mortal Peleus and the sea-goddess Thetis, parents of Achilles, Eris, goddess of Discord, threw a golden apple for the fairest goddess, which caused a dispute between Aphrodite, Athena, and Hera. Zeus intervened, calling on the handsome mortal Paris to resolve the divine question. Aphrodite took the title in exchange for granting him the love of Helen of Sparta, a woman noted for her beauty. The die was cast. The Trojan War soon erupted.

Some spoke of kidnap, others of infidelity. Heroes and gods took sides immediately. At the summit of Gargarus, Zeus turned the tide of war. Feeling the full wrath of Achilles and the Trojans' victorious attack, Poseidon, god of the sea, and Hera, wife and sister of Zeus, plotted to change the situation.

And so Hera charmed the father of the gods who fell into her amorous trap, and after satisfying his sexual desires, Zeus surrendered to a deep sleep. His brother Poseidon took advantage of this to help the forces of Agamemnon. When he woke, Zeus put things back in their place. In view of the imminent defeat, Achilles permitted Patroclus, at the head of the troops of Myrmidon, to help the Achaeans. His attack on the wall of Troy defended by the god Apollo provoked his anger, and he roused Hector, brother of Paris, to war.

The *Iliad* nears the end of the story with the death of Patroclus at the hands of Hector, which unleashes a fresh outburst of anger from Achilles, who, after being reconciled with Agamemnon, decides to return to battle. In the assembly of the gods there is free reign for everyone to support their mortal heroes. Achilles and Hector take the leading roles, appealing to their men during military action, on the eve of a singular battle at the foot of the large stone walls of Troy, where "the light-footed one" kills "the defender of the fatherland."

In the final song, Homer's tragic and heroic vein continues and ends in a gesture of compassion and mercy. From an Achilles who was a slave to his anger after the funeral of his friend Patroclus, and capable of insulting the lifeless body of Hector, followed another more sympathetic Achilles, ready to receive the pleadings of the Trojan king Priam and return to

him the body of his son. The *Iliad* ends in Priam's home with the celebration of the funeral rites of Hector, tamer of horses. The later *Odyssey* is also composed of 24 songs, although they are more optimistic and have a happy ending, narrating the adventures of Odysseus, head of the Cephalonians in the Achaean camp, during the hazardous journey back to Ithaca, his homeland, after his victory in the Trojan War.

## FROM POETRY TO ARCHAEOLOGY

This poetic story of success appeared to have some real basis when German Heinrich Schliemann (1822–90), with the *Iliad* as his guide, led a team of people on an excavation at the top of Mount Hissarlik, located on the northwest peninsula of Anatolia. They were lands belonging to the brother of Frank Calvert (1828–1908), an English consular civil servant who made his first trenches there, taking the instincts of Scottish journalist Charles Maclaren (1782–1866) into consideration, the first to put Troy in the region of Hissarlik. Using quite unorthodox excavation methods, Schliemann brought to light various layers superimposed over other Troys. With no reliable studies on archaeological strata, Schliemann decided that he had discovered Homer's Troy, and he mistook precious objects, which he wrongly took for the treasure of Priam. In 1882, he joined forces with German archaeologist Wilhelm Dörpfeld (1853–1940), who organized the different

## Was Helen the cause of the conflict?

The kidnapping of Helen initiated the fall of Troy. In the legend of Paris kidnapping Helen from her husband Menelaus's home in Sparta and taking her to his Trojan kingdom, the negative aspect of the seductress and the mortal danger of her beauty were highlighted, while few spoke of the wicked role played by the handsome, thoughtless seducer, Paris.

But was there, hidden between the lines of the Homeric verse, a war provoked by financial interests? In that world of perpetual metaphor, a great crisis arose in the second half of the thirteenth century BCE, when the Hittites lost control of the copper mines to the east of Anatolia at the hands of the Assyrians. To overcome this setback they seized Cyprus, which was rich in minerals, and established an economic blockade in the eastern Mediterranean that affected the ships of the Achaeans and Mycenaeans who were considered enemies.

Homer's "Mycenae rich in gold" was the swan song. Because of the Hittite blockade, Mycenaean civilization entered a period of decline, marked by internal wars which, at the end of that century, ended with piracy and expeditions to recover commercial trade routes. One of its main objectives may have been Troy, as it was an obligatory stop from the Aegean to the Black Sea. And the Homeric "to fight for Helen and all her treasure" may have been a simple justification that hid the real cause of the conflict.

→**Suitors**
Encouraged by the fame of her beauty, men from all over Greece tried to win Helen.

layers of deposits at Hissarlik until he had a total of nine from top to bottom: from the first New Roman Ilion of the first century to the last from c. 3000 BCE. In 1890, Dörpfeld located the city of the *Iliad* at Troy level VI, although his American colleague Carl Blegen (1887–1971), director of excavations carried out by the University of Cincinnati between 1932 and 1938, believed it to be Troy VII after observing the remains of fire as a result of the armed conflict that caused its destruction. From 1988, a multinational and multidisciplinary team recommenced the excavations under the direction of the German Manfred Korfmann (1942–2005), from the University of Tübingen, and the American Brian Rose, from the University of Cincinnati, and confirmed Blegen's observations.

Before his death in 2005, Korfmann echoed the advances made by his team that allowed them to respond positively to the question about whether or not the Trojan War actually took place. He even toyed with the idea that more than one armed conflict had occurred in the same place at the end of the Bronze Age. It was clear that Troy suffered several attacks and was obliged to defend itself over and over again, as shown by repairs made to the walls of the citadel and the efforts made to increase and fortify them.

### CHANGE OF IDEAS

The new excavations brought to light the remains of an urban settlement outside the permanent fortification, which became known as the "low city." As a result, there is a difference of opinion with respect to the size and population of Troy – until then limited to the region of the citadel. This increase, which agrees more with the source of the *Iliad*, also reinforced the idea that it was a kingdom of irrefutable geopolitical importance. Unlike Schliemann, Dörpfeld, and Blegen, who had placed Troy in Greek territory, Korfmann and Rose's team placed the Trojans as a power within the Hittite confederation to the northeast of Asia Minor—an alliance frowned upon by the Achaeans and Mycenaeans, the Hittites' rivals in the region. They each avoided direct confrontation, preferring to engage in wars against common allies. Troy, immersed in the "military games" of the superpowers, paid the price for this dangerous friendship.

In fact, Troy represented both a threat and a temptation to the Greeks (Achaeans and Mycenaeans) of the time. It was a dagger aimed at the heart of Greece and a bridge to the centre of the Hittite kingdom; it was also the most desirable prize and close on the horizon. It was a crucial point in the region, not least because it was an important trading station for Syria, Egypt, and, occasionally, the Caucasus and Scandinavia. It was clear to everyone that "it was not a fruit that was easy to pick," as Barry Strauss, Greek and Roman military history specialist at Cornell University, noted in the introduction of his book, *The Trojan War, A New History* (2006). On one side were the invaders who lived a wretched existence in tents and shelters. On the other were the Trojans, who basked in well-being, wealth, and refinement. But the Greeks had at least three advantages: they were less civilized, more patient, and more mobile, mainly thanks to their boats. Enough to win.

## Was the Trojan Horse real?

The Trojan Horse is mainly thought to be a fantastic construction of the poet Homer to hide the less suggestive force of a simple siege engine. Either way, there is no other horse in the history of war tactics as famous as the Trojan Horse. Homer referred to this cunning strategy retrospectively in song eight of the *Odyssey*, which narrates the adventures of Odysseus returning to his homeland Ithaca after having participated in the Trojan War.

The story of the horse came to light in the palace of Alcinous, king of the Phaeacians, where Odysseus was staying. He asked the blind singer Demodocus to sing about the "wooden horse built by Epeius with the help of Athena." It transpired that the Achaeans took to the sea after burning their own camps, while Odysseus and his men hid inside a wooden horse that the Trojans had dragged to the Acropolis. They first thought of destroying it, but finally decided to leave it as an offering to the gods. That was their undoing as "the bravest Argives causing destruction and death to the Teucers" came out of the horse.

**←Scientific data**
There is a great deal of archaeological evidence to support the existence of the Trojan War, after which there would have been a major fire that destroyed the city completely.

# A besieged city

Greek legend and myth intertwine in the events surrounding the tragedy of Troy. Narrated by Homer, the conflict between the coalition of Achaean armies against the city is one of the central axes of this Greco–Latin epic.

## The Bronze Age in the Aegean

During the second millennium BCE, Troy had reached the peak of its power. It maintained important relations with the Aegean world, which was succumbing to Indo-European invasions, and with the kingdoms of Asia Minor.

### The start of the conflict

Sent on a diplomatic mission to Sparta, Paris, a prince of Troy, fell in love with Helen, wife of the Spartan king Menelaus. He kidnapped her and took her to Troy. All the kings and princes of Greece united to destroy Troy.

**Homer, ninth century BCE**
Credited as the author of the two most famous epic works of ancient Greece: the *Iliad* and the *Odyssey*. His works narrated the tale of the Trojan War, the kidnapping of Helen by Paris, and the exploits of Hector and Achilles.

**❶**
**Agamemnon, king of Mycenae**
Son of King Atreus of Mycenae and Queen Aerope, and brother of Menelaus, he became the most powerful monarch in Greece. The *Iliad* made reference to his territories in the Peloponnese.

**❷**
**Menelaus, King of Sparta**
Menelaus became the King of Sparta after marrying Helen, the daughter of the King of Sparta, who was kidnapped by Paris, son of Priam, King of Troy.

Macedonia

Chalkidiki

Illyria

Epirus     Thessaly

Kerkira                          Iolcos ○

Ionian
Sea         Boeotia                    Euboea
            Lefkada Is.                        Avlida
            Ithaca Is.  Aetolia  Delphi ●  Gla ○
                ○                         Thebe ○
                 Alalcomenes                      Attica
            Cephalonia Is.                         Athens
                                     Mycenae        ○
            Zakynthos Is.  Arcadia  Argos ○  ❶
                           ●              Epidaurus
                Olympia         Tegea ○
                           Mesenia
                  Sparta ❷
               Pylos ○    Laconia      Sea of
                                       Crete

                              Cythera Is.

                                              Phaistos

## Chronology

The siege of Troy by the Achaeans lasted for ten years until it was finally conquered, during a period of change in the Aegean.

| 1730 BCE | 1550 BCE | 1479 BCE |
|---|---|---|
| **Troy VI** | **New Egyptian Empire** | **Battle of Megiddo** |
| The city occupied a strategic position as regards access to the Black Sea. Troy was rebuilt on more than ten occasions because of catastrophes and foreign occupations. | The governor of Thebes, Ahmose I, reunified Upper and Lower Egypt. His military campaigns against the Hyksos and Asia Minor lasted until 1070 BCE. | Thutmose III fought against the Canaanite coalition of the King of Kadesh in the city of Megiddo. The Egyptian victory granted him power over Canaan. |

## Is it true that Cassandra predicted the fatal destiny of Troy?

According to Greek mythology, Cassandra, the daughter of Priam and a priestess by trade, foresaw the destruction of Troy, the death of Agamemnon and her own fall from grace. However, she was unable to prevent these tragedies as Apollo, who was in love with her, placed a curse on her after she refused him.

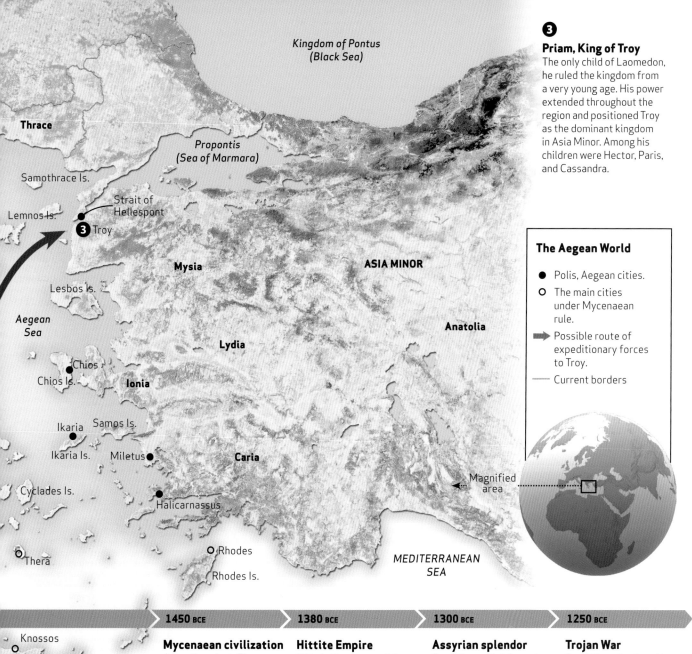

**❸**
**Priam, King of Troy**
The only child of Laomedon, he ruled the kingdom from a very young age. His power extended throughout the region and positioned Troy as the dominant kingdom in Asia Minor. Among his children were Hector, Paris, and Cassandra.

Kingdom of Pontus
(Black Sea)

Thrace

Propontis
(Sea of Marmara)

Samothrace Is.

Strait of
Hellespont

Lemnos Is.

❸ Troy

ASIA MINOR

Mysia

Lesbos Is.

Aegean
Sea

Anatolia

Lydia

Chios
Chios Is.

Ionia

Ikaria    Samos Is.

Ikaria Is.    Miletus●

Caria

Cyclades Is.

Halicarnassus

Thera

Rhodes

Rhodes Is.

MEDITERRANEAN
SEA

Knossos

**The Aegean World**

● Polis, Aegean cities.

○ The main cities under Mycenaean rule.

➡ Possible route of expeditionary forces to Troy.

— Current borders

Magnified
area

| 1450 BCE | 1380 BCE | 1300 BCE | 1250 BCE |
|---|---|---|---|
| **Mycenaean civilization** An earthquake in Thera caused a tidal wave that destroyed the Cretan navy. The sudden downfall of the Minoan culture saw the rise of the Mycenaeans and their dominance of the Aegean. | **Hittite Empire** Of Indo-European origin, the Hittites took up residence in Anatolia, Asia Minor, and reached the same level of power as Babylonia and Egypt. They introduced the use of iron. | **Assyrian splendor** From the capital, Assur, in the Tigris Valley, Assyrian king Tukulti-Ninurta I arrived in Mesopotamia and conquered Babylonia. He prevented the advance of the "sea peoples." | **Trojan War** Troy VII was besieged by Mycenae. Toward 1200 BCE began the downfall of the Mycenaean kings, and the start of the migration of Ionians and Aeolians toward the Cyclades and Asia Minor. |

# Priam's treasure

In 1873, during excavation work carried out at Troy, Heinrich Schliemann found a large number of objects that supposedly belonged to the mythical city, but that date back to the third millennium BCE.

## Long journey

Schliemann illegally transported the jewels he found to Greece. In 1874, he was accused of theft by the Ottoman Empire and ordered to pay a fine. Thus, he donated part of the collection to the Constantinople Museum in order to gain permission to continue excavating, with the rest being transported to Berlin, where it was confiscated by the Red Army at the end of World War II. Today, the treasures remain in the Pushkin Museum in Moscow, with Germany still seeking their return.

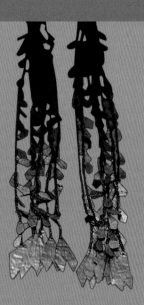

**Hidden jewels**
Before the Red Army took possession of them, they were hidden in a purpose-built shelter at the Berlin Zoological Garden.

**Diadems**
Made from gold with leaf- or flower-shaped dangling ends, they were found inside golden jars that were part of the treasure.

**Sophia, just like Helen**
Schliemann's second wife was Sophia, a 17-year-old Greek who was interested in the history and poetry of Homer. After the archaeologist found the jewels that supposedly belonged to Helen, Sophia was able to try them on and was even photographed wearing them.

## Frank Calvert, a pioneer

The region around Mount Hissarlik, where Schliemann found Priam's Treasure (the illustration recreates the dig), had already been excavated by another amateur archaeologist: around 1850, British consular official Frank Calvert was convinced that the archaeological remains of Troy were to be found at the site.

### Astonishing treasure

The objects found by Schliemann included a copper cauldron, gold and silver jars, 8,750 gold rings, buttons, and other small objects. Six bracelets, two chalices, and a number of glazed gold-plated bottles, a number of terracotta and electrum (a blend of gold and silver) cups, and six silver-covered knife blades were also found.

### Hatchets

These small handheld hatchets were made from lapis lazuli and nephrite.

## A thousand years before

Although the authenticity of Schliemann's discovery is not the subject of debate, the vast number of precious objects found (more than 10,000 pieces of gold) had been hidden some 1,000 years prior to the events narrated by Homer in his epic poems. However, Schliemann would never learn this; nor would he ever know that his Homeric Troy was not the second city, but the seventh, which he had barely touched at the start of his excavation work.

# CHAPTER 7

# Dead Sea Scrolls

The discovery of the Dead Sea Scrolls has shed new light on Judaism and early Christianity, although since the discovery was made public in 1947, they have been the subject of great controversy. Who wrote them? What secrets do they hold? Is there a hidden treasure?

Between November and December 1946, a Bedouin shepherd from the Ta'amirah tribe was looking after a herd of goats and decided to climb up one of the steep slopes of a cliff with the intention of rescuing some of his animals that had strayed too far from the rest of the flock. He found himself close to a place called Khirbet Qumran (meaning "Qumran ruins") in a desert valley of Judea some 1.2 miles/2 km from the western coast of the Dead Sea.

This was how Muhammed edh-Dhib came upon the entrance to a cave, one of many ancient caves carved into the landscape of a region in which all sorts of legends abound. His curiosity was aroused when, after throwing a stone into the cave, from out of the darkness came a sound as of a jug breaking. He imagined he had found treasure, but it was getting late and he abandoned the site. He returned the next day, together with his cousins Yuma Muhammed and Jalil Musa, to explore the place more thoroughly. The floor of the cave was covered in pieces of pottery, but along one wall they found several narrow jars that appeared to be intact, and some of which still retained their original seals.

## A DIFFERENT TREASURE

The Bedouin opened them and examined the contents, although they did not discover jewels or gold. To their disappointment, the vessels contained only old parchments, some of them bound in cloth, written in a language they could not understand. It is said that they decided to use some of them to make a fire to warm themselves up, and finally to take some of them to a local tradesman.

The parchments spent some time hanging from a post in a Bedouin shop, until they eventually ended up in the hands of a young Syrian orthodox bishop from St. Mark's Monastery in Jerusalem. Athanasius Yeshue Samuel, or Mar Samuel as he was known, thought that the parchments were older than the leading scholars he consulted had claimed, and he continued to search for someone to properly analyze the scrolls, which led the discoverers to think that there was indeed treasure hidden in the cave of Qumran, where the scrolls had been found. They returned again and discovered more jars and more scrolls. A specialist

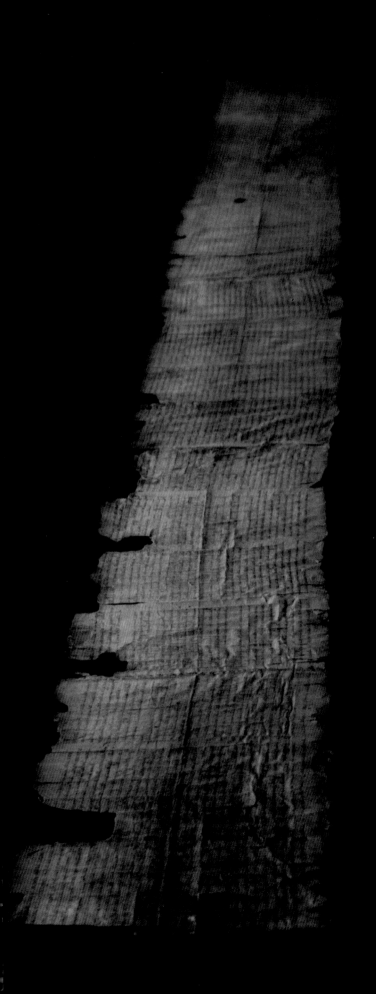

**Biblical scroll**
A large scroll of the Book of Isaiah, in a photo taken in 2008. This manuscript was the first to be discovered in cave 1 and is the best preserved.

bought three scrolls for seven pounds sterling and went to one of his partners in Jerusalem, a Christian Armenian, Nasri Ohan. It was Ohan who consulted another professor at the Hebrew University of Jerusalem, Eleazar Sukenik, a renowned expert in Hebrew epigraphy, who realized he was holding authentic and very ancient scrolls.

Four days later, on November 29, 1947 (the same day the United Nations General Assembly voted in favor of the division of Palestine into two states and the establishment of Israel), Nasri Ohan and Eleazar Sukenik traveled to Belén and returned with two more scrolls. Sukenik, who had very little money but a lot of time and patience, obtained more manuscripts over the next three months. Meanwhile, Bishop Samuel was not able to find anyone who believed in the authenticity of his scrolls until, in January 1948, he met Sukenik who, after examining them, concluded that they were the most valuable biblical manuscripts discovered so far. In 1948, the British mandate in Palestine was terminated and war was declared between the Arabs and the Israelis. The struggle lasted more than one year and ended with the armistice of 1949 and the victory of Israel.

In this confrontational environment, Bishop Samuel received "advice" not to deal with the Israelis and so, in his desire to study the manuscripts, he went to the Americans who managed the ASOR (American Schools of

Oriental Research) in Jerusalem. In this institution, the first photographs of the bishop's scrolls were taken (the Isaiah text: Regulation of the Community and the "Pesher" of Habakkuk). The word *pesher* comes from the Hebrew "to interpret" and is frequently used to introduce an explanation about a fragment of the scrolls. A short while later, on April 11, 1948, he produced the first report on the manuscripts under the auspices of the American Schools of Oriental Research in New Haven, Connecticut. All the important American and European newspapers reported the news immediately. Original versions of the Hebrew Bible, much older than those known to date, had been discovered.

The news spread like wildfire around the world and resulted in clashes and conflicts: among scholars for access to the scrolls and the first publications; between archaeologists and the Bedouin, who competed in the search for new caves and manuscripts; between Israel and Jordan for control of the Qumran area; and between Jewish and Christian experts who tirelessly argued about the interpretation and the ultimate meaning of the texts discovered. In this context, the ASOR director, archaeologist, linguist, and pottery expert, William Foxwell Albright (1891–1971) was entrusted with confirming the authenticity of the scrolls, and he reported that they belonged to a period spanning 250 BCE to 100 CE.

Effectively, these parchments, which would later come to be known as the Dead Sea Scrolls or Manuscripts, were the oldest of their type ever discovered. Until this point, the oldest Hebrew manuscripts of the Tanakh (the Hebrew Bible) were two medieval codices from 920 and 1008 CE (the Aleppo Codex and the Leningrad Codex, respectively). Therefore, these writings reset the record for the oldest Hebrew biblical manuscripts by more than 1,000 years.

The discovery encouraged fervent searches in the Qumran area, a narrow, arid strip of land 1,1230 ft/375 m below sea level where, between 1950 and 1960, hundreds of caves were explored, ten of which contained scrolls.

This land (like the other caves bordering Qumran) is located within the West Bank, which formed part of Jordan until 1967. That year, Israel conquered the West Bank during the Six Day War. Today, almost all the manuscripts are found in Israel and are under its control. Archaeologists have discovered a multitude of fragments, and with these they have been able to piece together 900 manuscripts in ancient Hebrew, Aramaic, and Greek, in which fragments of all the books of the Old Testament appear, with the exception of the Book of Esther. They also include texts about the history, statutes, and regulations of the enigmatic Jewish community that inhabited the site, in addition to the "Apocryphal" books, which were later omitted from the canon of the

Hebrew Bible. Were some of the writers and guardians of the manuscripts the Essenes, a Jewish community to which some say John the Baptist and, according to the most audacious, even Jesus, belonged? These questions are still controversial today.

## CLASSIFICATION METHOD

The researchers quickly found a way to classify the texts. Firstly, they gave each cave a number, then a Q (Qumran), then a number or letter referring to the fragment in question. For example, the first was 1Q1 and the last 11Q23. Cave 4 proved to be the most bountiful. It was discovered in 1952, and is actually two interconnected caves that contained 90 percent of the manuscripts and fragments discovered.

However, it was not only manuscripts and papyrus that were discovered. When two teams both in eastern Jerusalem, directed by Gerald Lankester Harding (who was then the director of the Antiquities Department of Jordan for the John Rockefeller Museum) and Roland de Vaux (of the École Biblique in Jerusalem, editors of the famous Jerusalem Bible), took charge of the excavations in the Qumran region from 1951, they found evidence that the caves had been used from the Chalcolithic period (around 4000 BCE). Exploration of the caves in the Nahal Darga, a fissure known in Arabic as Wadi al-Murabba'at, revealed, in addition to coins, objects, and

# Fragments of the New Testament?

In cave 7 of Qumran, fragments 7Q1 (Exodus 28: 4-7) and 7Q2 (Baruch verse of the Letter of Jeremiah) were found, and the rest were classified as "of probable biblical origin," until Spanish papyrologist Josep O'Callaghan (1922–2001), concluded in 1972 that four of the papyri (7Q5, 7Q6, 7Q7, and 7Q15) contained texts about the Gospel of Mark. This caused great controversy as the scientific consensus is that there are no texts of the New Testament in the caves of Qumran and, ultimately, the Spanish specialist was discredited. Some years later, however, German theologist and papyrologist Carsten Peter Thiede (1952–

2004) supported the validity of his work. O'Callaghan studied the 7Q5 fragment, written in the style of writers in the period of Herod, which contained five lines of writing, without spaces between words or phrases, and 20 letters. He trawled through the texts of the Old Testament without success, and then he tried the New Testament and discovered what he thought was a logical parallel with Mark 6: 52-53. The Greek text has 122 letters, the papyrus 20. Of these, eight appear to be in the right place. However, over the last few years some specialists have begun to think that the identification of these letters is not completely correct.

**→Controversy**
The fragment 7Q5 is a piece measuring just 1.5 x 1.1 in/3.9 x 2.7 cm. It has a few words in broken Greek, spread over four lines.

Arabic texts of the seventh to the fourteenth centuries CE, pottery and scarabs of the Middle Bronze Age (c. 2000 BCE) and an administrative papyrus written in Paleo-Hebrew that can be identified as belonging to the late Iron Age (around 650 BCE), the period of the last kings of Judah. This papyrus is written in the same ancient Hebrew that was preserved many centuries later in some scrolls from Qumran to write the sacred name of God (YHWH), as a sign that it should not be pronounced.

### MYSTERIOUS COPPER SCROLL

The so-called Copper Scroll (3Q15) is one of the most perplexing documents discovered in Qumran. It was discovered in poor condition in cave 3 in 1952 and is made up of two rolled sheets of copper. The state of corrosion of the metal prevented any detailed analysis. In 1956, a decision was taken to cut the roll into strips, and the resulting study revealed a list in Hebrew of 64 sites in Israel where, according to the document, valuable objects of gold and silver would be discovered. It was a wonderful treasure map. The list of treasure ended by mentioning a second scroll, called the Silver Scroll, which would contain additional details about the location of the sites.

However, none of the treasures of the Copper Scroll have been discovered. This could partially be due to the fact that the names of the sites recorded in the text no longer exist. Also, the text is deliberately ambiguous, although some believe that the treasure was removed at some point over the 2,000 years that have passed since it was written. It has also been argued that the Copper Scroll is a fraud of the

time, a rumor of the ancient Jewish people who wrote the scroll with the intention of misleading anyone trying to locate it. Strangely, this scroll was also written in a very unusual style of writing. Some paragraphs are written in a Hebrew some 800 years older than the scroll, and others in a version of Hebrew spoken at the time, and not at all like the other documents discovered at Qumran.

### WELL-KEPT SECRETS

The vast collection of religious and theological works discovered at the sites were largely written during the centuries before the destruction of the Temple of Jerusalem by the Romans in 70 CE, which put an end to the Great Jewish Revolt. Before the Romans had finished with Qumran, around 68 CE, the guardians wrapped the papyrus scrolls in several layers of cloth, stored them inside clay jars sealed with airtight lids and hid them in caves to protect them from destruction. Since their discovery, all sorts of speculations have been made about the ultimate intentions of their writers and compilers, although one thing is certain: the texts were extremely important to those who wrote them, copied them, and hid them, and they formed a large library of common use among the inhabitants of Qumran.

Through their care of the manuscripts, they ensured that the writings—with some help from the dry, arid climate of the region—would provide us with a marvelous legacy, an authentic treasure for the culture of humanity. A treasure that, for all the efforts of the researchers and scholars, continues to keep its secrets.

## The Essenes

The Essenes were a Jewish sect who lived close to the Dead Sea, to the south of Jericho and to the north of Ein Gedi. Their origins can be traced back to the times of Essen, an adopted son of Moses, who considered himself chosen by God to lead the fight against the "sons of darkness." No mention of them is made in the New Testament. This religious group, well documented by Romano-Jewish historian Flavius Josephus, flourished between the second century BCE and the first century CE. They were generally ascetic in nature and had an eschatological interpretation of contemporary history. They would have been the inhabitants of the ruins of Qumran, and the guardians of the Dead Sea Scrolls. Therefore, they would have been partly authors, partly copyists, and partly simple preservers.

Today, some scholars believe that the Qumran movement itself did not belong to the Essenes, but was a division of this group that had split around the mid-second century BCE. The Essenes were a tightly integrated and well organized community.

**↑Community hall**
Remains of what Roland de Vaux identified as the Qumran refectory.

**↑Qumran vessels**
These are the type of pots discovered in the caves of Qumran, inside which the manuscripts were found.

# The caves of Qumran

Papyrus manuscripts, scrolls, and a roll of copper with text have been found in these 11 caves. Many of the texts are biblical (canonical or apocryphal) while others are unique to the religious community who copied them.

## The manuscripts

The Dead Sea Scrolls are among the greatest manuscript discoveries of modern times. They were found between 1947 and 1956 on the northeast coast of the Dead Sea. In all there are about 900 texts on more than 15,000 fragments. Most are parchments, and written with a carbon-based ink.

## The Qumran Valley

At the foot of the Judean Desert, in the region of Qumran, hundreds of manuscripts were found hidden in caves, in pots, some rolled up. Most of the texts are written in Hebrew and Aramaic, and a few in Greek.

### The archaeological sites

Between 1951 and 1963, other scrolls were found nearby, and these are usually included under the general heading of the Dead Sea Scrolls.

Where the manuscripts were discovered
○

### Ruins at Qumran

The ruins were known before the discovery of the scrolls. From the beginning, the ruins were linked with the manuscripts.

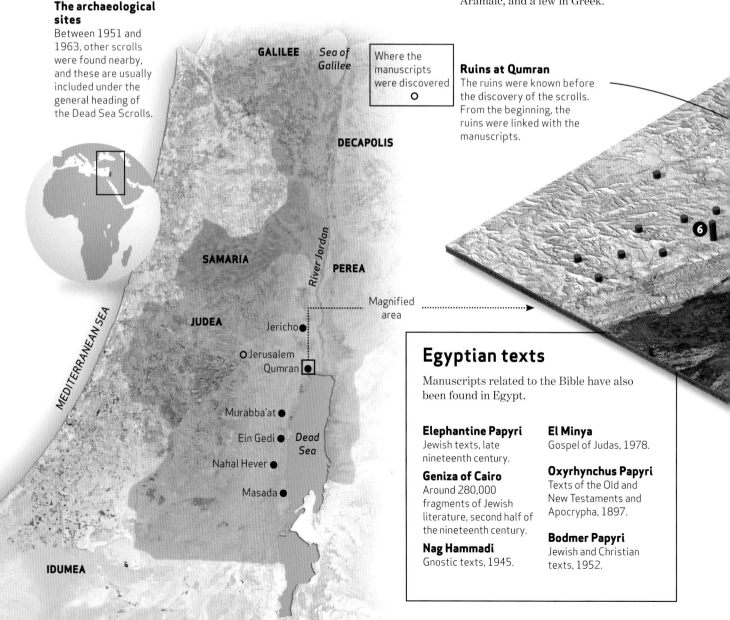

GALILEE
*Sea of Galilee*

DECAPOLIS

SAMARIA

*River Jordan*

PEREA

JUDEA

Jericho ●

○ Jerusalem
Qumran ▣

Murabba'at ●

Ein Gedi ● *Dead Sea*

Nahal Hever ●

Masada ●

MEDITERRANEAN SEA

IDUMEA

Magnified area

6

## Egyptian texts

Manuscripts related to the Bible have also been found in Egypt.

**Elephantine Papyri**
Jewish texts, late nineteenth century.

**Geniza of Cairo**
Around 280,000 fragments of Jewish literature, second half of the nineteenth century.

**Nag Hammadi**
Gnostic texts, 1945.

**El Minya**
Gospel of Judas, 1978.

**Oxyrhynchus Papyri**
Texts of the Old and New Testaments and Apocrypha, 1897.

**Bodmer Papyri**
Jewish and Christian texts, 1952.

## Why was the Book of Esther not found among the manuscripts discovered in the caves?

There are several possible explanations. First, there is evidence that the text originated among the "gentiles" (Babylonians and Persians) and second, although the text is important as a reaffirmation of Jewish identity, it has little religious value (in fact, the name of God is not mentioned).

### Caves with pottery fragments
Besides the caves with manuscripts, others were found containing thousands of broken pottery shards, similar to those that had contained the scrolls.

**Judean Desert**

**Judea**

### Parchments and papyrus
Around 80 percent of the texts are parchments made from goat or sheep skin, although others are made from gazelle or ibex skin. The rest are papyrus, made from plant material (only in cave 7) and one roll of copper (cave 3).

*Dead Sea*

### Caves with manuscripts
The caves were numbered in order of discovery. Caves 1 and 11 contained the best-quality items, while cave 4 had the most fragments.

# The ruins of Qumran

The explorations of Khirbet Qumran, between 1951 and 1956, attempted to find the possible relationship between the texts of the caves and the ruins. The citadel was occupied by the Romans and archaeological remains indicate a violent end.

## The Citadel

Located 2 miles/3.2 km from the western coast of the Dead Sea, on a cliff. The walls were demolished by the Romans. A layer of ash covers the entire citadel, where a number of arrowheads were found.

**Inkwell**
This bronze inkwell supports the hypothesis that some texts were copied at Qumran.

**Aqueduct**
Takes water from the Wadi Qumran stream.

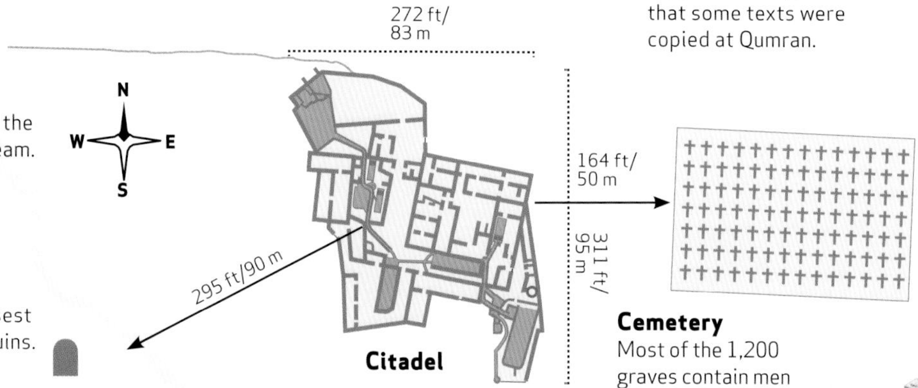

272 ft/ 83 m

164 ft/ 50 m

311 ft/ 95 m

**Cave 4**
The closest to the ruins.

295 ft/90 m

**Citadel**

**Cemetery**
Most of the 1,200 graves contain men and only a hundred women and children.

**Kitchen**

**Tower**

**Vases**
Those found in the ruins are identical to those containing the scrolls in the caves.

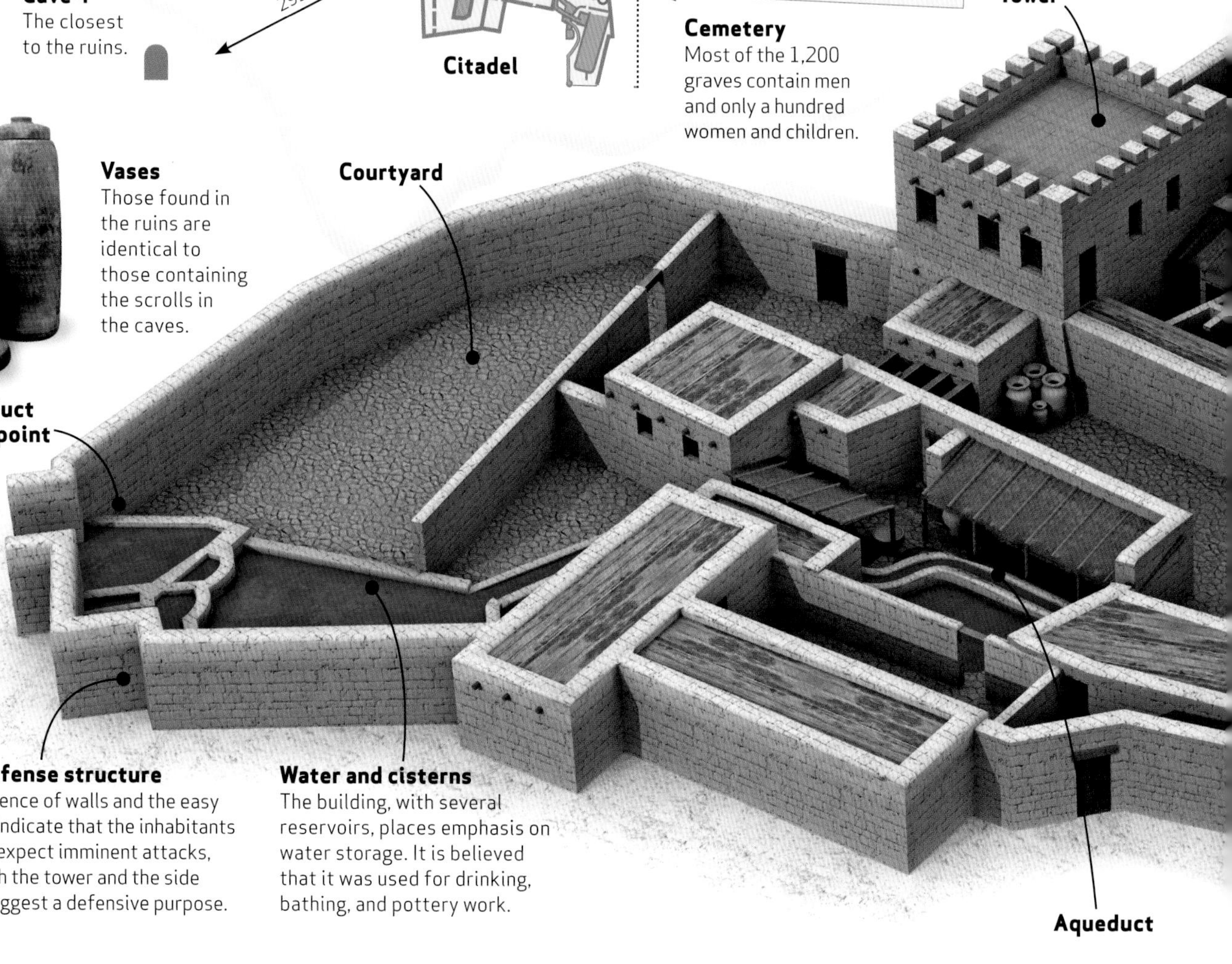

**Courtyard**

**Aqueduct entry point**

**The defense structure**
The absence of walls and the easy access indicate that the inhabitants did not expect imminent attacks, although the tower and the side walls suggest a defensive purpose.

**Water and cisterns**
The building, with several reservoirs, places emphasis on water storage. It is believed that it was used for drinking, bathing, and pottery work.

**Aqueduct**

# What was the war of the Sons of Light against the Sons of Darkness?

One of the most enigmatic documents in the caves is called the "War of the Sons of Light against the Sons of Darkness." It is a manual of military strategy that tells of a war between these two factions. The community that produced it called itself the "Children of Light," while the others could be Romans or other groups of Jews, who were considered corrupt.

**The scriptorium**
One of the main rooms in the daily life of the settlement. It is believed that rolls of papyri and parchments were written and stored here.

46 ft/
14 m

13 ft/
4.5 m

**Pottery workshop**

**Cistern for water**

**Refectory and assembly room**
The size of the room allowed the community to perform collective activities.

**Dispensary**

**The ruins today**
With a relief typical of the desert of Qumran, the ruins of the site are on a terrace of sand and clay. The area is now part of an Israeli national park.

**Cisterns for water**

**Stables**

# The *scriptorium* of Qumran

In the ruins of Qumran is the long room called the *scriptorium* (the "reading room"), where some of the texts found in nearby caves would have been copied. It could be a proof of the link between the citadel and the caves.

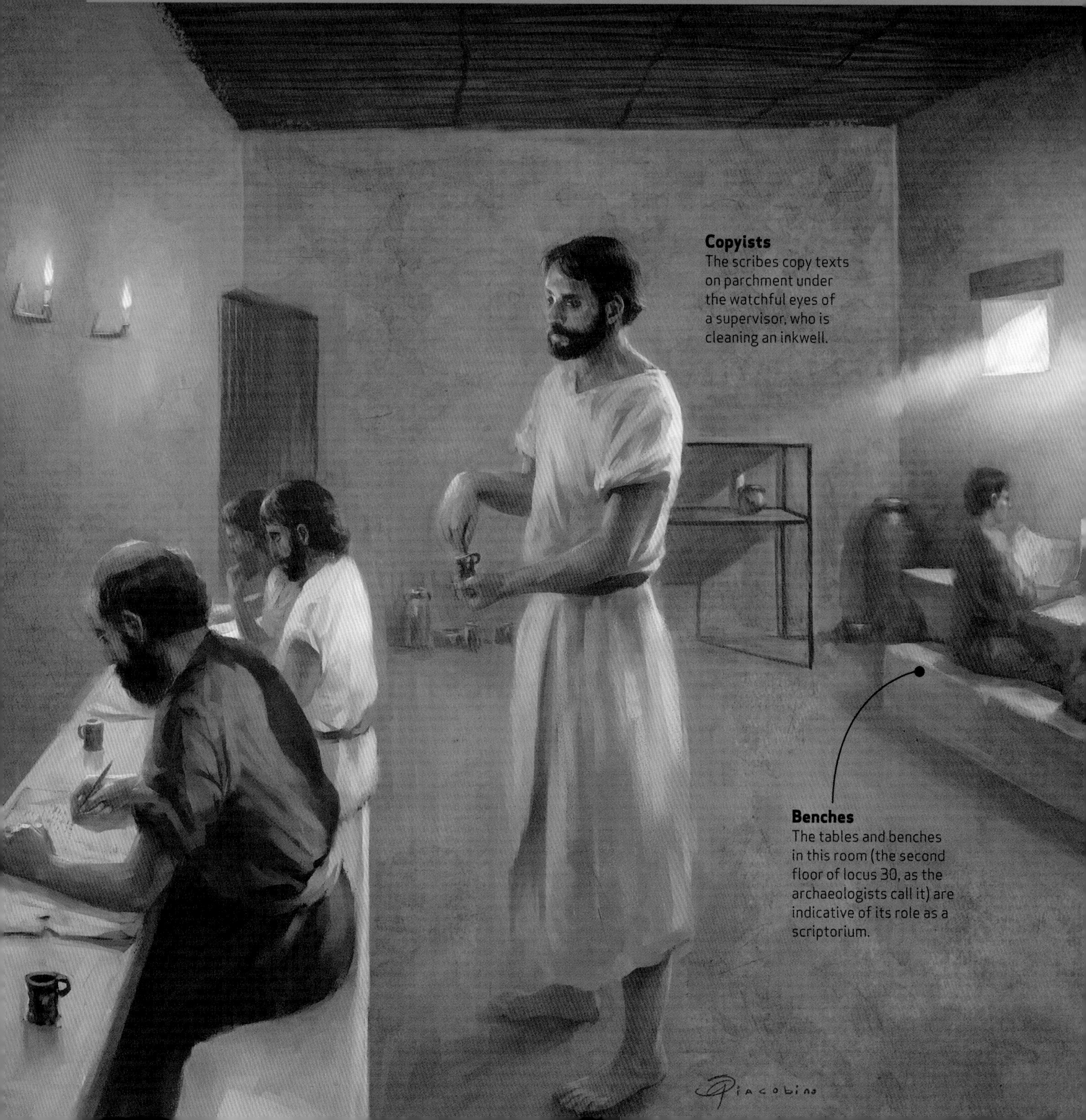

**Copyists**
The scribes copy texts on parchment under the watchful eyes of a supervisor, who is cleaning an inkwell.

**Benches**
The tables and benches in this room (the second floor of locus 30, as the archaeologists call it) are indicative of its role as a scriptorium.

Piacobino

## The origin of the texts

The benches and tables (pictured left) found on the second floor of the scriptorium of Qumran are archaeological remains that suggest that texts were copied there. There were no manuscripts, although there were inkwells and jars similar to those found in the caves. The ink in the inkwells matches the ink on the scrolls.

### Dictation
A community member dictates a sacred text to a scribe. The copyists had to be in a state of ritual purity for the job. Even the parchments had to come from "pure" animals and their preparation was done according to precise rules of hygiene.

# CHAPTER 8

# The Turin Shroud and other Relics

The Sindone is considered one of Christianity's most important relics. For believers, this was the shroud in which Christ was wrapped after the crucifixion. For skeptics, it is mere make-believe.

The Turin Shroud, also known as the Holy Shroud or Sindone (from the Greek *sindon*, meaning piece of cloth or sheet), is a rectangular piece of linen that currently measures 174 x 44 in/442 x 113 cm, although these measurements have been subject to slight variations throughout its checkered history.

At first glance, the only aspect that attracts attention is the tenuous double-sided human image: on one side the face and front part of a human body, on the reverse the shape of a human back, which has lightly stained the surface. Furthermore, several triangular-shaped patches and stains can be seen that mark the passing of time and events, such as fires in 1532 and 1997. Nothing special for a relic that is presumed to be "scientific" evidence of the foundational myth of Christianity: the resurrection of Jesus of Nazareth after his crucifixion at the hands of the Roman authorities in the first century of our era.

For centuries, the Turin Shroud was a relic that only concerned believers. In 1898, during preparations for the General Italian Exhibition in Turin, a semi-professional photographer, Secondo Pia, was authorized to take the first photographs of the cloth. While developing the negatives, Pia found that they displayed, although somewhat faintly, the image of a bearded man who appeared to have suffered violent injuries. Was this the genuine image of Jesus?

Following the birth of Christianity as a religion separate from the Jewish faith in the first century, relics and holy objects became extremely valuable tools for the new faith's hierarchy. In a violent and almost illiterate world, direct contact with anything related to Jesus and his disciples was useful in mobilizing popular faith. Relics "guaranteed" protection to those in possession of them, and served to unite Christian communities. The first Eucharists were celebrated at raised altars close to, or above, the crypts and graves of the holy martyrs.

The Catholic Church considers the worshipping of relics, in addition to visiting sanctuaries, pilgrimages, processions, the Stations of the Cross, religious performances, the rosary, medals, and a long list of other aspects as part of "popular religion."

Canonical relics are divided into three

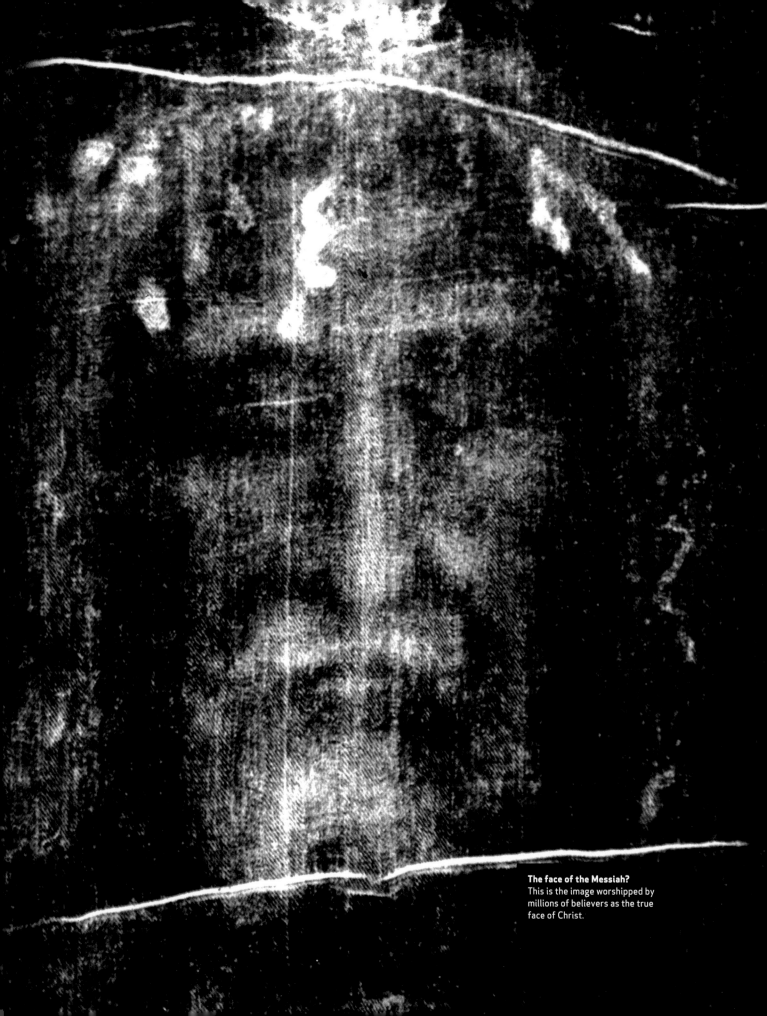

**The face of the Messiah?**
This is the image worshipped by
millions of believers as the true
face of Christ.

categories: bodies or body parts of holy people, including ashes and bones; objects that have been in physical contact with living saints or those sanctified in life, from robes to chains and other instruments; and pieces of cloth that have been in contact with first-class relics, from which the former are believed to have absorbed virtues.

The authenticity of the Turin Shroud has been the subject of heated debate since its "reappearance" in the fourteenth century. Those associating it with the Mandylion, a cloth on which the image of Jesus miraculously appeared, have traced its origin to Jerusalem, though Edessa (modern-day Urfa in Turkey), to Constantinople, where it arrived around 944, and from where it disappeared during the looting of the city by the Crusaders in 1204. The Shroud remained unseen for one and a half centuries. In 1349, French knight Godfrey de Charny asked for permission to build a church on his manor at Lirey to house the Turin Shroud; exactly how he came to be in possession of the Shroud was never established. He was granted permission and the Shroud was installed in this small town in Champagne in 1355.

In 1389, Pierre d'Arcis, bishop of nearby Troyes, wrote a letter to Pope Clement VII in which he stated that "the dean of Lirey, in an act of trickery and malice, motivated by greed, not by his devotion, but by avarice, submitted a cloth painted with an artifact to his church, asserting that it was the very same shroud as the one used to wrap our Savior, Jesus Christ, in the tomb. And this was not only spread throughout the kingdom of France but the entire world, attracting people from all over the world." However, there are doubts as to whether Pierre d'Arcis ever actually sent the letter, and no particular name is cited, which serves to weaken the bishop's accusations. It was Godfrey de Charny who took it upon himself to publicize the return of the Shroud by organizing the first expositions (displays of the relic in public), which attracted those "people from all over the world" who spent their money at inns and hostels. For the most part, the Shroud was hidden in his chapel, at first folded, before being rolled inside a silver reliquary box. It was not until 1998 in Turin that it was extended horizontally inside a special case.

### HISTORIC EVENT

When Secondo Pia obtained the negative image of the Shroud in 1898, he was accused of fraud. However, the Vatican received the news with satisfaction. In its June 14 edition, the official Vatican newspaper, *L'Osservatore Romano*, published an article entitled "A wondrous fact." The end of the nineteenth century was a particularly difficult period for the Catholic Church. The Bourgeois Revolutions and the Industrial Revolution had limited its influence in European society, and advances in positivism put all types of faith to the test. With the Turin Shroud, the Vatican

**←Pilgrimage**
The image has been preserved in Turin Cathedral since the end of the sixteenth century. Despite the controversy surrounding its authenticity, it is the most important relic of the Catholic faith, and it attracts millions of pilgrims.

**→1898 celebration**
Promotional poster of the 1898 exposition, during which the first photographs were taken of the Turin Shroud, which put the relic under a global spotlight.

believed it had found a weapon that could be used against its enemies. The relic experienced the strange paradox of having its authenticity doubted by Canon Ulysse Chevalier (considered one of the wisest men in France), while Yves Delage, self-proclaimed atheist and professor of zoology, anatomy, and physiology at the Sorbonne, was a supporter of its authenticity.

The controversy intensified in 1931 when Giuseppe Enrie took a second series of official photographs of the Sindone, which confirmed the existence of a negative image, invisible to the naked eye. One dissenting critic, Walter McCrone, asserted that there were traces of ocher-red and vermilion-colored paint on certain fibers, which sustained the theory that the relic was, in fact, a fake. Both pigments were very common during the Medieval period and would have been used to paint the body (ocher red) and to represent blood (vermilion). McCrone also referred to the existence of an 1847 book entitled *General painting practices during the 14th century*, which described methods of creating diffuse images, such as the one on the Shroud.

In 1988, the Holy See authorized an analysis of the cloth using the carbon-14, or radiocarbon, dating method. Three independent universities (the University of Arizona, the University of Oxford, and the Swiss Federal Institute of Technology in Zurich) carried out the examination, supervised by the British Museum. The result: the cloth had been created between 1260 and 1390, coinciding with the first mention of its appearance.

In 2008, a group of researchers at the Los Alamos National Laboratory asserted that they had found cotton fibers on other samples from the same part that served as a basis for the 1988 test, which, they claimed, annulled the findings of the carbon-14 test. The only answer would be a new analysis. However, the Holy See rejected this, given the destructive effect it would have on the fibers to be selected. In the eyes of the Vatican, the Turin Shroud must be left just as it is.

If the cloth used is medieval, then the image that it displays must be from the same period. So, how was it created? Certain scholars who support its authenticity state that a spontaneous and powerful nuclear radiation printed the image, which in reality does not possess the properties of a photographic negative, on the layers of cloth closest to the surface. This is the theory put forward by French biophysicist Jean-Baptiste Rinaudo. This would fit in with a hypothetical "resurrection."

The reasonable doubt about the suitability of carbon-14 dating methods and the continued appearance of studies and scientific articles on a variety of aspects (pollen analysis, photographic and physiological analysis, archaeological research, radiological projections, etc) have kept the controversy alive.

## The similarities of the Pray Codex

The documents comprising the Pray Codex, at the Hungarian National Library, were written between 1192 and 1195. They include two illustrations that both depict episodes after the crucifixion of Jesus. The first shows the anointing of the body, which holds great similarities to the image of the Shroud: longer than normal forearms, hidden thumbs, and three marks on the forehead. In the second, an angel announces the resurrection to the women who had arrived to collect Jesus's body from the tomb. At the angel's feet, the empty shroud can be seen. Here, it is possible to see the remnants of the cloth and four small circles forming an axis that corresponds to those found on the Turin Shroud, prior to the 1532 fire.

**↑Holes**
The Sindone has signs of burn marks. Their origins are unknown.

**↑Detail**
The medieval illustration reveals a striking similarity to the Turin Shroud.

### THE SURGE IN RELICS

The phenomenon of relics boomed as a result of the Crusades, a venture that had a significant religious, cultural, social, and economic impact. From the twelfth century, hundreds of knights returned from the Holy Land to their European homes with relics that they deposited in cathedrals, hermitages, and parish churches. These relics served to legitimize their authority and justify their military undertakings. They also attracted pilgrims when the relic in question was considered of great importance. In medieval Europe, almost no church was left relic-free. The multiplication of fragments of the True Cross, the "holy nails," the thorns from Jesus's crown, multiple samples of the Holy Lance with which the Roman centurion Longinus pierced Jesus's side, the chalices from the Last Supper, were deemed unimportant.

In Byzantium and the Near East, a rich artisan trade had flourished, providing Europe with everything it could ever want. Monarchs such as Louis IX of France (St. Louis), during the thirteenth century, and Philip II of Spain, during the sixteenth century, had extraordinary collections, which they built up by paying large fortunes for certain relics. Authorized copies were also created that served to satisfy famous guests of popes and monarchs, as well as to supply newly created Catholic places of worship. As a result, there are five replicas of the Turin Shroud in America, not to mention the other "Shrouds," whether full or partial, spread around Europe. The debates about its origin and authenticity aside, it cannot be doubted that its presence, popularity, and the fact that it remains topical to this day distinguishes the Turin Shroud from other relics with a more markedly mythical or legendary tone, the main reference to which tends to be literary or even cinematic.

This is the case of the Ark of the Covenant, for example, where the Jewish people stored the Tablets of Stone on which the Ten Commandments were inscribed, which, according to tradition, Moses received directly from God and which possessed powers capable of demolishing the city walls of Jericho. However, the Ark disappeared 2,500 years ago following the destruction of Jerusalem by the Babylonian king Nebuchadnezzar II. English researcher Graham Hancock, however, mantains that after a long journey the Ark ended up in Ethiopia and would have been taken to Aksum (the holiest city in the country), where he believes it has been preserved to this day, at the Church of Our Lady Mary of Zion (part of the Coptic Orthodox Church of Ethiopia). The Ark remains under the supervision of a priest, the only person allowed to see it.

As regards the Holy Grail, the chalice used by Jesus to offer the sacrament of the Eucharist during the Last Supper, the main candidate is the chalice held by Valencia Cathedral since 1437. However, since the twelfth century, literary tradition has created a genuine Europe-wide cultural myth, which has been kept alive for centuries and has surpassed the realms of religion.

Unlike these examples, the Turin Shroud enjoys a definite material existence. After ten years of silence, between April 10 and May 23, 2010, the Shroud had its most recent public viewing at the Cathedral of St. John the Baptist in Turin, the city in which it has been since 1578.

**↑ Waiting for the Grail**
The empty crypt waiting for the Holy Grail at Wewelsburg Castle.

## Himmler and the SS crypt

Himmler constructed what can only be described as an Aryan sanctum at his castle in Wewelsburg, located in west-central Germany. Himmler took possession of the castle, built at the beginning of the seventeenth century, in 1934 in order to convert it into an educational center for the SS. Although he did not accomplish this objective, important changes were made to its structure, most notably on the northern tower. There, two new rooms were created: the so-called General's Hall, which was fitted with a mosaic of a "Black Sun," the mystical SS symbol, similar in appearance to a swastika, but with 12 arms, and a crypt (see

above). This circular room had 12 alcoves, reminiscent of King Arthur's Round Table. A large swastika adorns the top of the room's dome. In the center of the room, an empty space was left, apparently for the Holy Grail—a weapon that would be definitive in the battle between Europe and the savagery that, according to Himmler, was imminent.

**→ Cathar sanctuary**
Some people believed the Holy Grail was hidden in Château de Montségur, in southern France.

## Did the Nazis covet the Grail?

After defeat at the end of World War I, there was an upsurge in pan-Germanist organizations that sought to build a mythology with fully nationalistic roots; these entities took an interest in including the Holy Grail in their doctrine.

Within the Nazi hierarchy interested in this myth, Heinrich Himmler, head of the SS, was most prominent; he believed that the Holy Grail was a physical object with supernatural powers. Himmler entrusted various specialists with the task of finding the Grail, and he himself even went to Spain to find it. Using the pretext of a meeting held between Adolf Hitler and Francisco Franco in Hendaye on October 23, 1940, Himmler and some of his collaborators traveled to the monastery at Montserrat, close to Barcelona, where he found no trace of the precious relic. Before leaving, Himmler made it clear why he was so interested in the Holy Grail: the Nazis, manipulating the Biblical legend about Jacob and Esau, argued that the Aryan race descended from the former, chosen by God, and Jews from the latter. It was essential that the Holy Grail, a symbol of divine power, came under the protection of the new Messiah: Adolf Hitler.

# The route of the relics

The Holy Shroud, the Holy Grail, and the Ark of the Covenant are the three relics that have generated the most fascination in the Christian faith. This is a possible route that they traveled from Jerusalem to the present day.

Magnified area

FRANCE

Lirey

SWITZERLAND

Chambéry

**Turin**

ITALY

Rome
(St. Peter's)

Monastery of San Juan de la Peña (8th century)

Zaragoza (14th century)

Huesca (3rd century)

**SPAIN**

**Valencia**
(15th century to present)

GREECE

ATLANTIC
OCEAN

In 2002, the "Way of the Holy Grail" between San Juan de la Peña and Valencia was opened—a distance of over 300 miles/500 km—which aims to promote Catholic devotion and tourism.

MEDITERRANEAN
SEA

LIBYA

## Holy Grail

### TECHNICAL SPECIFICATIONS

**Principal candidate:** The Holy Chalice of Valencia.

**Biblical reference:** Mentioned in the Gospels of Matthew (26: 26–29), Mark (14: 22–25), Luke (22: 15–20) and 1 Cor. (11: 23–27).

**Current location:** Valencia, Spain.

**Description:** This is the name of a legendary sacred vessel, also identified as the Eucharist chalice used by Jesus at the Last Supper.

**Weight:** No data.

3.75 in/
9.5 cm

2.75 in/
7 cm

6.7 in/
17 cm

5.7 in/
14.5 cm

### References
⮕ Route of the Holy Shroud
⮕ Route of the Holy Grail
⤍ "The Way of the Holy Grail"
⮕ Route of the Ark of the Covenant
○ Current location

N

0    300 km

# What shape was the Holy Grail originally? Is it certain it was a kind of cup?

In the chivalric romances the Grail is described in very vague terms and only later identified as the chalice from the Last Supper and the one in which Joseph of Arimathea caught the blood of Christ. But in the same legends it is also described as a plate or tray (the word "grail" comes from the Latin *gradalis*, meaning "wide and shallow dish"), or as a stone fallen from heaven, usually an emerald.

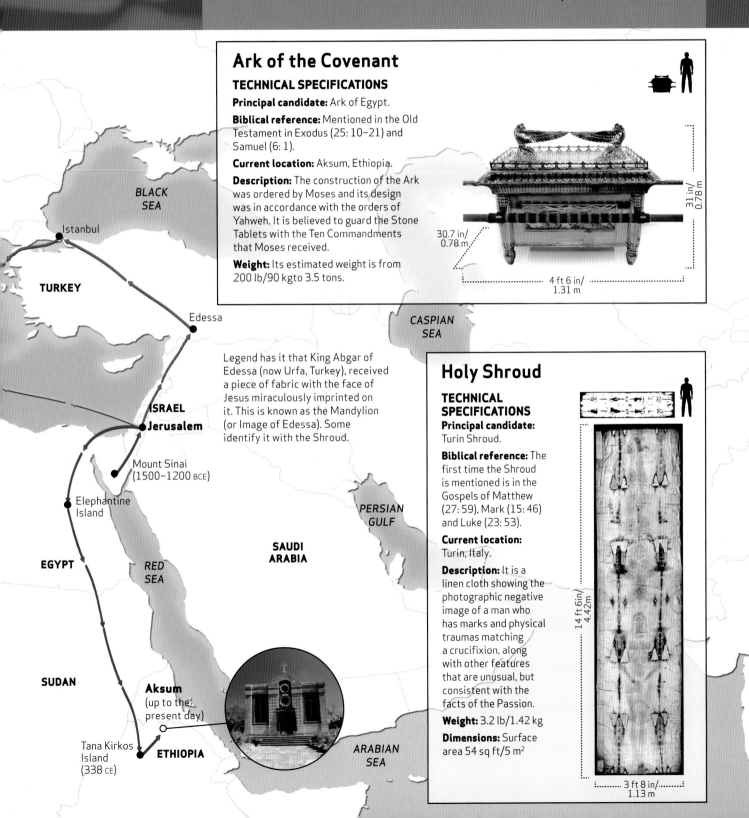

## Ark of the Covenant

### TECHNICAL SPECIFICATIONS

**Principal candidate:** Ark of Egypt.

**Biblical reference:** Mentioned in the Old Testament in Exodus (25: 10–21) and Samuel (6: 1).

**Current location:** Aksum, Ethiopia.

**Description:** The construction of the Ark was ordered by Moses and its design was in accordance with the orders of Yahweh. It is believed to guard the Stone Tablets with the Ten Commandments that Moses received.

**Weight:** Its estimated weight is from 200 lb/90 kg to 3.5 tons.

31 in/ 0.78 m

30.7 in/ 0.78 m

4 ft 6 in/ 1.31 m

BLACK SEA

Istanbul

TURKEY

Edessa

CASPIAN SEA

Legend has it that King Abgar of Edessa (now Urfa, Turkey), received a piece of fabric with the face of Jesus miraculously imprinted on it. This is known as the Mandylion (or Image of Edessa). Some identify it with the Shroud.

ISRAEL

**Jerusalem**

Mount Sinai (1500–1200 BCE)

Elephantine Island

PERSIAN GULF

EGYPT

RED SEA

SAUDI ARABIA

SUDAN

**Aksum** (up to the present day)

Tana Kirkos Island (338 CE)

**ETHIOPIA**

ARABIAN SEA

## Holy Shroud

### TECHNICAL SPECIFICATIONS

**Principal candidate:** Turin Shroud.

**Biblical reference:** The first time the Shroud is mentioned is in the Gospels of Matthew (27: 59), Mark (15: 46) and Luke (23: 53).

**Current location:** Turin, Italy.

**Description:** It is a linen cloth showing the photographic negative image of a man who has marks and physical traumas matching a crucifixion, along with other features that are unusual, but consistent with the facts of the Passion.

**Weight:** 3.2 lb/1.42 kg

**Dimensions:** Surface area 54 sq ft/5 m²

14 ft 6 in/ 4.42 m

3 ft 8 in/ 1.13 m

# The marks of the Shroud

The Shroud has a number of marks of different backgrounds and different ages that have been identified in its study. Some traces left in the fabric, however, remain controversial for researchers.

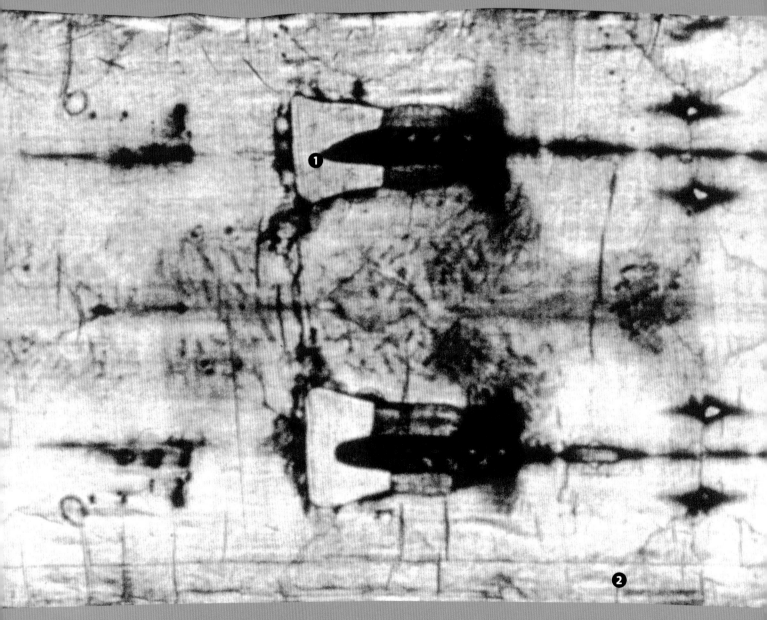

**❶**

### Fire
In the fire of 1532, a drop of molten silver burned one corner of the Shroud (which was kept folded) leaving a series of triangular holes. Two years later patches were applied to the fabric. The burns that form an "L" (to the left) occurred prior to this fire.

**❷**

### Thin strip
According to some scholars, a strip along the bottom edge of the canvas is a later addition. It still forms part of the shroud, but in the 2002 restoration led by Professor Flury-Lemberg, the 30 triangular patches sewn on in 1534 by nuns of the Order of St. Clare were removed.

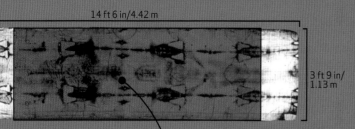

14 ft 6 in/4.42 m

3 ft 9 in/
1.13 m

## Conservation

A study conducted in June 1998 suggested that the Shroud be kept stretched out instead of rolled or folded. It is in a case (with laminated and bulletproof glass) filled with a compound of 99.5 percent argon and 0.5 percent oxygen, which maintains a constant temperature and humidity.

**❸**

#### Blood stains

There are signs of high blood flow on the front of the image and in its left side, where Christ received a lance on the Cross. The stain spreads through to the back of the canvas, and the back of the figure. The face is swollen, as if as a result of beatings.

**❹**

#### Iron nails

The arms are outstretched, with the hands crossed on his body. The right hand is above the left, and there is clearly a blood stain on the wrist, caused by an iron nail. Blood stains are also visible on the feet, as if caused by another nail.

# The relics of Christ

Throughout history Christian devotion has preserved a number of relics attributed to Christ. Although science has revealed that many are not from the time of Jesus, for believers their symbolic value remains.

## Iron Crown

Preserved in the Cathedral of Monza, Italy, there is an item of jewelry made at the end of the sixth century and used by the Lombard kings at their coronations. Charlemagne, Charles V, Napoleon, and in 1805 the King of Italy were crowned with this. Its name is derived from the thin sheet of metal around the inside of the crown, where there is a nail that is identified with one of the nails of the Crucifixion. Tests carried out on the jewel in 1993 showed that the nail is silver and mid-fourteenth century.

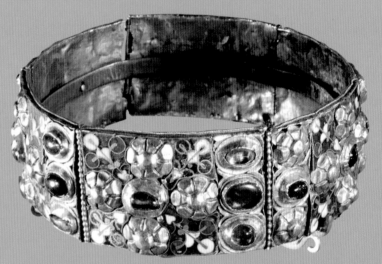

## Nail of the Cross

It is kept in the cathedral of Trier, Germany, the oldest church in the country. The nail is protected by a richly decorated reliquary from approximately 980 CE. This relic, like many others, was collected by St. Helena, the mother of Constantine. The cathedral also has the Holy Tunic (considered to be the clothing worn by Jesus on the Way of the Cross), the body of St. Matthew, St. Andrew's sandal, and a tooth of St. Peter.

**Blood of Jesus**
Stored in the Basilica of the Holy Blood in Bruges, Belgium. According to tradition, it was collected by Joseph of Arimathea.

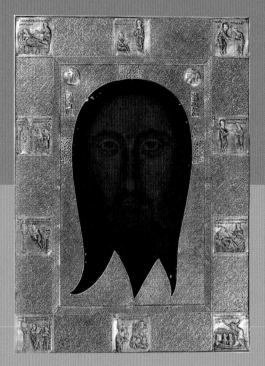

## The Holy Face of Genoa

It is in the church of St. Bartholomew of the Armenians, in Genoa, and is identified with the Image of Edessa, or Mandylion. The frame around the image is from the fourteenth century, although no dating tests have been performed on the image. There is another relic that also claims to be the historic Mandylion—the Holy Face of St. Sylvester—in the Vatican.

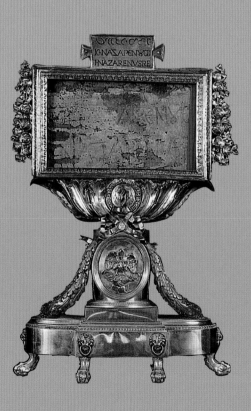

**Titulus crucis**
This is part of the plate that marked the judgment of Jesus on the Cross. It is written in three languages and the text (abbreviated as "INRI") is read from right to left. It is kept in a basilica in Rome.

**Spear of Longinus**
Also known as the "Holy Lance." It is located in the Schatzkammer, in the Hofburg Palace, Vienna. In 2003, it was dated to the seventh century.

**Fragment of the cross**
Reliquary containing one of the many fragments of the Cross spread throughout the world. This is in the Church of the Holy Cross in Rome. The church has other relics supposedly belonging to Christ.

# CHAPTER 9

# In Search of the Real Jesus

The Gospels do not describe everything. Other primitive writings from outside the canon of the Catholic Church fill in the voids with images of a more human Jesus, capable of falling in love and hating. Perhaps they are a more truthful representation of Christ.

I f we close our eyes and try to imagine Jesus as a child, the image of a blond cherub with pale skin, perhaps with wavy hair and blue eyes, comes to mind. We would most likely have to think twice to suppress this idealized image and convert it into the small Palestinian boy with caramel-colored skin and dark hair that is probably a more accurate depiction. Everything would seem to suggest that his mother, a young girl of just 15 years of age as explained by the Scriptures, was also a woman with Arabic, or at least, Mediterranean features.

### A MORE REALISTIC JESUS?
For the first time in history, during the seventeenth century, the Enlightenment shone the spotlight on the gap between the historical Jesus and the religious portrayal of Jesus that forms part of both Western and global culture.

The Catholic Church proposes immersing oneself in the Gospels of Matthew, Mark, Luke, and John, which narrate the life of the Messiah, as a way of better understanding his life. These depict a heavenly Jesus, concentrated on his mission as the Son of God and detached from passions of the flesh.

However, other texts written by the first Christians offer different versions that fill in the voids left by the Bible, describing a more human Jesus, a special person who had to learn to control his power, who suffered outbursts of rage and who was capable of loving a woman. There are those who believe that this Jesus, as represented by the Apocryphal Gospels, is closer to the real Jesus.

It is important to bear in mind that all the Gospels were written as propaganda for the new religious current that was

starting to take hold at the time. Historical accuracy does not have priority, and the writers of the Gospels simply wanted to leave a written account of Jesus's message, about a Jesus who varied depending on the interests of each person. The original form of Christianity was not a homogeneous movement, as it comprised different groups, each with their own reference texts.

### AN OFFICIAL FAITH
Theologians such as Albert Schweitzer, Rudolf Karl Bultmann, Ernst Käsemann, W. D. Davies and E. P. Sanders have suggested that the Christ depicted by the Catholic Church is a made-to-measure product created by Paul the Apostle. He was able to connect with the powerful elite and convert a marginal sect into a wide-reaching religion.

**Jesus of Nazareth**
Statue of Jesus located on
a black marble tomb in a
cemetery in Aachen, Germany.

After a difficult struggle for the leadership, Paul managed to establish himself as leader; it was under his guiding hand that the movement gained followers and considerable wealth. The Roman powers, who had initially fiercely persecuted Jesus's followers to the point of including them in circus shows with lions, eventually embraced the new faith. The emperor Constantine, son of Helena, a Christian, declared religious freedom for Christians throughout the Roman Empire.

However, Christianity remained a heterogeneous movement, with different ideologies at play. To unite them, the founding fathers of the Church met at the Council of Nicaea, in Turkey, in 325 CE, and there they decided which religious texts had been "inspired by God" (as they are still known to this day) and which were not, with all those falling under the latter category being deemed "heresy."

Thus, the New Testament, as we know it, was born. In 392, Emperor Theodosius proclaimed that Christianity would be the new religion of the empire, with all other religions being forced underground as a result. Many texts that did not resonate with the new faith were destroyed, just like others that, even though they defined themselves within the scope of Christianity, did not pass the filter at Nicaea. And so, the control and implementation of an official discourse arrived at a point under which possession of writings considered heresy became a crime.

## PARALLEL STORIES AND MISSING DATES

In theory, the authors of the canonical Gospels reconstructed Jesus's life based on their own memories and the testimony and memories of other people about direct witnesses, especially the apostles. Years after Jesus's death, tales about his life stopped being mere oral narratives, and were documented on paper and, to an extent, reinterpreted. Today, researchers trying to reconstruct the real Jesus study the Gospels in a different light, given that texts are always a product of the time in which they were written, the context, and the intentions of those who wrote them.

In the Gospel According to Matthew, for example, there is a palpable attempt to demonstrate that Jesus was sent by God, rather than just one of many prophets in the vibrant Palestine of the first century. This biography is adapted to fulfill the prophecies of the Old Testament. The Gospels According to Matthew and Luke are the only ones that describe the birth of the Messiah, and their description matches the circumstances of other deities: Mary sought a place to give birth, just as did the mother of Apollo; also, he was born on December 25, the same day on which it is claimed Horus, Mitra, Dionysus, Krishna, and Buddha were born.

In addition to single facts that are subject to question, there are entire black holes. Through Luke, we know that Jesus attended the Temple in Jerusalem with his entire family when

**← A genuine couple?**
This 1520 painting by Lucas Cranach (c.1472–1553) found at Friedenstein Castle in Gotha, Germany, illustrates the possible relationship between Jesus and Mary Magdalene, upheld by certain scholars.

**→ The parents of Jesus**
Mary married Joseph while pregnant with Jesus, as shown in this oil painting by Bartolomeo Gennari (seventeenth century). According to ancient texts, the High Priest, Annas, wanted to report her.

he was 12, as part of the Jewish Passover ritual. After the group completed the day-long journey to return to Nazareth, his parents discovered that he was nowhere to be found. They returned to Jerusalem and found him at the Temple, debating law and theology with experts. Having been reprimanded by his parents, Jesus asked whether they were unaware that he was obliged to address matters relating to his Father. As the Son of God, it was his duty.

Thereafter, there is a gap in the Gospels until Jesus is almost 30 years old, when he begins his life in the public eye. Matthew directly connects the story to the point just after the birth of Jesus. The Gospels According to Mark and John make no mention of his infancy nor his adolescence.

The truth is that, between the episode as a lost child at the Temple and when Jesus starts to preach, there is a lapse of two decades during which nothing is known of him. Scholars refer to these years as "the unknown years." What did he do during this time? Presumably, he continued dealing with matters involving his Father, but Matthew, Mark, Luke, and John remain silent on this. Some believe that during these years he traveled to Tibet.

**CHANGES TO THE TEXTS**
Furthermore, there are a number of discrepancies between the four Gospels accepted by the Church as being "inspired by God." At the time of the crucifixion, the Gospel According

to Matthew states that Jesus was accompanied by Mary Magdalene, Mary, mother of James the Less (Mary of Clopas), and the mother of Zebedee's children, Salome. In the Gospel According to Mark, the same three women are listed as being present. In the Gospel According to Luke, however, they are just "the women who had followed him from Galilee," and in the Gospel According to John, they are cited as being the Virgin Mary, Mary of Clopas, the sister of the Virgin, and Mary Magdalene. This example has no consequences, but it is representative of how the texts differ from one another.

It must also be remembered that the texts have undergone amendments as a result of censorship over time. In 1958, U.S. researcher Morton Smith found a letter from Clement of Alexandria, who lived around 200 CE, to Theodore, whose identity is unknown, in which he states that sections of the Gospel According to Mark appeared to have been censored. According to Clement, Mark had written two Gospels: the canonical Gospel, addressed to the whole world; and another secret Gospel, to which only the most devoted believers could be granted access. He claimed that this contained, among other aspects, two sections that had "disappeared," which suggest that Jesus had a homosexual relationship with a young man he had resuscitated, although experts consider that this text could also be read as an initiation rite to Christianity, similar to others performed at the time in the

# Did he visit Tibet?

Where was Jesus between the ages of 12 and 30? Did he work in Joseph's carpentry business? There is another possible explanation: during those "unknown years" of which the Church does not speak, he was not in Nazareth, but in the Himalayas. This was the proposal of Russian author Nicolas Notovitch in his book, *The Unknown Life of Jesus Christ*, published in 1894 in French. According to his account, while he was staying at a Buddhist monastery in northern India, in Kashmir, Notovitch received word of documents that spoke of an ancient sage known as Issa (the Koran uses the name Isa to refer to Jesus), who shared many of the same characteristics as the young Messiah. Notovitch was given access to the documents, 244 paragraphs grouped under the title "The life of Saint Issa," and translated them. The texts explained that Issa, "son of God, born of a virgin," had left Israel at a very young age and had traveled eastward in search of the ten lost tribes that had disappeared after the fall of the kingdom in 722 BCE.

Following the trade route through Persia, India, and the Himalayan region, Issa had lived with members of different eastern religions and had learned from them and from the basic aspects of their philosophy, before returning to Israel aged 29.

**↑ Eastern religions**
During his travels to the East, Jesus may have lived with different religious communities—Jains, Brahmins, and Buddhists—who would have shaped his message.

East, with no sexual connotation whatsoever. Some experts even cast doubt on the authenticity of the letter, given that the one found by Smith is a copy from the eighteenth century and, photographs taken by the researcher aside, nobody else has ever seen them. In any case, if the letter were authentic and the sections had been censored, other sections could equally have been censored.

### TRANSLATION AND INTERPRETATION
We should also not overlook the "accidents" that the text may have experienced during its translation into Coptic, Aramaic, Greek, and Spanish. In the Gospels According to Matthew and Luke, Jesus is claimed to have said: "It is easier for a camel to go through the eye of a needle, than for a rich man to enter into the kingdom of God." The phrase gained popularity, although some nitpicking translators assert that Jesus was not referring to a camel, *kamelos* in Greek, but a *kamilos*, a thick string. Which would change the phrase to: "It is easier for a thick piece of string to go through the eye of a needle, than for a rich man to enter into the kingdom of God."

Furthermore, the possibility of misinterpretations must be considered. Thus, for example, the *koiné* of Jesus have been controversial: James, Joseph, Thomas, and Judas. *Koiné*, in Greek, translates as "brother," which, to some extent, could contradict the theory that the mother of Jesus was a virgin, as asserted by the Catholic Church. However, the Protestant Church accepts that Mary may have had more children after Jesus. In any case, it is true that *koiné* may translate as "brother," but also as "half-brother," or "cousin".

### APOCRYPHAL TEXTS
Throughout the twentieth century, different researchers have debated whether the Gospels are a reliable source of information on historical Jesus: first, the Gospel According to John (analyzed by David Friedrich Strauss), then the Gospels According to Matthew and Luke (by Christian Hermann Weisse and Christian Gottlob Wilke), before finally the Gospel According to Mark (by Wilhelm Wrede and Karl Ludwig Schmidt, in addition to Wilke). However, authors like Bultmann opened a new approach by stating that it is irrelevant whether the Jesus reflected in the Gospels is real or not; what is important is his message.

In 1945, a new element was added to the debate. In Nag Hammadi, Upper Egypt, a clay vase was found that contained documents belonging to the New Testament—in other words, documents on the life of Jesus. Carbon-14 analysis proved their age, but what really caused controversy was the content of some of the texts, which spoke directly of Jesus. What was most surprising was that they described a very human Jesus, who experienced emotions such as love, hate, and rage—a person who evolved as a result of his experiences until he became the catalyst of an extraordinary religious movement. The authenticity of these writings may be subject to debate. However, they offered a vision of a Jesus held by other Christians which had, until then, not found its place within the official Church. If only because of this fact, their discovery was most interesting. Nor would it be unreasonable to suggest that they may also have influenced the texts accepted by the Church.

# Did he marry Mary Magdalene?

In the Gospels, there are 18 mentions of Mary Magdalene that place her in the foreground in many of the most important passages in Jesus's life: she mourns his death at the foot of the cross and enters his tomb at dawn to anoint his body. From this, it may be concluded that she was very close to him. She is also the person to discover the empty tomb and, as described by the Gospel According to John, the first to discover the Messiah following his resurrection. However, the Gospels offer no information about the age, occupation, or family of Mary Magdalene. They do not specify whether she was a mother, sister, or daughter of anyone, whereas these qualifications were commonly used in the Gospel when referring to women. Why would a mere disciple occupy such an important place next to the cross? In fact, she is the only person to consistently appear at the crucifixion across all canonical Gospels.

Researchers Michael Baigent, Richard Leigh, and Henry Lincoln, authors of the book, *The Holy Blood and the Holy Grail*, have suggested that the famous wedding at Cana, Jesus's first public miracle, could actually have been the wedding between the Messiah and Mary Magdalene. Among other aspects, the basis of their argument is that it would be strange for the Virgin Mary to have directly informed Jesus that they had run out of wine, and not the bride and groom. Furthermore, the name of the newly married couple is never mentioned.

**↓ The Magdalene with the Smoking Flame**
This oil painting by Georges de La Tour (c. 1640) depicts Mary Magdalene meditating at the tomb following Jesus's death.

# Rivalries and chauvinism

Certain authors believe that the chauvinism of early Christians and their desire to debunk a potential rival represented the perfect opportunity to sully the image of Mary Magdalene. The Gospel of Philip, found in 1945 among the Nag Hammadi manuscripts, supports the theory that she was Christ's partner and the person to whom he entrusted his message. The text states, "They asked him why he loved her more than all the disciples, and used to kiss her often on her ..." Ants seem to have eaten the missing word, although some cryptographers assert that it was "mouth." The mystery will go unresolved forever. Earlier, in 1896, German scholar Karl Reinhardt found a manuscript dating back to the third century which he named the Gospel of Mary Magdalene as Mary appears therein as Christ's chosen disciple. Peter asks: "Sister, we know that the Savior loved you more than the rest of the women. Tell us the words of the Savior which you remember, which you know (but) we do not, nor have we heard them." Mary responds that everything that is hidden will be revealed to them, and encourages them to spread Christ's message. In this, and other apocryphal tests, there appears to be a clear rivalry between Peter and Mary Magdalene. "Did He then speak secretly with a woman, in preference to us, and not openly? Are we to turn back and all listen to her? Did He prefer her to us?" Peter asks at one point. Another of his followers defends her: "But if the Savior made her worthy, who are you indeed to reject her? Surely the Savior knows her very well. That is why He loved her more than us."

# Biblical geography

Jesus was born in Bethlehem in Judea, at the end of the reign of Herod the Great. Judea and Galilee are alleged to have been the regions of Jesus's preaching, although some believe he traveled as far as India.

## The main stages of Jesus's journey

Orthodox Catholics argue that after fleeing to Egypt in childhood, Jesus lived in Galilee until age 30, when he began to preach. Other theories speak of prior learning journeys to distant lands and of death perhaps in Japan or in the Himalayas.

**❶ Bethlehem**
Birth and early days of Jesus's life. Tradition says that Herod the Great ordered the killing of all children born in Bethlehem under two years old, to avoid having one of them displace him as King of the Jews.

**❷ Egypt**
According to the Gospel of Matthew, an angel told Joseph: "Get up, take the child and his mother and flee to Egypt." The family remained there until the death of Herod.

**❸ Nazareth**
Mary, Joseph, and Jesus stayed here on their return from Egypt, thus fulfilling the prophecy of the Old Testament: "The Savior will be called the Nazarene." Herod Antipas ruled in Galilee.

**❹ Jerusalem**
There were two major events for Jesus in Jerusalem: at age 12, when he debated with the sages in the Temple, and at 33, when he entered the city riding a donkey, shortly before he was crucified on Mount Calvary.

**❺ India**
According to some researchers, Jesus traveled to India at 12 or 13 years of age, and lived there before returning to Palestine. Others believe that his actual grave is in Kashmir, where he died at an age of over 100 years.

**❻ Qasr el Yahud**
This place by the River Jordan was where, according to tradition, John baptized Jesus, marking the beginning of his public life.

**❼ Capernaum**
A town where Jesus, after spending 40 days in the desert, began his preaching and conducted his first miraculous cures.

**❽ Cana**
According to the Gospel of John, this is where the first miracle of Jesus, turning water into wine at a wedding, took place. The Apocrypha claim that that was his own marriage ceremony with Mary Magdalene.

**❾ Mount Tabor**
Close to Nazareth, this is where the Transfiguration of Jesus took place, when he changed his appearance. With him came the prophets Moses and Elijah, who had died long before.

## Power in Jesus's time

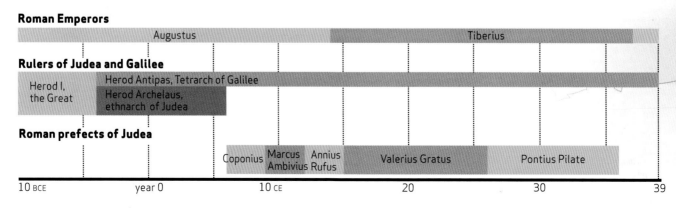

**Roman Emperors**

| Augustus | Tiberius |

**Rulers of Judea and Galilee**

Herod I, the Great
Herod Antipas, Tetrarch of Galilee
Herod Archelaus, ethnarch of Judea

**Roman prefects of Judea**

Coponius | Marcus Ambivius Rufus | Annius Rufus | Valerius Gratus | Pontius Pilate

| 10 BCE | year 0 | 10 CE | 20 | 30 | 39 |

# Why is it said that Jesus was born in a stable in the village of Bethlehem?

There is no agreement about whether Jesus was born in a stable, a cave, or a house, or why it was in Bethlehem. The Gospel of Matthew says that Joseph and Mary lived there, but Luke says he traveled from Nazareth to register, since Joseph was from Bethlehem. Finding no inn, it is said that Mary gave birth in a stable, perhaps attached to an inn.

**PROVINCE OF SYRIA**

Sidon

Zarephath

Damascus

*Perea*

Tyre

Paneas
(Caesarea Philippi)

*Phoenicia*    *Ulatha*

*Trachonitis*

Lake Huleh

*Gaulanitis*

Acco

*Batanea*

Capernaum

Gennesaret    Bethsaida **7**

*Galilee*    Magdala    Sea of

*Aurantis*

Tiberias    *Galilee*

Cana    **8**

Nazareth    **3**    **9**

Nain    Mount
Tabor    Gadara

Cesarea

*Decápolis*

Salim

Aenon

*India*
(2,175 miles/3,500 km away)    **5** →

Gergesa

Samaria

*Samaria*    Sychar

Antipatris

Joppa    Arimathea

*Peraea*

Efraum

**ARABIAN
DESERT**

Lydda

Mount of
Olives    Jericho

Emmaus    **6**    Qasr el Yahud

Ashdod

Jerusalem    **4**    Bethphage

Betania    Julias

Ascalon    **1**    Bethlehem

*Judea*

Gaza

*Idumaea*

Dead
Sea

**MEDITERRANEAN
SEA**

*River Jordan*

### Israel at the time of Jesus

- ● Kingdom of Herod the Great, 6 BCE
- ○ Places associated with Christ
- ···· Places associated with other New Testament figures
- Roman administration
- Tetrarchy of Philip
- Tetrarchy of Herod Antipas

**2**
**EGYPT**

N
0    MILES    125

*Nabatea*

EUROPE    Caspian
Sea

● Rome    Black Sea

ASIA

*Mediterranean Sea*

● Jerusalem

Magnified
area

Roman Empire 1 CE

# Jesus and his associates

Jesus was accompanied by 12 chosen men, the Twelve Apostles, and often by his mother, family members, and faithful followers such as Mary Magdalene. It is said that the group followed the customs of the Essenes, living in community and sharing all expenses.

## The family

Jesus's immediate family were his parents, Joseph and Mary, his aunt and uncle, Elizabeth and Zechariah, his cousin, John, and, according to the apocryphal Gospels, also Mary Magdalene, as his partner. Several brothers and sisters are also mentioned.

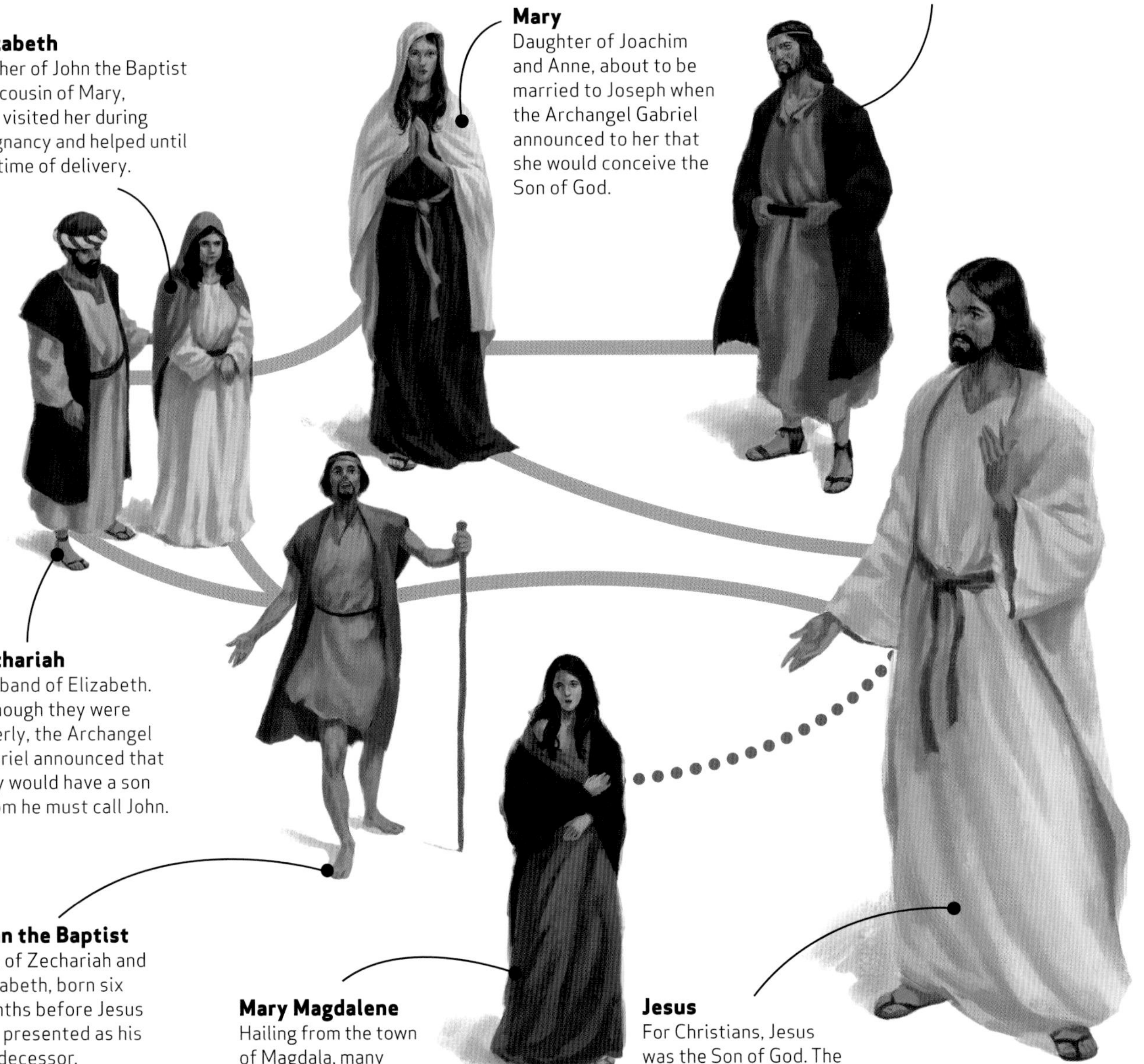

**Joseph**
Jesus's earthly father. On the point of repudiating Mary, an angel warned him that the child she expected was conceived without stain.

**Elizabeth**
Mother of John the Baptist and cousin of Mary, who visited her during pregnancy and helped until the time of delivery.

**Mary**
Daughter of Joachim and Anne, about to be married to Joseph when the Archangel Gabriel announced to her that she would conceive the Son of God.

**Zechariah**
Husband of Elizabeth. Although they were elderly, the Archangel Gabriel announced that they would have a son whom he must call John.

**John the Baptist**
Son of Zechariah and Elizabeth, born six months before Jesus and presented as his predecessor.

**Mary Magdalene**
Hailing from the town of Magdala, many scholars consider her as Jesus's consort.

**Jesus**
For Christians, Jesus was the Son of God. The canonical Gospels narrate much of his public life.

**Is it possible that the Apostle Thomas was the identical or fraternal twin brother of Jesus?**

He was called Judas Thomas, and the name Thomas, *Te'oma* in Aramaic, means "twin," or also *Didymus* which is Greek for "twin." His name matches that of one of the brothers of Jesus mentioned in the Bible, and in the Acts of Thomas it is said of him that he was "twin brother of Christ, apostle of the high However, the Catholic Church considers him only Jesus's cousin.

# The Apostles

They were the people chosen by Jesus to preach his teachings. Initially, there were 12. After the death of Judas Iscariot, Matthias was chosen to replace him, although some consider that the replacement for Judas was really Paul of Tarsus.

**5. Andrew, the first**
Peter's brother, he was the first of the 12 apostles. Disciple of John the Baptist when he baptized Jesus.

**1. Judas Iscariot, the traitor**
Matthew tells how he delivered Jesus to the authorities in exchange for 30 pieces of silver.

**3. Philip, the supplier**
Disciple of John the Baptist, he used to mediate between Jesus and the inhabitants of the towns through which they passed.

**4. Peter, the spokesman**
A fisherman, like his brother Andrew, he was the voice of the apostolic group. He was the first pope of the Catholic Church.

**2. Bartholomew, the sincere**
Friend of Philip and considered a true Israelite, sincere and faithful.

**6. John, the beloved disciple**
The youngest of the apostles. With his brother James and Peter, the closest to the Messiah.

**11. Simon, the nationalist**
Activist in a Jewish faction that fought against Roman rule.

**12. Judas Thaddeus, the Judaist**
Considered one of the strictest followers of the Jewish tradition within the apostolic group.

**7. James the Older, the closest**
Brother of John, he was one of the closest to Jesus. He was present at the Transfiguration.

**8. Matthew, the tax collector**
Before becoming an apostle he was a publican, a tax collector for Rome: one of the most detested professions.

**9. James the Younger, the respected**
Jesus's cousin, they were very similar. After the Crucifixion he was one of the most respected members.

**10. Thomas the Doubter**
Cousin, or according to some, brother of Jesus, who did not believe in his resurrection until he saw the wounds on his body.

# Domestic life

The canonical Gospels are not very informative about the daily life of Jesus, although the apocryphal texts fill the gaps. These, together with works such as the painting by Millais, help to give an idea of how his life could have been in childhood.

## The Holy Family at home

There are many artistic representations of the Holy Family in the privacy of their home, and they offer different interpretations. On these two pages, the mystical spirituality of Francisco de Zurbarán (left) from the seventeenth century, is contrasted with the prosaic realism of the painting by Millais (below).

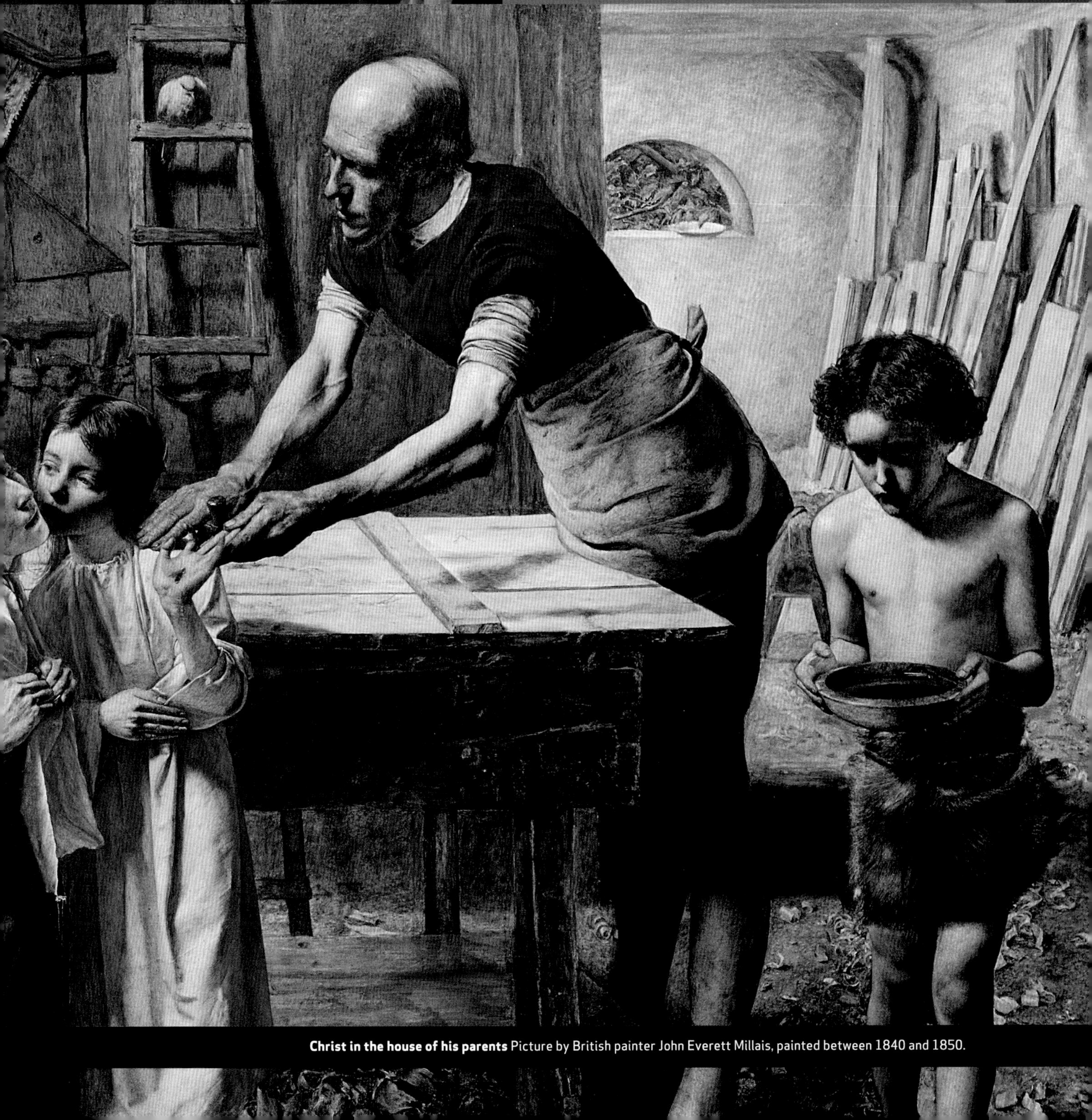

**Christ in the house of his parents** Picture by British painter John Everett Millais, painted between 1840 and 1850.

# Biblical archaeology

Since they started, excavations in the Holy Land have frequently brought science and religion together. The weight of these two elements is not always balanced.

## Tools

Current archaeological research uses a variety of tools to carry out fieldwork. Two of the most important are aerial photography and magnetometers.

### Aerial photography
A complement to images taken in the field, aerial photography provides a very important viewing angle for archaeological research since, among other things, it can detect structures that are difficult or impossible to see from the ground. On the left, the remains of the fortress of Masada in the Judean desert, used by Herod the Great as a refuge.

### Magnetometer
This is used to detect magnetic fields produced by certain elements found in the ground and forming part of archaeological deposits. It is very useful in areas that cannot be protected or excavated. The picture shows an archaeologist with a magnetometer at the site of Marib (ancient kingdom of Sheba).

## 200 years of research in the Holy Land

**1838**
American geographer Edward Robinson traveled to the Holy Land to locate the biblical cities. His study is still a reference work today.

**1865**
The British Palestine Exploration Fund created to boost archaeological excavation. The Temple of Jerusalem was studied for the first time.

**1890**
British Egyptologist William Matthew Flinders Petrie first applied stratigraphic analysis to date findings in the deposits of the Holy Land.

**1892**
First issue of the prestigious *Revue Biblique*, associated with the École Biblique et Archéologique Française de Jérusalem, founded in 1890.

## A science for the faithful?

The first archaeologists came to the Holy Land seeking scientific justification for the stories from the Bible: on the left, the tomb of Lazarus at Bethany, around 1890. However, from the 1970s, a new trend has arisen that opposes that idea and suggests that the Bible should not be read as a historical account.

### Fishing boat

The discovery of unique remains, such as this ship from the Sea of Galilee in the time of Jesus, is a reward for biblical archaeology, as they help to confirm or refute hypotheses that had no archaeological evidence to sustain them.

## Documents

The manuscripts found in the archaeological excavations are mostly papyrus or parchment. Papyrology reconstructs the fragments found, and interprets the data for other scholars to use in their research.

### Papyrus

Made from leaves of the plant from which it takes its name and used as a writing medium until the second century.

### Parchment

More durable than papyrus, as it is made from leather, and was used in the West until the arrival and popularization of paper.

### Codex

Codices (books made of papyrus or parchment) are the oldest preserved texts about the life of Jesus, such as the Sinaiticus (above), dating from the fourth century.

| 1914 | 1918 | 1948 | 1952 | 1967 | 21st century |
|---|---|---|---|---|---|
| The outbreak of World War I forced the Allied archaeologists to leave the area, which would remain in Ottoman hands until the end of the conflict. | Resumption of excavation in Palestine; William Foxwell Albright provided a detailed chronology linking archaeology and biblical stories. | After the proclamation of the State of Israel, the Zionist archaeologists tried to use their research to prove the Jews' right to the territory of Palestine. | British archaeologist Kathleen Kenyon studied the ancient city of Jericho and failed in her attempt to link the actual date of its destruction with the biblical account. | The occupation of Gaza, Sinai, and the West Bank by Israel in the Six-Day War offered a new field of study for archaeologists in the Holy Land. | The work still continues, although even the twenty-first century tools have not yet been able to establish the historical accuracy of many Bible passages. |

# CHAPTER 10

# Lost Cities of the Amazon

The Amazon, one of the largest unexplored territories on Earth, has begun to reveal its secrets. Recent research seems to confirm the existence of civilizations that would have brought together thousands of people.

Until quite recently, it was believed that the impenetrable jungles on the shores of the world's longest and mightiest river would only have provided shelter to small tribes of hunter-gatherers. However, evidence began to emerge just a few years ago suggesting that they may have been home to thousands of people in the past, who lived in complex, structured societies that may have inhabited this vast area for hundreds, or perhaps even thousands, of years.

### NEW EVIDENCE

Scientists and researchers such as Dr. Anna C. Roosevelt, from the Anthropology Department at the Field Museum of Natural History in Chicago; Brazilian archaeologist Dr. Eduardo Neves, from the University of São Paulo; Colombian anthropologist Augusto Oyuela-Caycedo, from the University of Florida; and Michael Heckenberger of German nationality from the same institution, have explored and studied faraway places such as San Martín de Samiria, close to the Ucayali River, in Peru; the banks of the Madeira River, in northeast Bolivia; Manaus, at the center of the Brazilian Amazon; the lands of the Xingu people, in southern Brazil (close to the river of the same name); and the island of Marajó, at the mouth of the Amazon.

In all these places they found evidence of advanced cultures that could have sustained thousands of people on what had until recently been considered infertile land, incapable of generating sufficient resources and food supplies for complex societies to evolve.

In San Martín de Samiria, Augusto Oyuela-Caycedo found remains of orchards that may have been worked by humans, movement of agricultural land, and mounds of earth enriched with coal, phosphorus, and calcium, dated to 900 CE using carbon-14 analysis, that could have fed up to 5,000 people.

In northern Bolivia, American, Finnish, and German archaeologists have also found mounds of fertile soil, raised fields, large paths, and water channels constructed around 1200–1300 CE, in addition to evidence of settlements that may have been home to more than 2,500 people. Furthermore, in this area, jungle deforestation has made it possible to identify several enigmatic geoglyphs;

**Xingu village**
Aerial view of a typical Xingu village, set out in a circular shape, on the shores of the Xingu River, a tributary of the Amazon River, in Brazil.

**→ El Dorado**
A 1599 illustration of the mythical city of El Dorado, located on the shores of the imaginary Lake Parima, close to the River Essequibo in Guyana.

**→→ Excavation of Terra Preta**
Extremely fertile plots of land have been uncovered in the Amazon Basin. This is attributable to the *terra preta* ("dark earth"): an extremely rich manmade mixture of nutrients.

large shapes and linear and geometric structures, mostly circular or rectangular, but occasionally triangular or polygonal, that are only visible from the air. These forms are reminiscent of the Nazca lines in Peru, and seem to represent evidence of a very ancient human presence.

In Manaus, in addition to apparently intensively worked orchards, Eduardo Neves has excavated soils artificially fertilized using charcoal, human waste, and other organic materials. He has also discovered the remains of what appears to be a large square and other works dating back to between 970 and 1440 CE. Very close by, at the Pedra Pintada cave, some 6 miles/10 km from the Amazon River and halfway between Manaus and Belém, Dr. Anna C. Roosevelt made a discovery in 1992 that revolutionized theories about population on the continent: she found around 30,000 specimens, including fossils, that were studied in depth and revealed that the caves were occupied up to 10,000-11,200 years ago.

Finally, along the Xingu River, one of the many Brazilian tributaries of the Amazon, Michael Heckenberger found and completed an in-depth study on what appeared to be networks of ditches, embankments, pathways, channels, and remnants of a civilization that, according to the researcher, existed around 800 CE, much earlier than the arrival of the Spanish conquistadors in the New World. These findings, together with the remnants of ceramics produced on the island of Marajó,

where the foundations of buildings and evidence of advanced agriculture, capable of feeding more than 100,000 people, have been found, give strength to a theory that the Amazon was inhabited by one or more cultures—developed and well-structured societies that were able to "tame" this wild landscape and provide food and accommodation for thousands of people, who would have lived in wooden constructions built in urban centers interlinked by wide avenues.

### DISCREPANCIES
Not all researchers agree with this theory. Betty J. Meggers, until her death in 2012 Director of the Latin American Archaeology Program at the Smithsonian Institute and author of the book, *Amazonia: Man and Culture in a Counterfeit Paradise* (1971), asserted that the Amazon is not, and never has been, suitable for housing communities of people. In her opinion, theories formulated to this end are based more on well-intended yet improbable hypotheses than scientific evidence. She publicly accused certain archaeologists of trying to put an end to previously accepted theories in order to "promote their own professional careers." However, other scientists, such as Eduardo Neves from Brazil, believe that the recent discoveries "are giving a new sense to Amazonian evolution," and that it is no longer the "black hole" of South American history.

## IN SEARCH OF "EL DORADO"

The search for cities in the Amazon is nothing new. In fact, in a bid to locate El Dorado, the mythical and fantastical kingdom in which the streets were believed to have been paved with gold, Spanish and English explorers undertook missions that have become great legends. In 1535, Spanish explorer Sebastián de Belalcázar searched the southwestern part of the Northern Andes, close to Colombia, as did Gonzalo Jiménez de Quesada, who the following year traced the territory of the Muisca population.

However, the most famous expedition was undertaken in 1541 by Gonzalo Pizarro (the governor of Quito at the time) along with Francisco de Orellana, traveling east from Peru. After dividing into two groups, Pizarro and his men returned to Quito, ordering Orellana to continue his journey in search of provisions down the Napo River. He continued with a group of 50 men toward the confluence with the Trinidad River and, driven by the currents, on to the Amazon River, which he himself named, reaching its mouth in 1542. He traveled with Dominican missionary, Gaspar de Carvajal, who would enter history as the author who narrated the expedition. The work entitled *Relación del nuevo descubrimiento del famoso río Grande que descubrió por muy gran ventura el capitán Francisco de Orellana* ("Account of the recent discovery of the famous Grand River which was discovered by great good fortune by Captain Francisco de Orellana") provides invaluable information on rituals, customs, tools, and war tactics of the indigenous peoples he found along the way. The friar spoke of "sparkling cities," "canoes in which dozens of warriors sailed," "straight and well-laid-out avenues," and "very fertile lands."

The testimony of Gaspar de Carvajal was disparaged for years, and described as the result of the fantasy and exaggerations of a man who sought to attract his compatriots to such places. However, recent discoveries in the Amazon have confirmed the sixteenth-century writings of the missionary: there really were large and straight roads; communities of hundreds, perhaps thousands, of people; fertile lands (with the recent discovery of the so-called *terra preta*— land enriched by humans). But were there actually cities? Perhaps there were, although they were not made of stone. From his viewpoint on the river, perhaps what Gaspar de Carvajal really saw were large wooden buildings that seemed to stack up on top of one another, behind large stockades.

## PAITITI: FACT OR FICTION?

Another site, searched for time and again in the mountainous jungles of southeast Peru, north Bolivia, and southeast Brazil, is Paititi, a fantastical city or kingdom, whose name has been written in a variety of ways, and whose etymology and meaning have been the subject of numerous debates. It is believed that

## A great civilization in the Amazon?

Until recently, the Amazon had been considered a virgin jungle, populated by tribes who arrived during the Stone Age. However, this theory is changing, as was proposed in 2009 by *Science* magazine, in which archaeologist and anthropologist Michael Heckenberger stated "under the canopy of jungle trees there is evidence of a complex pre-Columbian society."

The archaeologist, in collaboration with the Kuikuro (the largest indigenous population in Upper Xingu, north-central Brazil), excavated a network of towns and villages, interconnected by roads, that once sustained a population "perhaps 20 times greater than today," possibly up to 50,000 people, the organization of which would suggest that they implemented a regional planning system.

Communities were grouped into settlements of around 148 acres/60 ha, scattered throughout the jungle, surrounded by high stockades. His team compiled maps of groups divided into settlements, each of which had a main ceremonial center and several satellite villages located in very specific positions around the center. It is estimated that the ancestors of today's Kuikuro may have started to alter the structure of the jungle up to 1,500 years ago.

**←The same model**
Kayapo settlement, from the Xingu culture, beside the Iriri River.

during the Incan Empire, the jungle that crossed the Madre de Dios River was called Antisuyu, and its settlers the Anti (from which the name of the Andes originated). Legend also has it that a sovereign from Cusco may have gained control of this region in which several Amazonian tribes lived, worshipping him with gold offerings. Incan legend states that the Andean god Inkarri created a city akin to Cusco in the jungle, a long time before the arrival of the Spanish conquistadors, ten days' walk east of the Incan capital. It is also said that after the arrival of the Europeans in 1533, Prince Huascar and a number of Incan priests transferred enormous wealth to Paititi, making it the final stronghold of the civilization after the fall of Vilcabamba and the execution of Túpac Amaru. Finally, another version places Paititi much farther east, on the modern-day border between Bolivia and Brazil, an area that for centuries was inhabited by the Moxo, in whose language, Arawak, *paititi* means "white and sparkling." It is precisely in this area of the Bolivian Amazon (the Moxo plains) that geoglyphs have recently been discovered, in addition to canals and walls, attributed to an ancient confederation of Amazonian tribes.

### SOURCES
There are a range of written testimonies. One of them was left by Jesuit missionary Andrea López, who, around 1600 CE, reported the existence of a large city, rich in gold, silver, and jewels, located in the middle of the jungle, "close to the waterfall called Paititi by the natives." Another, from 1618, is also attributed to a Jesuit, Blas Valera, presumed to be the author of *Exul Immeritus Blas Valera Populo Suo*, which includes two engravings in which the city of Paititi is depicted from the jungle and the mountain. Both testimonies are recent findings: the first, discovered by Italian archaeologist Mario Polia in 2001, is in an archive in Rome; the second, in 1999, was found by Italian scholar Laura Laurencich Minelli.

Researchers have not ruled out the possibility that there were Incan constructions much deeper into the forest than is currently generally accepted. It is known that those who built the Tawantinsuyu—the Old Incan Empire—maintained an active presence in the western Amazon jungle and that the links between the coast, mountains, and jungle were more common than had previously been accepted by most scholars. There are a variety of paved routes into the jungle and many more are discovered daily. However, there are people, such as Juan Álvarez Maldonado, who participated in jungle explorations in Peru in 1568, who still believe that Paititi was merely the name of a great river—the Amazon.

Another of the lost mythical cities of the Amazon is cited in "Manuscript 512," a Brazilian document from the eighteenth century, for which English explorer Percy Fawcett diligently searched and baptized "Z." This document describes the city but does not name it. Fawcett lost his life during his quest.

It is highly likely that the geoglyphs, the remains of the "garden-cities" found in the Xingu region, and the Marajó culture are not directly related, as perhaps the *terra preta* may be. Nonetheless, these findings serve to demonstrate that vast sections of the Amazon were densely populated prior to the arrival of the first European colonizers in the New World.

## The Muribeca mines

In addition to El Dorado and Paititi, the Europeans also searched for the legendary Muribeca mines that have been inscribed in the history books thanks to none other than "Manuscript 512." In 1753, an expedition of *bandeirantes* (colonial Brazilian explorers), headed by Francisco Raposo and João da Silva Guimaraes, ventured into the jungle covering the modern-day Brazilian state of Bahía in search of the fantastical Muribeca mines. They found no riches, but rather a lost city, describing its Cyclopean and Greco-Roman architecture in a report later sent to the viceroy. The document disappeared until it was stumbled upon among the shelves of the Rio de Janeiro court library, in 1839. It was submitted to the Brazilian Historic and Geographic Institute, and this organization assumed responsibility for publishing it. Shelved in the "Manuscripts, strange works" section of the Rio de Janeiro National Library, the document appeared under its present name in 1881 in the Brazilian Historical Exposition catalog. Percy Fawcett believed that with this manuscript he had found the route to the lost city of "Z."

Current local road

Embankment
Ditch
Mound

## Who is responsible for the Acre geoglyphs?

In Acre, a region of Brazil, deforestation has revealed a number of strange symbols carved into the soil, similar to the Nazca lines. To date, 210 of these geoglyphs have been classified, such as those described by Alceu Ranzi, a geologist and paleontologist at the University of Acre, who discovered the symbols from a plane during the 1980s, in an area of Brazil close to the border with Bolivia and Peru. An investigation that he led suggested that a complex pre-Columbian society had existed in the area of the upper Purus River, a tributary of the Amazon. The geology itself, combined with the size of the geoglyphs—some measure up to 985 ft/300 m in diameter—are proof of the existence of a sedentary and organized society. Although the purpose of these figures is unknown, it has been calculated that the society that created them may have included at least 70,000 people. The carvings are between 3-13 ft/1-4 m deep. Although analysis has dated the geoglyphs to the eighth century, it is believed that the culture responsible for them inhabited the Amazon 1,000 years before.

**↑Fazenda Colorada**
Discovered in Rio Branco, Brazil, the Fazenda Colorada geoglyph is one of the most complex figures discovered as it is made up of three geometric figures.

**←Prodigious city**
Image of "Manuscript 512," preserved in Rio de Janeiro.

# Remnants of civilization

Since the 1960s, the rich archaeological finds of the Amazon seem to support the researchers who argue for the existence of a complex civilization in the Amazon River Basin.

## Findings in the jungle

Conquerors, explorers, and adventurers have ventured into the Amazon in search of lost cities, built by a civilization that disappeared without leaving any trace in history. The archaeological remains found in recent years are, for many archaeologists, evidence that there was a complex, developed civilization that learned to live with and even dominate the forest.

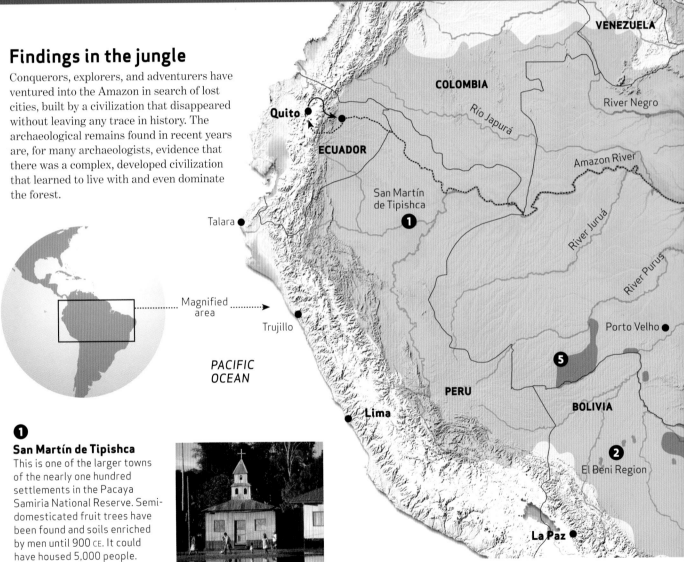

Magnified area

Talara

Trujillo

PACIFIC OCEAN

Lima

Quito

ECUADOR

San Martín de Tipishca ❶

COLOMBIA

VENEZUELA

Río Japurá

River Negro

Amazon River

River Juruá

River Purus

Porto Velho

❺

PERU

BOLIVIA

❷ El Beni Region

La Paz

### ❶ San Martín de Tipishca

This is one of the larger towns of the nearly one hundred settlements in the Pacaya Samiria National Reserve. Semi-domesticated fruit trees have been found and soils enriched by men until 900 CE. It could have housed 5,000 people.

### ❷ El Beni, Bolivia

Archaeological work in this region of northern Bolivia has discovered paths, high ground for cultivation, and channels built in rivers around 1200 CE. It is estimated that between then and 1600 CE, the population may have reached 25,000.

### ❸ Xingu National Park

Located in the state of Mato Grosso, Brazil, this park was created to protect various indigenous tribes and houses the remains of a series of interconnected circular cities, which are one of the main evidences of an ancient civilization in the region.

**Is there linguistic evidence that confirms the thesis of a separate civilization?**

It is known that indigenous groups of Llanos de Mojos (Bolivia), settled on plots of *terra preta* soil and used words for cultivated crops such as "maize" and "cotton" that were 2,000 years old. This linguistic peculiarity suggests a local origin in a very ancient culture.

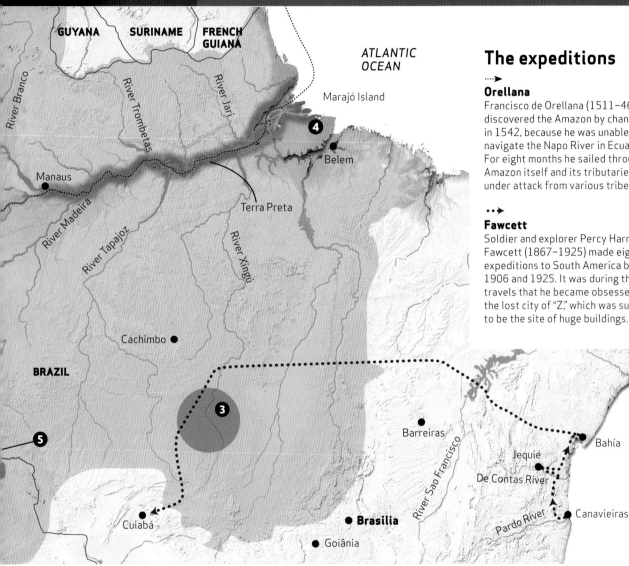

GUYANA  SURINAME  FRENCH GUIANA

ATLANTIC OCEAN

River Branco

River Trombetas

River Jari

Marajó Island

**4**

Manaus

Belem

River Madeira

Terra Preta

River Tapajoz

River Xingú

Cachimbo

**BRAZIL**

**3**

**5**

Barreiras

Bahía

Jequié

De Contas River

River Sao Francisco

Cuiabá

**Brasilia**

Pardo River

Canavieiras

Goiânia

## The expeditions

····▶

### Orellana
Francisco de Orellana (1511–46) discovered the Amazon by chance in 1542, because he was unable to navigate the Napo River in Ecuador. For eight months he sailed through the Amazon itself and its tributaries, coming under attack from various tribes.

··▶

### Fawcett
Soldier and explorer Percy Harrison Fawcett (1867–1925) made eight expeditions to South America between 1906 and 1925. It was during these travels that he became obsessed with the lost city of "Z," which was supposed to be the site of huge buildings.

**4**

### Marajó Island
Important findings of pottery shards were discovered on the world's largest river island. The pottery's unique style, compared with other ceramic styles found in the Amazon, suggests that it was a key urban center that may have housed up to 100,000 people.

**5**

### Geoglyphs
Deforestation in Bolivia and Brazil has uncovered geoglyphs made up of geometric shapes up to 330 ft/100 m wide. Many are interconnected by roads, and it is believed they were traced out by a sophisticated culture.

# Amazon urban planning

Archaeological finds belie the supposed "Stone Age" character of the Amazonian peoples. Their social structures were advanced and hierarchical, as evidenced by local tribes in the Upper Xingu.

## Circular cities

The first inhabitants of Mato Grosso came from the west about 1,500 years ago. Before the arrival of Europeans they already coexisted in a complex urban system of interconnected centers that was remarkable for its circular cities, protected by high palisades of logs, which may well be the "walled cities" that Francisco de Orellana referred to in 1542.

### Extension

Today, the remains of about 20 population centers have been located, which, if they were put together, would occupy an area similar to that of Maryland and would house about 50,000 inhabitants.

### Types

In the area studied, three types of centers were found: cities and ceremonial centers; towns or villages; and centers without any construction.

### Orientation

The centers are connected by a series of paths. The main paths run east-west, with secondary paths going north-south.

### Avenues

The main "avenues" that are preserved measure about 65 ft/20 m wide, but some may have reached 130 ft/40 m.

### SOUTH AMERICA

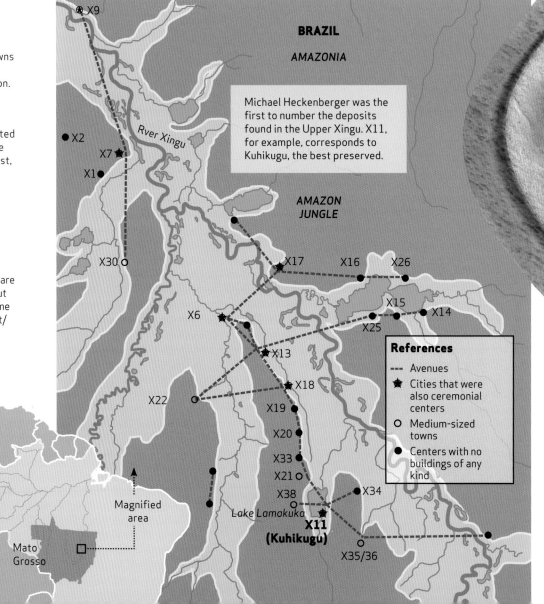

X9

**BRAZIL**

*AMAZONIA*

Rver Xingu

X2

X7

X1

Michael Heckenberger was the first to number the deposits found in the Upper Xingu. X11, for example, corresponds to Kuhikugu, the best preserved.

*AMAZON JUNGLE*

X30

X17  X16  X26

X15

X6  X25  X14

X13

X18

X22  X19

X20

X33

X21

X38  X34

*Lake Lamakuka*

**X11 (Kuhikugu)**

X35/36

Magnified area

Mato Grosso

#### References

- - - Avenues
★ Cities that were also ceremonial centers
○ Medium-sized towns
● Centers with no buildings of any kind

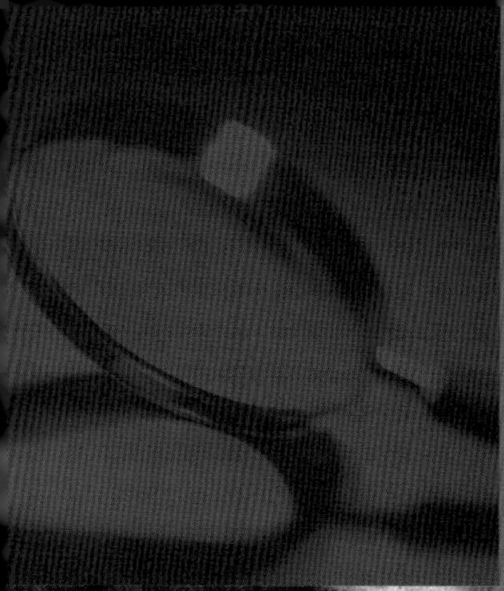

## What determined the size of the urban centers?

The towns were large or small depending on the particular features of the land where they were located, although another theory refutes this topographic explanation. It argues that the greater the "political" weight of its indigenous leaders, the greater the size of the town with respect to others.

## Kuhikugu, the best preserved

Of all the cities, Kuhikugu has provided the most details about the way of life of the ancestors of the tribes that now inhabit the Mato Grosso. It reveals that the largest expansion of the indigenous population of Upper Xingu took place between 1200 and 1400.

### The Kuikuro

It is believed that the Kuikuro, one of the tribes of Mato Grosso, who are descendants of the Caribs, once occupied Kuhikugu. The ceramic remains found seem to support this theory.

Palisade

Double palisade

**Fertile soils**
The garden and grounds show that these tribes were able to make the Amazon soil more fertile and productive.

Chief's house

Central Square

Homes

Avenues

Orchard

Access to the lake

**Powerful families**
The most influential families of the tribe were distributed to the northeast and southwest of the city, with the chief always in the center. Their houses were larger than others.

**Protection**
The presence of fences is still unexplained. What did they protect the inhabitants from? If it was from rival tribes, why leave the side open to the lagoon without protection, as in Kuhikugu?

# CHAPTER 11

# Giant Sculptures of Easter Island

Striking stone giants protect Easter Island, at the heart of the Pacific Ocean. Over centuries, the world's most isolated population developed a culture whose secrets, for the main part, remain unsolved.

In 1722, Dutch sailor Jacob Roggeveen traveled deep into the Pacific Ocean, into previously uncharted territory, in a convoy of three vessels. Almost 2,240 miles/ 3,600 km from the South American coast, he stumbled across a small triangular-shaped island and anchored in a bay on its northern shore. The date of his arrival was April 5: Easter Sunday.

The island was populated, although the food supply of its inhabitants was sparse: hens, rats, and the few vegetables they were able to produce. Rapa Nui residents were unable to go out to sea in order to fish as they did not have the material required to make boats. What most caught the sailor's attention were the giant sculptures—the moai—almost all of which had been knocked over, that lined the coastline on enormous stone platforms. The

difference between the handful of inhabitants with scarce resources and the exaggerated features of the sculptures was evident. As if the figures were not striking enough, and the manner of transporting them to their resting place a complete mystery, the real enigma was how such a complex society could have existed, capable of such feats, while being so isolated from the rest of the world.

The original name of the island remains unknown to this day. Among the names traditionally used, the most frequent was Henna, "Navel of the Earth." The current natives call the island Rapa Nui (Great Rapa). However, the island's official name is Easter Island, as it appears on modern-day maps of Chile, to which it has belonged since 1888; the translations of the island's names include *Isla de Pascua* in Spanish, or *Île de*

*Pâques* in French. Although studies have been able to shine a light on its history and culture, it has not been possible to unveil all the island's mysteries. Rapa Nui, the most isolated inhabited island on Earth, is located at the heart of the Pacific Ocean, 2,236 miles/3,599 km from continental Chile and 2,517 miles/4,050 km from Tahiti. Pitcairn, 1,398 miles/2,250 km away, is the nearest inhabited island.

The island's location, halfway between America and Polynesia, has fueled speculation about the origin of its inhabitants; as a result, researchers have looked in both directions. However, although some Incan legends mention expeditions that may have reached some Polynesian islands, it has been impossible to scientifically prove the presence of indigenous Americans in the Pacific.

**At the foot of the volcano**
Surrounding the Rano Raraku volcano, on the east side of Easter Island, there are dozens of complete and incomplete moai. It was from here that the raw materials to make the enormous statues were obtained.

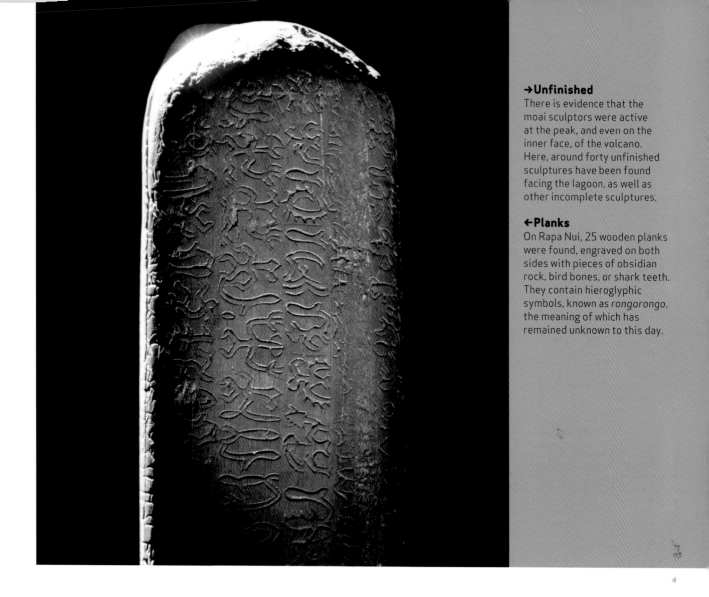

Furthermore, the distribution of two American crops in Polynesia, sweet potatoes and pumpkins, is most probably attributable to Polynesian sailors having brought them from America. In fact, there is solid evidence (chicken DNA from 1300–1400 CE) to support the arrival of Polynesian sailors in southern Chile, where they would have had contact with pre-Colombian Mapuches. It is believed these sailors would have arrived in Rapa Nui from the Marquesas Islands or from Mangareva between 800 and 1000 CE. Chilean archaeologist José Miguel Ramírez Aliaga, based on a number of shared cultural features, formulated the hypothesis that Polynesians, as part of their exploration of the eastern Pacific, reached the southern or central Chilean coast after discovering Easter Island. Between the ninth and eleventh centuries, the Polynesians embarked upon a period of expansion that lasted for centuries. Their boats, double canoes with a mobile sail that they invented, enabled them to navigate against the wind and reach impressive speeds. Their knowledge of the sea and the stars helped them to steer on their voyages.

### THE FIRST ENIGMAS

The Europeans who first made contact with the island in the eighteenth century did so sporadically and for a short period of time. Nonetheless, they were all in agreement that they had encountered an extraordinary phenomenon that was difficult to explain. Initially, they asked themselves how and from where the Rapa Nui people had come to inhabit this remote island. With the sailing instruments and boats the Europeans found when they landed on the island, it was impossible to explain how the inhabitants had arrived there, just as it was impossible to decipher what the giant sculptures represented and how and who had moved the rocks that weighed tons.

The Rapa Nui's open-air workshop, a quarry located on the Rano Raraku volcano, was the only place on the island where the compact form of ash, known as "tuff," could be found; this was the raw material of choice for carving the images that incarnated the spirits of the islanders' ancestors. Around 900 moai have been identified throughout Easter Island. Only 288 were associated with the *ahu*, the "ceremonial platforms" of the different clans, which were generally located on the coastline. Around 400 never made it out of the quarry where they were sculpted. The remainder have been found dotted all over the island. Some figures are located in their designated position, whereas others were abandoned for various reasons during transportation.

Those left at the quarry are the best source of information with which to reconstruct the entire sequence of their creation, given that the level of completion of those left unfinished varies widely. Some moai were left abandoned shortly after the sculpting process had begun, while others were left completed and ready to be transported to their final resting-place.

## THE WORKING PROCESS

Work began by cutting a piece of lapilli-tuff stone equal in size to the final moai. This material was used as its relative softness made it easy to carve. The quarry site, on the face of the volcano, made it possible for the stonemasons to work on the sculpture with relative ease. The moai was sculpted while laid flat, facing upward. The carving process started with workers cutting around the sides of the chosen piece of rock. A 24-in/60-cm wide channel was left on either side of the stone, in which the sculptors positioned themselves. This enabled several stonemasons to simultaneously carve the head (on which the nose and ears were particularly prominent), arms, hands, and the rest of the moai's body. Part of the underside of the stone was also cut out, although not totally. Thus, it remained attached, perfectly still in its place, helping work on the sculpture without it moving.

The main tools used by the craftsmen to sculpt were basalt hoes; this material was much harder than the stone out of which the moai were carved. At this very same site on Rano Raraku, a large number of these tools have been found. Once the figure was completed, it was removed from the mountainside by gently chipping into the joint that connected the sculpture to the mountain. However, the arduous task of transporting the moai still lay ahead. Given the significant difficulty involved in this task, logically the routes that best

eased the transportation of these heavy sculptures, in many cases over considerable distances, were chosen. It is likely that over time the Rapa Nui developed different techniques for transporting the moai, depending on their size and weight and the resources available. Old Rapa Nui legends aside, which state that the *ariki* (ruler) moved them, using the strength of *mana* (spiritual power), there is no doubt that, based on research undertaken, the moai were positioned, whether upright or lying face down (with plants used as protection to prevent damage) on a base of tree trunks joined together as a sled. Once they were stable, they were then slid over other transverse trunks, to reduce wear, using ropes to pull them.

Archaeologist Sergio Rapu maintains that they were transported upright, following the tradition that the moai walked, while other researchers consider that the position in which they were transported depended on their size. Levers were most likely used throughout the process, especially when lifting the figures onto the platform, in addition to ropes made from plant fibers. The marks left by a large number of trunks installed on both sides of pathways throughout the island seem to support this theory. The transportation process was always completed before installing the sculptures' coral eyes. Once the figure had been installed on its designated ahu, decorations were then carved on the moai's back. All the evidence seems to suggest that the *pukao*—the statue's

## The Polynesian clues

In 1774, British sailor, explorer, and cartographer, James Cook, visited Easter Island for four days. To his surprise, the Tahitian that accompanied him on his travels was able to communicate with the Rapa Nui. The language they spoke was related to a dialect used on the Marquesas Islands.

The tools used by the Rapa Nui (harpoons, stone hoes, hooks, basalt tools, and coral files) were also similar to others used on different Polynesian islands, as were the fishing techniques. The domestic animal they raised—chickens—also came from Polynesia, as did many of the crops on which they depended: for example, sweet potato, taro, sugar cane, and certain varieties of banana. In addition to this, recent DNA analysis on 12 human skeletons must be taken into consideration: its results provided data similar to the data obtained from the remains of Polynesians from other islands.

The Rapa Nui also shared part of their symbolic world with Polynesians: their belief in mana, the power that emanated from one's spirit, and the *tapu*, or "taboos." Polynesians started sailing around 40,000 years ago; however, their efforts grew in strength around 1000 CE, and in just 200 years, they colonized all the archipelagos in the Pacific.

**↑Sailors**
The innovative double-hulled canoe, or catamaran, was fundamental in the Polynesian conquest of the Pacific.

"headdress"—was also added at the end, once it was installed on the ahu. These cylinders, carved from the Puna Pau quarry, measured 3–6.5 ft/1–2 m wide and 6.5–10 ft/2-3 m in diameter. To test the theories about how they were moved, the entire task was performed under similar conditions. The test consisted of placing the moai vertically on a wooden sled, which was then pulled on rails with lubricated supports and fixed sleepers which generated relatively little friction. The best alternative, however, appeared to involve placing the statue face down on a sled, with the base toward the front, and pulling it on parallel trunks. With the assistance of ropes and levers, 50 or 60 people would have been able to move a moai that weighed several tons. These two alternatives were both tested successfully.

### PROGRESS AND DECADENCE

Analysis of pollen deposited on the island thousands of years ago, and studies on charcoal remains that were used to cook food, have demonstrated, for example, that much taller trees than those seen by the Europeans at the beginning of the eighteenth century originally grew on the island. Despite its isolation, the Rapa Nui lived in a period of flourishing growth that lasted a number of centuries, while they were organized into a stratified society. During this period, the population grew and may have reached 10,000 inhabitants. In the later stages of Easter Island history, around the seventeenth century, when the construction of the moai ceased and those erected were torn down, the ahu were altered to house mass burial sites, or *avanga*. This solution was adopted as a necessity, when it was impossible to continue incinerating the dead because of the lack of firewood. The high population levels exhausted the island's resources as part of an unstoppable process. The destruction of plant life made the scarcity of food supplies worse, as the volcanic soil, deprived of vegetation, was unable to retain water. The output of the island's orchards reduced dramatically.

The battle for food resulted in clashes among the 12 different clans on the island, who were divided into two groups. Their organization, progressively more military, not only crushed the opposing clans, but was also responsible for toppling the symbols that represented them—the moai. Women, children, and the weakest groups took refuge in caves. The violence caused a large environmental crisis, despite ongoing work to maintain the soil's productivity using technological advances that involved even greater efforts than constructing and transporting the moai.

The most significant impact was the loss of trees, which inhibited the continued construction of the ahu, moai, and even canoes. The Rapa Nui made efforts to adapt to these new circumstances, both economically and ideologically, until, in 1862, an international company, the Seven Friends Society, including Chilean and Peruvian businessmen, recruited them to work on farms in Peru. From the 2,000 Rapa Nui that left the island at different stages, just 15 survivors returned. Many of them caught smallpox, tuberculosis, and other diseases that transformed into epidemics, and brought the islanders to the brink of extinction. In 1877, just 110 inhabitants remained on the island. The Rapa Nui people started to recover, as a tourism-based economy, during the mid-twentieth century.

# Why were the moai destroyed?

The construction of statues at the request of the different clans that comprised Rapa Nui society became a crazed competition to see who could build the largest figures. This was the situation at the end of the seventeenth century, when the over-exploitation of arable land had exhausted the soil, which was no longer able to produce enough food to feed the island's population. Clashes over food were inevitable and rivalries between clans became more acute and polarized: two groups were left in a confrontation about an inefficient political and religious system that was unable to mitigate the food-shortage crisis.

The theocratic monarchy, which used the influential priestly class for support, was replaced by the power of military aristocracy—the *matato'a* or "warriors." The fight for survival only served to catalyze the violence. To avoid the struggle, the weakest took refuge in underground caves. The outbreak of tension swept away not only the rival clans, but also what came to symbolize them—the moai. The moai were first destroyed around 1680, and the process lasted until the nineteenth century. The last moai was destroyed in 1836.

**→ Doubts and certainties**
Whether transported vertically or horizontally, there is no doubt that entire mountains were exploited to produce the moai on Easter Island.

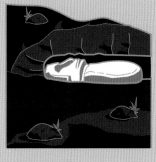

### 1. Carving the moai
The moai were carved facing upward, from the volcanic rock. Their backs were not carved so that they could be pulled down the mountainside.

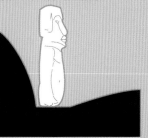

### 3. Opening the pit
Having smoothed its back, the pit into which the moai was pulled, was opened to allow the statue to continue its journey.

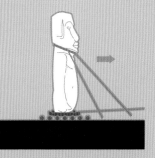

### 4b. Vertical transportation
A wooden sled was placed underneath the moai, which was transported in a swinging fashion, using ropes for assistance.

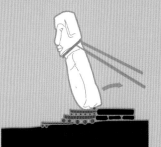

### 6. Lifting stones
Using ropes, and additional tree trunks placed beneath the sculpture, the moai were lifted onto the ahu.

### 2. Burrowed-out pit
Once the statue was detached from the rock, it was dragged to a pit burrowed into the mountain, to stand it upright using ropes and levers.

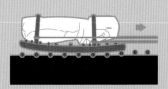

### 4a. Horizontal transportation
The sculpture was placed and transported faced down, on a sled that was pulled over tree trunks.

### 5. Positioning
Once the moai had been transported to the ahu, preparations were made to hoist it onto the platform.

### 7. Coronation
Once the statue was erected on the ahu, the stones were removed and the moai were consecrated: the final details were carved into their backs and faces; their coral eyes were inserted; and they were crowned with a *pukao*.

# Easter Island

Located in Oceania, 2,236 miles/3,599 km west of South America, the massive sculptures known as moai are the main trace left by its first inhabitants. There are about 900 of them scattered around this beautiful, enigmatic island.

## The navel of the world

The first inhabitants of the island called it Te Pito O Te Henua, meaning "The Navel of the World." In 1722, the Dutch named it Easter Island. The current inhabitants call it Rapa Nui, meaning "Great Rapa."

### LOCATION

| | |
|---|---|
| **Country** | Chile |
| **Capital** | Hanga Roa |
| **Population** | 5,800 inhabitants |
| **Density** | 91.7 inhabitants/sq mile (35.4 inhabitants/km²) |
| **Surface area** | 63.2 sq miles/163.7 km² |

Path
Track or trail
Urban center
Area with moai

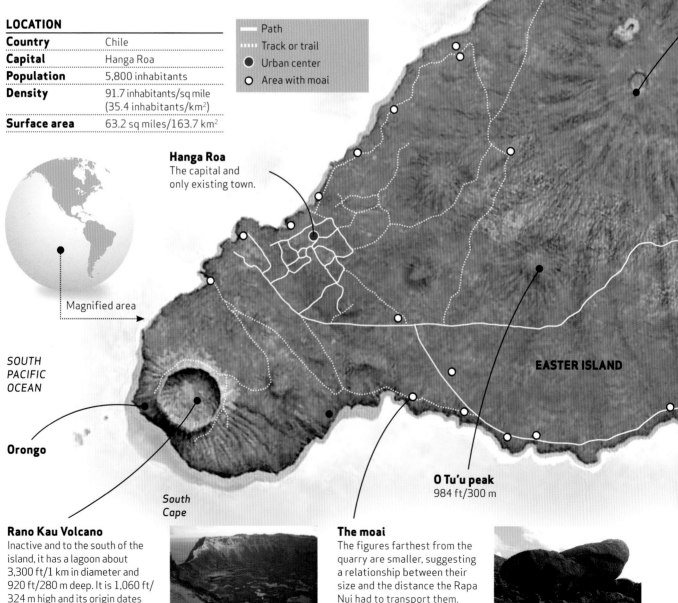

Magnified area

**Hanga Roa**
The capital and only existing town.

SOUTH PACIFIC OCEAN

**EASTER ISLAND**

**Orongo**

**O Tu'u peak**
984 ft/300 m

South Cape

**Rano Kau Volcano**
Inactive and to the south of the island, it has a lagoon about 3,300 ft/1 km in diameter and 920 ft/280 m deep. It is 1,060 ft/ 324 m high and its origin dates back some 2.5 million years.

**The moai**
The figures farthest from the quarry are smaller, suggesting a relationship between their size and the distance the Rapa Nui had to transport them.

## Was the Rongorongo writing system invented by the Rapa Nui?

The recurring symbols on the tablets found in Rapa Nui are the birdman, birds, and fishhooks. There are doubts whether the Rongorongo writing system was invented by the Rapa Nui. Some people define it as a rudimentary phonetic writing system, without sentences.

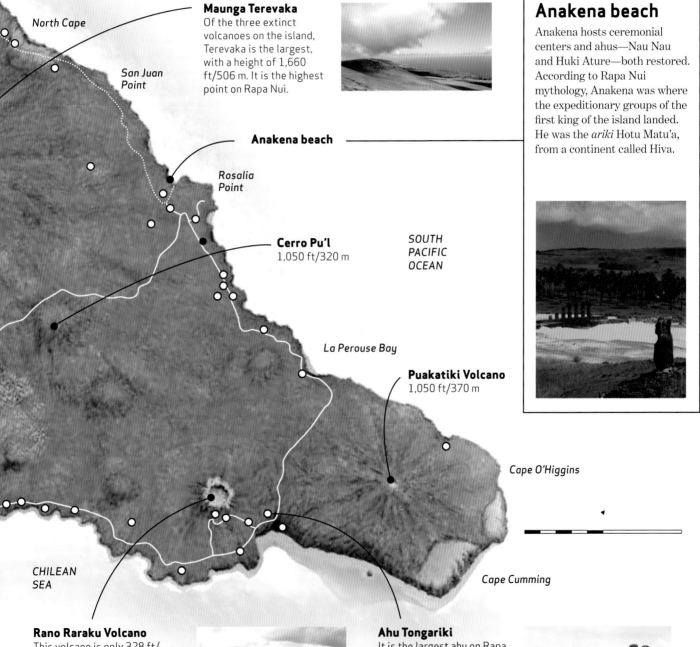

**Maunga Terevaka**
Of the three extinct volcanoes on the island, Terevaka is the largest, with a height of 1,660 ft/506 m. It is the highest point on Rapa Nui.

*North Cape*

*San Juan Point*

**Anakena beach**

*Rosalia Point*

**Cerro Pu'l**
1,050 ft/320 m

SOUTH PACIFIC OCEAN

*La Perouse Bay*

**Puakatiki Volcano**
1,050 ft/370 m

*Cape O'Higgins*

*Cape Cumming*

CHILEAN SEA

### Anakena beach

Anakena hosts ceremonial centers and ahus—Nau Nau and Huki Ature—both restored. According to Rapa Nui mythology, Anakena was where the expeditionary groups of the first king of the island landed. He was the *ariki* Hotu Matu'a, from a continent called Hiva.

**Rano Raraku Volcano**
This volcano is only 328 ft/ 100 m high and has a lagoon inside it. It is a volcanic crater formed of compacted ash, and is 300,000 years old.

**Ahu Tongariki**
It is the largest ahu on Rapa Nui, and has 15 moai. In 1960, it was devastated by a tsunami. The moai were recovered and restored.

# Anatomy of the Moai

No two moai are the same. All are carved from volcanic rock (about 800 from tuff), are often crowned with a headdress (*pukao*) of red scoria, and may have coral or obsidian eyes. On average, they measure 13 feet/4 m and weigh 12 tons.

## Distribution

Of the nearly 900 moai on Rapa Nui, 397 are concentrated in the Rano Raraku quarry, 288 are associated with the ahu and the rest are scattered around the island. Most ahu are on the coast, although there are 20 or so farther inland.

### Orientation
The ahu are positioned so that their moai turn their backs to the sea and look at the towns of their descendants, as it is believed that they are statues of dead leaders.

### Coral and obsidian eyes
All the moai with obsidian and coral or, in some cases, painted, eyes have been restored. Until 1978, when Sergio Rapu and Sonia Haoa found fragments of an original eye, nobody knew they had inlaid eyes.

## Tahai ceremonial center

About 1 mile/1.5 km from the center of Hanga Roa is Tahai, the most important monumental center of Rapa Nui, restored between 1968 and 1970 by William Mulloy. It consists of three ahu near the sea: the ahu Vai Uri has the first group of moai, beside which a canoe ramp paved with stones goes into the sea; to the right of this is the ahu Tahai, with a solitary moai without a pukao; and nearby, there is the ahu Ko Te Riku, also with just one moai, this one with a pukao.

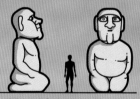

**Moai of the ahu Vai Uri**

**Moai of the ahu Tahai**

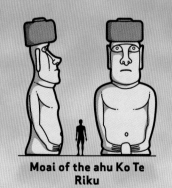

**Moai of the ahu Ko Te Riku**

**Paro: the tallest moai on an ahu**
The moai Paro is the highest. Today, it has been demolished and lies broken into three parts. A moai of the ahu Hanga Te Tenga measures a little more, but must have fallen during erection because its eye sockets have not been carved.

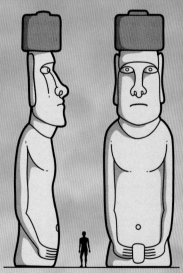

**Moai of the ahu Te Pito Kura**

## Moai Paro: technical data

| MATERIAL | WEIGHT | HEIGHT |
|---|---|---|
| Volcanic tuff of Rano Raraku | 82 tons | 32 ft/9.8 m |

## Why was the moai called "the Giant" not finished?

The largest moai on the island (68 ft/21 m high and weighing 270 tons) lies on its back on the slopes of Rano Raraku. It is not known if the Rapa Nui had no time to finish it or if they left it half-done because they saw that they would not be able to erect it.

## Ahu Ko Te Riku

The moai Ko Te Riku, standing alone in this ahu, has been restored. Eyes were added (not in the original material). It measures 17 ft/ 5.2 m and is thought to have been carved in the ninth century CE.

### Pukao
There are 58 moai on Rapa Nui with pukao. The average weight of this headdress, which some specialists think represents a hairstyle (a bun) and others a hat, is 10 tons.

### Eyes
The gaze symbolized the protection provided by the moai. After a war, the statues of the defeated tribes were pulled down and the eyes removed, to destroy their power.

### Ears
These are usually very elongated, to represent the look of the natives. In the statues from the earliest times, the ears were shorter and wider.

### The quarry of the pukao
The headdresses were carved from red scoria from a quarry at Puna Pau, 9 miles/15 km from Hanga Roa.

# The raising of the Moai

Although there is no consensus on how the moai were erected, the prevailing theory is the one depicted in this illustration. There is no doubt that great skill was needed to erect such heavy sculptures.

## On stone ramps

Once the moai were transferred to the ahu, the Rapa Nui would have gradually raised them by stacking an accumulation of stones beneath the sculpture, to make an increasingly sloped ramp. The operation was completed with the use of wooden levers, the other key element in the process of elevation. Building the ramps would have required a significant amount of additional work for the Rapa Nui, both while raising and in the subsequent clearing away.

**The levers**
They placed one or more levers on each side of the moai, between the ramp of stones and the sculpture. With these they swung the moai up toward its platform.

## Crowning of the sculptures

Most researchers believe that the pukao (left) in the crater of Puna Pau were put on each moai after it had been placed on its ahu, although others argue that they would have been raised with the moai "glued" on to it. Interestingly, the pukao placed in restorations had to be lifted by cranes.

**Control**
Skilled craftsmen who were part of the caste of nobles controlled the progress of the work.

# Unusual Moai

Among the more than 900 moai found on Easter Island, there are some that stand out. They are distinguished either by the material they are made from or by their position, their features, their decorations, or their meaning.

### Ava Rei Pua

Its torso was recovered in Anakena during Norwegian Thor Heyerdahl's expedition in 1956, while the head, unusually long, was found during the Kon Tiki Museum's expedition of 1987. When the two parts were put together, the islanders baptized the figure as Ava Rei Pua, this being the name of the sister of Hotu Matu'a, first king of the island in Rapa Nui mythology. It is one of the few moai made of basalt (there are only ten of them) on the island.

**Moai Tukuturi**
It is located on the slope of Rano Raraku, and is the only kneeling moai (in a praying position). Its naturalistic style betrays its age.

**Moai Ko Te Riku**
Located in the area of Tahai, birthplace of King Nga'ara, this moai has eyes in coral and red scoria, which were placed a few years ago when it was restored.

**Titahanga-o-te-Henua**
This tuff moai marked the axis of the territorial divisions of the clans from Motu Nui.

## Bas-reliefs

Some moai have raised symbols on their backs. The design of these images, present in figures from the ahu Nau Nau of Anakena, resembles an Egyptian cross, although any relationship has been ruled out. It is likely that this mark is a sign of rank, or the fastening of the *hami* ("loincloth"). Other reliefs are in spiral, M, or Y configurations.

**Decorated back**
Its back, richly carved with figures associated with the cult of the birdman, make it a unique and very valuable piece. It dates from 1000 CE, although it is believed that the designs are later.

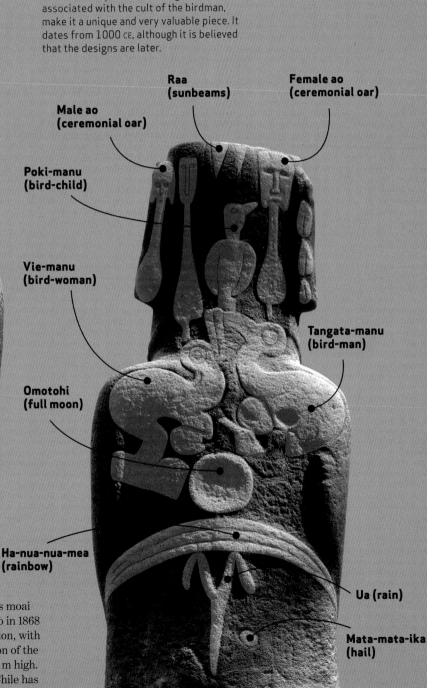

Raa
(sunbeams)

Female ao
(ceremonial oar)

Male ao
(ceremonial oar)

Poki-manu
(bird-child)

Vie-manu
(bird-woman)

Tangata-manu
(bird-man)

Omotohi
(full moon)

Ha-nua-nua-mea
(rainbow)

Ua (rain)

Mata-mata-ika
(hail)

## Hoa Hakananai'a

Although it is believed that it was originally outside, this moai was found in a house in the ceremonial center of Orongo in 1868 by the crew of a British ship. It was transferred to London, with the help of the islanders, and is now part of the collection of the British Museum. It weighs 4 tons and measures 8 ft/2.5 m high. Its name means "stolen friend" in Rapa Nui language. Chile has repeatedly demanded its return.

# The end of the Mayan Culture

The Mayan culture, still surrounded in the mystery of its rise and fall, is an open book in which history continues to be deciphered. Archaeologists and anthropologists leave no stone unturned in their attempts to reach the end of the world.

The Mayan civilization reached extraordinary cultural and material heights in pre-Columbian Mesoamerica. It wasn't a united empire; instead, it developed alliances and rivalries between city-states. The scene of their magnificence and decline included the Mexican states of Yucatán, Campeche, Tabasco, Chiapas, and Quintana Roo, and the highlands and lowlands of northern Guatemala, a part of Belize, and part of Honduras.

Its origins date back more than 4,000 years in a region of high cultures that Americanists call Mesoamerica, located between a line that runs from east to west, north of the capital of Mexico, and another that crosses

Guatemala, Honduras, Nicaragua, and Costa Rica. In the beginning, there was a developmental period known as the Preclassic period, which gave way to the rise of the Classic period (250–900 CE) and finally its decline in the Postclassic period, the end of which coincided with the arrival of the Spanish in the sixteenth century.

The Maya, in constant contact with other Mesoamerican cultures, formed a multiethnic, pluralistic society, governed by complex ideological and cosmological concepts. Some of their achievements in art, writing, and architecture, as well as mathematics and astronomy, rivaled those of ancient Egypt and Classical Europe. Their pyramids are among the largest in the Americas; their paintings, in the frescoes of Bonampak, for example, show high

artistic sensibility, and their writing (as well as their calendar) is considered the most advanced in the Americas. They were an agricultural people, possibly the first to plant maize, were great observers of the environment in which they lived and worshippers of many gods related to the earth.

They also developed ingenious cultivation techniques within the constraints imposed on them by the environment. In the jungle they practiced slash-and-burn techniques on the vegetation, which then served as a fertilizer, and in other regions they farmed terraces. They also understood crop rotation on the lands they cultivated. According to archaeologist and anthropologist Miguel Rivera Dorado, Professor of the Madrid Complutense

**Mayan Pyramid**
The Temple of the Great Jaguar, standing 147 ft/45 m high, towers over the Great Square of the city of Tikal, in the Guatemalan forest.

University and specialist in ancient Mayan culture, "Mayan theocracy was based on a monopoly of religious activities along the principal lineage of the chief as priest and supreme ruler, and the founder of the lineage as god and legitimating source of all encompassing authority." The peasantry, unlike the chief and his lineage who lived in the ceremonial centers, lived in huts dispersed over the jungle. This appears to indicate that Mayan political organizations began shaping themselves from approximately 800 BCE, in the Preclassic period. It was a multiple process, which took place in different areas, such as El Mirador, Tikal, and Calakmul.

During the Classic period, the center of the Mayan civilization was the Petén region, which today is part of Guatemala. In Petén several city-states with a refined culture flourished, of which Tikal is most notable for being one of the largest and most populated, with temples that rise above the jungle vegetation. The Maya quickly developed a complex system of writing carved on stelae and other stone monuments. Thanks to its partial decipherment, a series of historical events, dates, and names have been decoded with some accuracy. A new reading of Stela 31 from Tikal has revealed that a high-ranking military man called Siyah K'ak ("Fire is Born," also called "Lord of the West" in reference to his Teotihuacán origins) captured the city on January 16 of the year 378. It seems that this figure was lieutenant to

the Lord of Teotihuacán. At that time, and until the seventh century, Teotihuacán exerted a significant influence on the valley of Mexico and nearby regions. From then on, Tikal was more influential through the entire Mayan territory.

## GREAT POWERS

From fragmented city-states a kind of superpower was established: Tikal, which gained allies and enemies. New kingdoms were forged under the reign of "Fire is Born." Even newcomers to the throne stopped to write their own history, as reflected in the city-state of Copán in Honduras. According to the text engraved on altar Q, another Lord of the West was regarded as the founder of the "Copan" dynasty, under the name K'inich Yax K'uk Mo', or "Great First Sun Quetzal Macaw," in 426. But later a stela was deciphered that mentioned a first ruler from the year 159, which exposed the Teotihuacán's revision of history to take exclusive credit for the cities incorporated under his area of influence.

Over time, the city-state of Calakmul, located in the Mexican lowlands of Campeche, became the main enemy of Tikal. This confrontation divided the Maya and contributed to the extinction of five centuries of magnificence. For example, the kingdom of Palenque, an ally of Tikal, began to decline after being defeated by Tonina, an ally of Calakmul,

← **Art in Wood**
Bas-relief on a wooden lintel of the Tikal Temple IV. Considered one of the most elaborate of the Mayan culture, it shows a king on a palanquin, celebrating a military victory.

→ **Under the Forest**
Lithograph by Frederick Catherwood illustrating the main temple of Tulum, covered by vegetation. Catherwood accompanied John Lloyd Stephens on his expeditions; together they began the systematic study of Maya sites.

around 800. In the region of Chiapas, which marked the western boundary of Mayan territory, the tomb of King Pakal (603–683) was discovered. His jade death mask, located in the Temple of Inscriptions, was discovered in 1952. In the final stage, the Mayan population decreased rapidly; they stopped writing on stelae and monumental buildings were abandoned. Why? No one knows for sure, but researchers think that it was the result of a combination of factors: drought, overpopulation, resource depletion, and war.

**ENVIRONMENTAL CRISIS**

In this sense, Marcello Canuto, an anthropologist from Yale University, believes that "the load capacity of the ecosystem reached its limit." Historian David Christian points out that this is a typical characteristic of the early farming civilizations: "When important innovations emerge, the population can grow until it goes beyond the final demographic ceiling. Then there is a sharp decline as the land is exhausted, famine takes the hungry, diseases finish off the malnourished, and wars, often organized by governments competing for scarce resources, kill the soldiers and inhabitants of the towns and cities."

American biologist and physiologist, Jared Diamond, author of the book, *Collapse: How societies choose to fail or survive*, considers the decline of the Mayan civilization from

↑ **Writing system**
The Maya developed the only complete writing system in the Americas using logosyllabic characters, which combined logograms and phonetic symbols. In addition to narrating the history of their kings, much of Mayan writing, both in books and on stone, is concerned with astronomical events.

## The end of the world?

According to American astronomer and anthropologist, Anthony Aveni, as he explains in his book, *The End of Time: The Maya mystery of 2012*, the Maya thought of time as cyclical, which coincides with a mythical concept of time. Apocalyptic beliefs of Judeo-Christian tradition, however, hold the theory of a linear concept of time.

The Maya observed time in large cycles that ended and began with significant changes in the transition periods. Hence, the fear associated with the end of one cycle and the beginning of another, as in 2012. But Aveni stated that the Mayan inscriptions related to the prophecy should be understood more as a way to preserve political power and stability than as a literal prophecy.

Either way, the cycle that ended on December 21, 2012 was a date of great importance for the ancient Maya, as it ended "the long count calendar" that they established, which began in August 3114 BCE.

**←Final Judgment**
The god Kukulcan (or Quetzalcoatl), representation of Venus and creator of humanity, in the form of the morning star arises out of the jaws of serpents of the earth.

the perspective of an environmental crisis caused by human activity. Massive deforestation caused a drought that was aggravated by general global warming. After the erosion of the hills caused by systematic dismantling, acid soils were washed away by floods into the valley, where fertile soils were coated with sterile sediment. A desolate panorama: "At the beginning of the year 800, about five million Mayans lived on the plains of the south over an area as large as Switzerland. They ended up lacking everything; food, water, firewood, while the kings fought each other for the best land and the farmers did the same to keep a piece for cultivating."

After the fall of cities in the south, the Mayan civilization changed the course of its decline in the Yucatán Peninsula, now in the Postclassic period. There they developed two neighboring kingdoms, this time under the influence of another foreign people, the mysterious Toltecs, who spread the cult of Quetzalcoatl, the Plumed Serpent, known in local languages as Kukulcan or Gucumatz. First was Chichen Itza, which flourished as a commercial and religious center after 1000. It was suddenly abandoned around 1200, perhaps overcome by its successors. Later, not far away, they established the town of Mayapan, which fell in the mid-fifteenth century. A short time later, in the sixteenth century, the Spanish conquistadors penetrated the Yucatán Peninsula and reigned over the decline of the Maya.

Scattered in small kingdoms, the plant cover swallowed the monumental remains of this stunning civilization. The conquest lasted 19 years, from 1527 to 1546. The conquest of Guatemala was practically complete in 1530. Pedro de Alvarado's troops, with the support of the Cakchiquel, confronted groups of Quiche (both of Mayan origin). But the last pocket of Mayan resistance in the Guatemalan region of Petén was not quelled until 1697. By 1839, the Maya began to emerge from obscurity, thanks to a special U.S. ambassador in Central America called John Lloyd Stephens (1805–52), inveterate explorer and travel writer. It all started the day he read a report on the ruins of Copán, Honduras, with no maps or drawings, which proved a powerful inspiration to him. Stephens made the trip and found the cities of Palenque, Labná, Kabah, Uxmal, Chichen Itza, and Tulum, among others. He wrote about them all in two books: *Incidents of travel in Central America, Chiapas and Yucatán* (1841) and *Incidents of travel in Yucatán* (1843). But it would never have been the same without the drawings of the monumental ruins in the landscape, using photographs and daguerreotype images taken by English architect, Frederick Catherwood (1799–1854), his long-suffering jungle companion. That Anglo-American work, especially Catherwood's series of color lithographs, was an iconographic model par excellence, which raised a plethora of questions, fantasies, and mysteries.

The time of romantic explorers gave way to that of the first archaeologists. From 1881 to 1894, Englishman Alfred Percival Maudslay (1850–1931) made seven expeditions to Mayan lands. In addition to photographs, drawings, and descriptions, he made plaster casts of reliefs and inscriptions and took priceless objects that eventually formed part of the collection of the British Museum in London. He was the first to take photographs and draw a map of Tikal. However, there are still many gaps in our knowledge about the Maya.

## How did they attain their knowledge?

Perhaps because of their status as farmers, the Maya were forced to measure the passage of time very precisely in order to develop the crop cycle successfully. To do this, the priests turned their gaze to the domed sky and watched the movements of the stars, becoming scholars of astronomy. They set up observation centers on top of the temples, where they had a chamber on which they arranged two pieces of crossed wood to give them a fixed point of observation. From this vantage point, using just their vision, they took note of the movement of the sun, moon, and planets, thereby establishing a 260-day ritual calendar and a 365-day solar calendar. The first was the Tzolkin,

a period of twenty 13-day periods, which was used to predict the future and know the feast day of each deity, where each day was named corresponding to its number. The second calendar, the solar calendar, was known as Haab, and was made up of 19 months. In fact, it was a cycle of 18 months of 20 days and one additional month of five days to complete the solar cycle.

In addition, every four years a day was added to make up for the fact that they were six hours behind each year. They combined the two calendars, which produced a new 52-year cycle—the "Calendar Wheel"—the dates of which were repeated every 52 years. Thus, they had enough

temporal space to give a date to any event with a calendar that was even more accurate than the Gregorian calendar.

The accuracy of their mathematical calculations is stunning, and this was because arithmetic, which is derived from astronomical observations, was no secret to the Maya. In ancient times, probably between the fourth and third centuries BCE, a 20-period numerical system, starting from zero, was devised. It is still unclear whether the Maya invented the concept of zero, or if they inherited the knowledge from the Olmecs. In any case, the first written record among the Maya precedes the first historic appearance in the Old World, in India, by several centuries.

# Mayan civilization

Over the course of thousands of years, the Maya spread themselves across Central America independently. They founded several cities, while maintaining wide-ranging contacts, not always peacefully, with the rest of the region.

## Many towns, a single origin

Today, there are seven million Maya spread across Guatemala, Mexico, Honduras, and Belize. They form part of a population that dates back over 4,000 years in Guatemala; it was from there that they moved around Mesoamerica, creating different towns, each with its own language and culture. Today, 31 Mayan languages are still in existence; the most important are K'iche' and Yucatec.

Mayan
Culture

### Pyramids

The Maya left evidence of their architectural excellence during the Classic period, although the most colossal constructions are from the Preclassic period and can be found in the city of El Mirador. The volume of La Danta, a pyramid 236 ft/72 m high, is greater than that of the Pyramid of Khufu (also known as Cheops), in Egypt. It is considered the highest pyramid in pre-Columbian America, although the Pyramid of Cholula is an even greater size.

### Cities and periods

- Preclassic
- Classic
- Postclassic
- Modern cities
- ★ Modern capitals

Chiapa
de Corzo

| **Great Pyramid of Giza** | **La Danta** | **Cholula** | **Pyramid of the Sun** | **Tikal Temple IV** | **El Tigre** |
|---|---|---|---|---|---|
| Egypt | Guatemala | Mexico | Mexico | Guatemala | Guatemala |
| 450 ft/137 m | 236 ft/72 m | 217 ft/66 m | 213 ft/65 m | 210 ft/64 m | 180 ft/55 m |

### The Mayan period: Preclassic to Postclassic

Archaeologists have identified three main periods in Mayan history: Preclassic (a formation period), Classic (where the culture reached its peak) and Postclassic.

**300 BCE**
The Maya adopted the concept of a hierarchical society, ruled by noblemen and kings.

**1 CE**

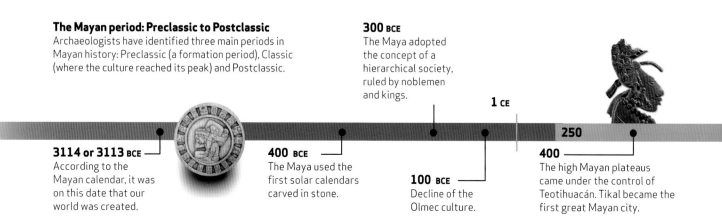

**250**

**3114 or 3113 BCE**
According to the Mayan calendar, it was on this date that our world was created.

**400 BCE**
The Maya used the first solar calendars carved in stone.

**100 BCE**
Decline of the Olmec culture.

**400**
The high Mayan plateaus came under the control of Teotihuacán. Tikal became the first great Mayan city.

## What was the purpose of the ball game played by the Maya and other Mesoamerican populations?

The game consisted of players hitting a rubber ball without using their hands or feet, although there were a number of different variations. Although kings made huge bets on games, there was also a ritual side as they recreated a Maya myth. Sometimes, the losers were killed in a sacrificial ritual.

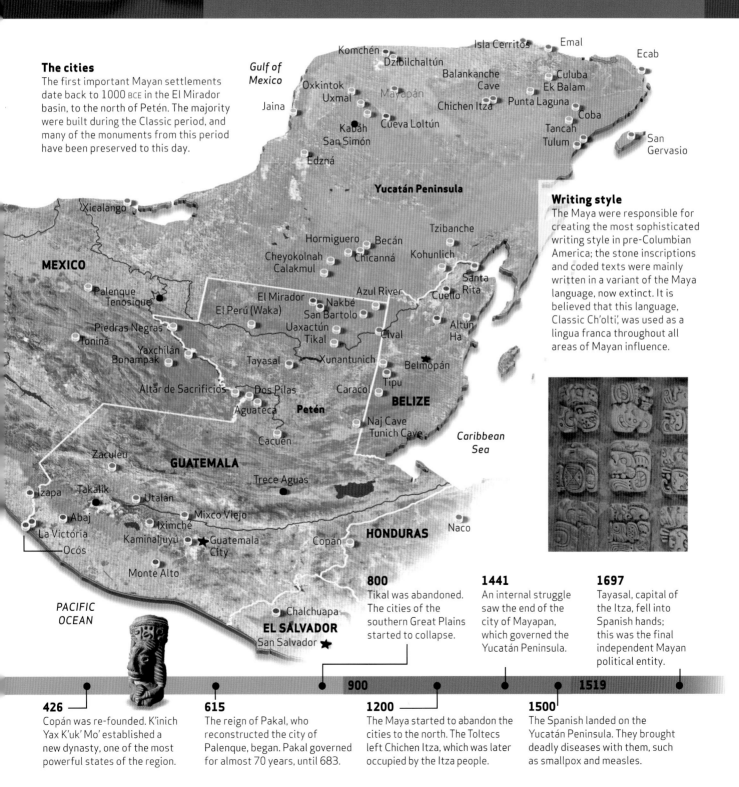

### The cities

The first important Mayan settlements date back to 1000 BCE in the El Mirador basin, to the north of Petén. The majority were built during the Classic period, and many of the monuments from this period have been preserved to this day.

Gulf of Mexico

Komchén
Dzibilchaltún
Isla Cerritos
Emal
Ecab
Oxkintok
Uxmal
Mayapán
Balankanche Cave
Culuba
Ek Balam
Jaina
Chichen Itza
Punta Laguna
Kabah
San Simón
Cueva Loltún
Coba
Tancah
Tulum
San Gervasio
Edzná

**Yucatán Peninsula**

Tzibanche

### Writing style

The Maya were responsible for creating the most sophisticated writing style in pre-Columbian America; the stone inscriptions and coded texts were mainly written in a variant of the Maya language, now extinct. It is believed that this language, Classic Ch'olti', was used as a lingua franca throughout all areas of Mayan influence.

Xicalango

Hormiguero
Becán
Cheyokolnah
Chicanná
Kohunlich
Calakmul

**MEXICO**

Palenque
Tenosique

Santa Rita
Azul River
Cuello
El Mirador
Nakbé
El Perú (Waka)
San Bartolo
Uaxactún
Cival
Altún Ha
Tikal

Piedras Negras
Toniná
Yaxchilán
Bonampak

Tayasal
Xunantunich
Belmopán

Altar de Sacrificios
Dos Pilas
Tipu
Caracol
Aguateca
**Petén**
**BELIZE**
Cacuen
Naj Cave
Tunich Cave
*Caribbean Sea*

Zaculeu
**GUATEMALA**
Trece Aguas

Izapa
Takalik
Utalán
Abaj
Mixco Viejo
Naco
La Victória
Iximché
Kaminaljuyú
Guatemala City
Copán
**HONDURAS**
Ocós
Monte Alto

*PACIFIC OCEAN*

Chalchuapa
**EL SALVADOR**
San Salvador

**800**
Tikal was abandoned. The cities of the southern Great Plains started to collapse.

**1441**
An internal struggle saw the end of the city of Mayapan, which governed the Yucatán Peninsula.

**1697**
Tayasal, capital of the Itza, fell into Spanish hands; this was the final independent Mayan political entity.

**426**
Copán was re-founded. K'inich Yax K'uk' Mo' established a new dynasty, one of the most powerful states of the region.

**615**
The reign of Pakal, who reconstructed the city of Palenque, began. Pakal governed for almost 70 years, until 683.

**900**

**1200**
The Maya started to abandon the cities to the north. The Toltecs left Chichen Itza, which was later occupied by the Itza people.

**1519**

**1500**
The Spanish landed on the Yucatán Peninsula. They brought deadly diseases with them, such as smallpox and measles.

# The Chichen Itza complex

World Heritage listed since 1988 and one of the New Seven Wonders of the World since 2007, it has the largest ball-game court in Mesoamerica, a sacred cenote for sacrificial purposes, and an astronomical observatory.

## Chichen Itza

This Mayan city was founded between 435 and 455 CE. Around the ninth century, it was considered one of the most important political centers of the Maya, and was the main power center in the Yucatán around the tenth century.

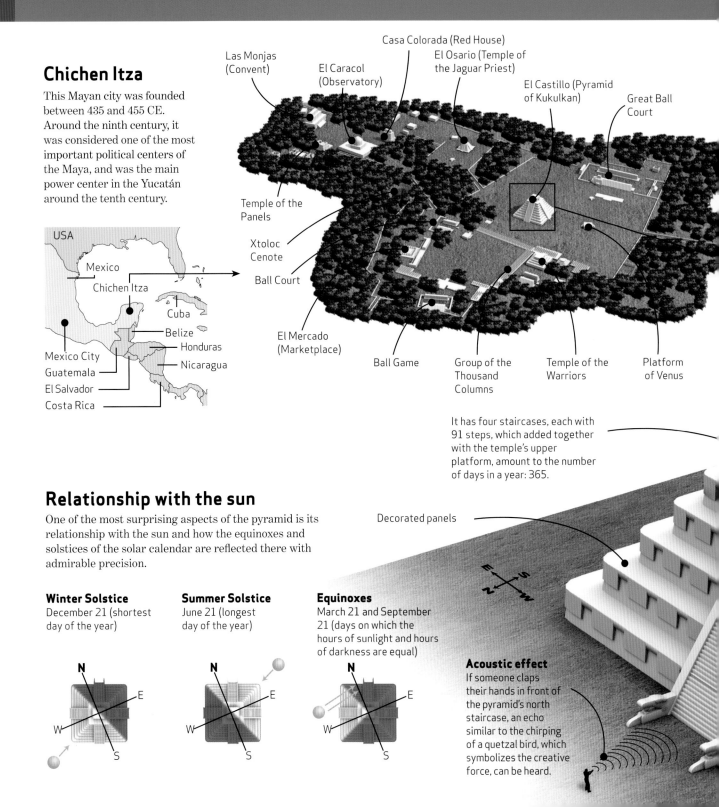

USA
Mexico
Chichen Itza
Cuba
Mexico City
Guatemala
El Salvador
Costa Rica
Belize
Honduras
Nicaragua

Las Monjas (Convent)
El Caracol (Observatory)
Casa Colorada (Red House)
El Osario (Temple of the Jaguar Priest)
El Castillo (Pyramid of Kukulkan)
Great Ball Court
Temple of the Panels
Xtoloc Cenote
Ball Court
El Mercado (Marketplace)
Ball Game
Group of the Thousand Columns
Temple of the Warriors
Platform of Venus

It has four staircases, each with 91 steps, which added together with the temple's upper platform, amount to the number of days in a year: 365.

Decorated panels

## Relationship with the sun

One of the most surprising aspects of the pyramid is its relationship with the sun and how the equinoxes and solstices of the solar calendar are reflected there with admirable precision.

**Winter Solstice**
December 21 (shortest day of the year)

**Summer Solstice**
June 21 (longest day of the year)

**Equinoxes**
March 21 and September 21 (days on which the hours of sunlight and hours of darkness are equal)

**Acoustic effect**
If someone claps their hands in front of the pyramid's north staircase, an echo similar to the chirping of a quetzal bird, which symbolizes the creative force, can be heard.

## Who were the Toltecs and how, if at all, were they related to Chichen Itza?

The Toltecs ruled most of Mexico between the tenth and twelfth centuries. From Tula, their capital, they conquered Chichen Itza, although whether this involved an invasion, or merely a cultural influence, is a subject for debate. Recent studies assert that they were, in fact, influenced by the Aztecs.

## A stone calendar

The Maya had an advanced understanding of mathematics and astronomy. The Kukulkan pyramid is testament to their knowledge.

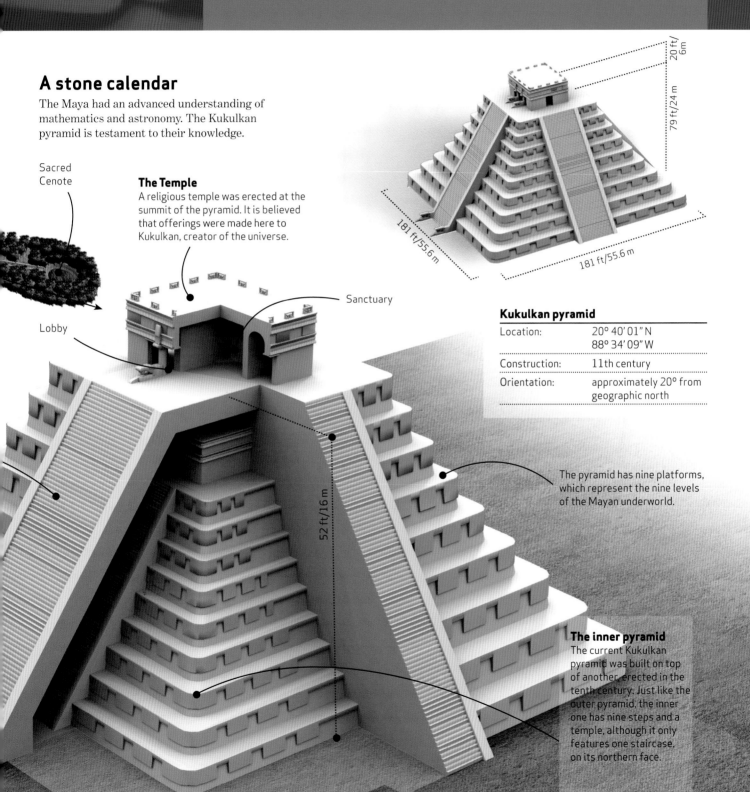

Sacred Cenote

**The Temple**
A religious temple was erected at the summit of the pyramid. It is believed that offerings were made here to Kukulkan, creator of the universe.

Sanctuary

Lobby

20 ft / 6 m

79 ft / 24 m

181 ft / 55.6 m

181 ft / 55.6 m

52 ft / 16 m

### Kukulkan pyramid

| | |
|---|---|
| Location: | 20° 40' 01" N 88° 34' 09" W |
| Construction: | 11th century |
| Orientation: | approximately 20° from geographic north |

The pyramid has nine platforms, which represent the nine levels of the Mayan underworld.

**The inner pyramid**
The current Kukulkan pyramid was built on top of another, erected in the tenth century. Just like the outer pyramid, the inner one has nine steps and a temple, although it only features one staircase, on its northern face.

# Mayan treasures

The Maya brought an original style to their artwork, whether mud statuettes, heavy stone stelae, or simple vases and jars. Jade, which had a high symbolic value, was the most sought after and precious stone.

## Pakal mask

The death mask of the king of Palenque (Chiapas, Mexico), who ruled during the twelfth century, is made up of 340 pieces of carefully assembled jade. Its eyes are made from mother-of-pearl and obsidian. King Pakal is the only Mesoamerican sovereign whose tomb, discovered in 1952, is inside a pyramid (Temple of the Inscriptions). He is famous because the lid of his sarcophagus depicts him in a pose interpreted by some as resembling that of an astronaut.

### Dazzling jar
Given its beauty, this is known as the "dazzling jar." Crafted in a Teotihuacán style, it is from the Margarita Tomb at Copán, Honduras, and belonged to the wife of one of the city's kings.

### Jade ornament
Delicate ornament made from jade, representing a god, accompanied in the upper section by two heads. It belongs to the Classic period.

### Ritual vase
Cylindrical Tikal vase in polychrome ceramic, from the Classic period. It is decorated with a scene depicting members of the aristocracy.

## Sovereigns of the earth

This terracotta statuette (left) depicts a nobleman or king sitting on a throne. Its style is typical of Jaina Island and dates back to the Classic period. The lavish headdress and elaborate clothing suggest he belonged to the Mayan elite. Like many ritual masks, ceramic statuettes tend to depict characters accurately and in detail.

### Stelae
They depicted kings or governors, and always included glyphs with historical information. Some of the most elaborate and interesting examples can be found in Copán, Honduras. The image right, known as Stelae H, represents King Uaxaclajuun Ub'aah K'awiil.

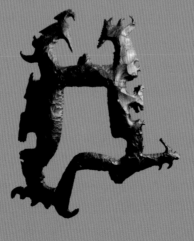

### Pendant
Ornament made from a seashell (an attribute of nobility). The image above represents a warrior, perhaps a god. These pendants were used by both men and women.

### Eccentric
These strange figures, known as "eccentrics," were made from silex (like the ones in the image) or obsidian. Human profiles were carved around their edges.

# The splendor of Copán

Copán, one of the most prosperous and powerful cities during the Mayan Classic period, was a populous and dynamic metropolis, full of artistic representations that are considered among the most beautiful pieces of art left by this civilization.

## Feast of the king

The center of Copán (in modern-day Honduras) is located on an artificial hill. The city was established at the beginning of the fifth century CE, although other important settlements date back even farther in time. One of the kings who brought this location to the peak of its splendor was Uaxaclajuun Ub'aah K'awiil, shown with his back to us in this painting, observing a ball game with his family. His servants can be seen offering him food and drink, using an umbrella to provide him with shade. The king himself ordered the construction of the ball court in 738. Shortly after, the 43-year reign of Uaxaclajuun was brought to an end when he died at the hands of a rebellious vassal.

## Who was the "Red Lady"?

In 1993, a tomb in Temple 13 at Palenque was discovered that contained the richest Mayan female burial remains ever discovered. She was named the "Red Lady" as her bones were covered in red pigment. She is believed to be the wife of the founder of the Copán Dynasty.

**Absolute sovereign**
Here the king, dressed in clothes that highlight his superior status, is watching a ball game.

# The Incan City of Machu Picchu

During the short history of the Incan state, Machu Picchu was a sacred citadel that grew strong in the shadow of Cuzco. American historian Hiram Bingham uncovered its hundred-year-old ruins for the world in 1915.

Between Lake Titicaca and the Cuzco valley at the foot of the Andes, a culture was born which, in just a few years, extended over most of the Andes mountain range. At the height of its development, it reached limits barely dreamed of by any of the states that followed in ancient Peru. It spanned Ecuador, through Peru and Bolivia, to Chile and northern Argentina. This was an immense territory nearly 2,500 miles/4,000 km long and 250 miles/400 km wide in which lived from ten million to thirty million people (there is no common consensus) under the rule of a dynasty established around 1200 in the city of Cuzco.

According to Incan chronicler Garcilaso de la Vega (1539–1616) in the *Primera parte de los Comentarios Reales* (1609),

Cuzco "in the language of the Incas, means center of the Earth," but of Machu Picchu, which was finished in the fourteenth century, he took no notice at all. Legend has it that Manco Cápac and Mama Ocllo, both brother and sister and husband and wife, mythical founders of the Incan Dynasty, emerged on the Island of the Sun on Lake Titicaca (located 12,500 ft/3,810 m above sea level) . This legend maintains that Manco planted his lance of gold 11,200 ft/3,400 m high in the middle of an ancient settlement of the tribes of the Huallas, the Poques, and the Lares, flanked by the Huatanay and Tullumayo rivers. Thus, Cuzco was born and, from 1200 to 1438, the so-called legendary "Incan Empire" consisted of a dynasty of eight sovereigns: Manco Cápac, Sinchi Roca, Lloque Yupanqui, Mayta

Cápac, Cápac Yupanqui, Inca Roca, Yáhuar Huácac, and Hatun Topa or Viracocha (which had the same name as the main Incan god). The Chanca nation threatened the hegemonic power of the Cuzcan dynasty in the final stretch of Viracocha's reign. Only military resistance led by one of his sons, Inca Yupanqui, prevented the fall of Cuzco.

The ninth Inca, Pachacutec, was the first ruler of the historic empire, Tawantinsuyu, which in Quechuan means "the four parts (or regions) of the world," coinciding with the four cardinal points. During his reign he must have built Machu Picchu: the architectural, engineering, and town-planning jewel of the Incas, built in secret, perhaps to preserve their political or religious nature of incalculable value. In 1471

**Hidden**
The ruins of Machu Picchu are located at an altitude of 7,875 ft/ 2,400 m, between the summits of the Andes and in the shadow of Huayna Picchu.

**← Royal tomb**

This natural cave under the Temple of the Sun was called the Royal Tomb by Bingham although no mummy was found there. There is a staircase carved into the rock and some hand-shaped stones.

**→ Andenes**

The classical terraces, or agricultural "andenes," have a marked presence in Machu Picchu. In the photograph, a channel through the terraces, framed by a row of houses, can be seen.

Pachacutec abdicated in favor of his son Topa Inca Yupanqui, who was a great conqueror and statesman for 22 years. The eleventh Inca, Huayna Cápac, continued the policy of his father, although he was obliged to suppress the frequent uprisings that occurred over the vast territory. In 1525, he died in Quito, possibly as a result of a virus introduced by the Spanish.

### CIVIL WAR

After Huayna Cápac's death, there was a fight for power between his sons, who had been conceived by different women: Huáscar, supported by the Cuzco nobility, and Atahualpa, who had a mighty army from the north. In 1532, Atahualpa's troops occupied the city of Cuzco and Huáscar was taken prisoner. The victor showed no mercy. He ordered the entire family of his brother, which was largely his too, as well as leaders and personal friends, to be put to death.

In the middle of the Civil War, Spanish conquistador Francisco Pizarro, commanding a group of just 200 men and 70 horses, landed at Tumbes in April 1531. On November 15 of the following year, Atahualpa and Pizarro were preparing to meet in Cajamarca. Before the meeting of the representatives of the two kingdoms, the Dominican friar Vicente de Valverde, with a cross and a book in his hands, went to the Inca to proceed with the reading of the "Requirement," a type of ultimatum that urged the indigenous population to recognize the sovereignty of the kings of Castile, receive their envoys in peace, and accept the faith that they were going to preach. Atahualpa ended up taking a swipe at the book, and Valverde, shouted 'the chief has thrown to the ground the book of our holy law,' which led to artillery fire and a cavalry charge. The fate of the Incas was cast. There was nothing Atahualpa could do; he was taken hostage. Three rooms filled with gold and silver were given in exchange for his freedom, but the Inca was sentenced to death on August 29, 1533, for ordering the death of his brother Huáscar, among other alleged crimes.

### THE DECLINE OF THE INCAS

On November 15 that same year, the Spanish conquistadors took Cuzco without opposition. The extraordinary network of Incan roads helped the devastating success of the foreign forces. Cuzco was the mighty Incan Empire's axis and it led to its rapid decline. Its strong political and social organization, divided between the ruling priestly nobility and the peasant tributary farmers, was notable for the absence of strong class conflict. Social organization was related to specific communities and lineages and the functions to be fulfilled by individuals within each group. Machu Picchu was located at the top of the social pyramid; it may have been a residential retreat for Pachacutec, and then it possibly became his mausoleum. It was a high-ranking sanctuary, housing a palace, temples, and altars as well as terraces, livestock, and workshops, in the middle of a unique site between

two hills, with abundant water and vegetation, seven days on foot from the capital Cuzco. And despite the network of roads that American archaeologist John Hyslop noted in his book, *The Inca Road System* (1992), as being some 14,408 miles/23,187 km, although it may have been 24,850 miles/40,000 km, the Spanish never reached Machu Picchu.

### AN ABSOLUTE SOVEREIGN
Everything appears to indicate that the decline of a region so carefully hidden as Machu Picchu occurred during the Spanish occupation of Cuzco. It has not been ruled out that, once uninhabited, it suffered the fiery wrath of the friar soldiers who soon ravaged the Vilcabamba area, next to the sanctuary. Within the Spanish Empire in the Americas, the "Inspector General of Idolatry" was in charge of approaching the locals to encourage them to leave their polytheistic worship and denounce sinners. Most of the Incan rebels took refuge in Vilcabamba led by Manco Inca Yupanqui, son of Huayna Cápac, who arrived to lay siege to Cuzco for 12 months and establish his headquarters at Tambo (today Ollantaytambo), at the gates of the capital of Tawantinsuyu. This focus of Incan resistance, which at the death of Manco Inca Yupanqui was continued by his children, Tito Cusi and Túpac Amaru, lasted over 40 years. In 1572, the Inspector General Viceroy Francisco de Toledo ordered the final assault on Vilcabamba, and beheaded Túpac

**↑ Aligned cities**
Cajamarca, Machu Picchu, Ollantaytambo, Cuzco, and Tiwanaku are aligned in a northwest-southeast direction, in a diagonal of sacred importance that is present in numerous Incan crafts and objects.

Amaru in the Cuzco square and stuck his head on a spike. Thus ended Tawantinsuyu. Vilcabamba became a kind of Incan myth, but it was also the most searched for place by adventurers, explorers, and writers, mainly from Europe and the United States. The American, Hiram Bingham (1875–1956), associate professor of South American History at Yale University, first went to this remote region in 1909. He is famous for having traveled a large part of South America on foot. In 1906, he went from Venezuela to Colombia, along the same Andean path taken in 1819 by Simón Bolívar. Two years later, he followed the old Spanish trade route from Buenos Aires to Lima, through the Andes. His Peruvian adventure led him to search for the remains of a site called Choquequirao which, according to his native guides, was the last capital of the Incan rebels. The lost city of the Incas had always aroused the greed of many men who swept through the region of Vilcabamba in the hope of finding hidden treasures. Bingham was able to say that Choquequirao was not the place they were looking for.

In 1911, the historian returned to Cuzco as director of an archaeological expedition from his university and dug in the valley of Urubamba. On the morning of June 24 that same year, accompanied by a Civil Guard sergeant, he climbed the cultivated terraces of some farmers, whose son was responsible for showing them the ruins covered in vegetation where they used to play, which he called Machu Picchu. In 1912 and 1915, Bingham, supported by Yale University and the National Geographic Society, returned to Machu Picchu with a team of experts with different specialties to carry out excavations. Bingham believed that Machu Picchu was the last stronghold of the Incan resistance. Today, we know that it was not. It was a royal residence, a sanctuary, a fortress, and finally a lost city, hidden from the eyes of the world. His discovery raised a range of questions, many of which are still unanswered.

## Was it a sanctuary?

The Spanish chronicler Juan de Betanzos (1510–76), in the *Suma y Narración de los Incas* (1551), was the first person to link the first Inca of Tawantinsuyu with Machu Picchu and went on to confirm that his mummy was in a town called Patallacta, which the same sovereign had ordered to be built. In that region, abundant with *patallacta* ("high village" in Quechuan), Betanzos may well be referring to Machu Picchu. Machu Picchu, the patallacta of Pachacutec, appears to have been a resting-place before becoming a mausoleum. Betanzos also announced that the Inca's mummy was usually carried on a platform to the city of Cuzco to celebrate certain holidays, where other royal mummies were exhibited, and to take part in the ritual worship of dead Incas, established by the same Pachacutec.

There they held a ceremony of the living and dead, as if there were no difference between them, with songs, stories of warlike deeds and public works, food, drinks, and even changes of clothes. On returning to the sanctuary of Machu Picchu, the mummy was returned to the Royal Tomb, located below the turret. From June 21 to 24, the winter solstice in the southern hemisphere, the sun's rays entered the windows of this temple, announcing the new agricultural cycle.

### ↑ Temple of the Sun
The only circular construction at Machu Picchu was a solar observatory. Its architecture is one of the finest works of all the Incan constructions.

## Was it built in nature's image?

Some researchers have indicated the possibility that the Incas often closely followed natural models in their constructions. As can be seen in the photograph, the sacred stone known as "Intihuatana" could be in the shape of the mountain Huayna Picchu, located behind it. Not far away is the collection of the Sacred Rock, marked by a monolithic piece that also appears to be copied from the mountains opposite. From this rock, toward the west up a steep path with steps cut into the rock and which passes between small agricultural terraces, the top of Huayna Picchu can be accessed. There, on the heights of the "young mountain," a large stone stands out like a throne, and is known as "the Inca's chair." From it there is a breathtaking view onto the sanctuary, the canyon of the Urubamba, and the sacred mountains. On the northern slope, the hill has a cave, similar to the royal crypt of the Temple of the Sun, connected to another above, which contains walls made with stone blocks, trapezoidal niches, and alcoves. This set of caves is known as the Temple of the Moon.

**↓Intihuatana**
Its raised location makes this stone an excellent place to make astronomical observations.

## Where is the treasure of Machu Picchu?

The material removed from Machu Picchu by Bingham (now in Yale University) is a mystery. It comprises about 5,000 artifacts, but recently the government of Peru reclaimed more than 46,000 pieces. Confusion arises because many of the objects are made up of numerous fragments. It is believed that only 350 objects are exhibition pieces. The university pledged to return these objects (and an unspecified number of fragments) in a 2008 agreement, as long as they are housed in a proper museum, according to specifications required by the university.

# Urban structure

Divided into two large sections, rural and urban (at the heart of the latter was the main square), Machu Picchu had an "upper part," the Hanan (sacred area), and a "lower part," the Hurin (residential area).

## Imperial Residence

Most researchers agree that it was the Inca Pachacuti, founder and first sovereign of Tawantinsuyu (the Inca Empire), who ordered the construction of this citadel as a place for recreation and refuge during winter.

**Location**
About 73 miles/118 km from Cuzco, the ancient capital of the Inca Empire, and 745 miles/1,200 km from Lima, the modern-day capital of Peru.

**Distribution**
A step, a wall, and a moat, which also served as a drainage channel, separate the rural area from the urban area.

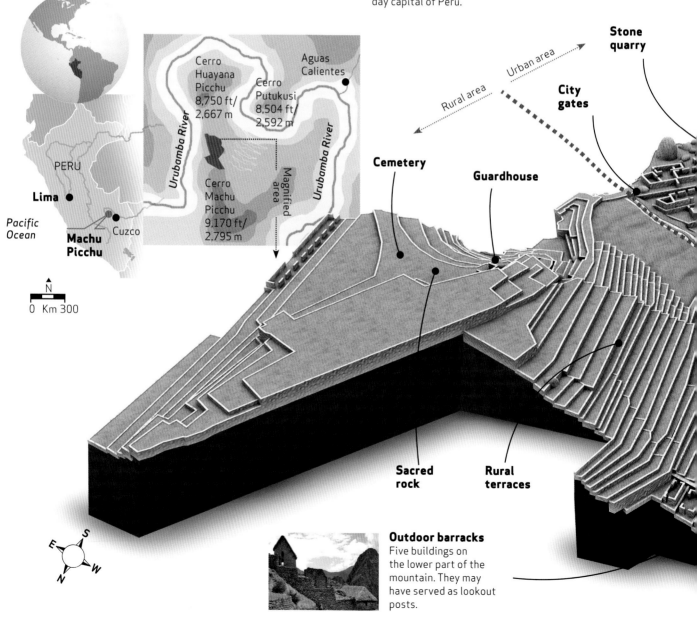

Cerro Huayana Picchu 8,750 ft/ 2,667 m

Cerro Putukusi 8,504 ft/ 2,592 m

Aguas Calientes

Urubamba River

Magnified area

Cerro Machu Picchu 9,170 ft/ 2,795 m

PERU

Lima

Pacific Ocean

Machu Picchu

Cuzco

N

0 Km 300

Stone quarry

Urban area

Rural area

City gates

Cemetery

Guardhouse

Sacred rock

Rural terraces

**Outdoor barracks**
Five buildings on the lower part of the mountain. They may have served as lookout posts.

## What purpose did the Funeral (or Ceremonial) Rock at Machu Picchu serve?

The large stones held significant religious meaning to the Incas. The Funeral Rock, also known as the Ceremonial Rock, has a smooth surface, with steps and a ring carved into the rock. Certain theories suggest it was used for mummification, although in reality its purpose remains unknown to this day.

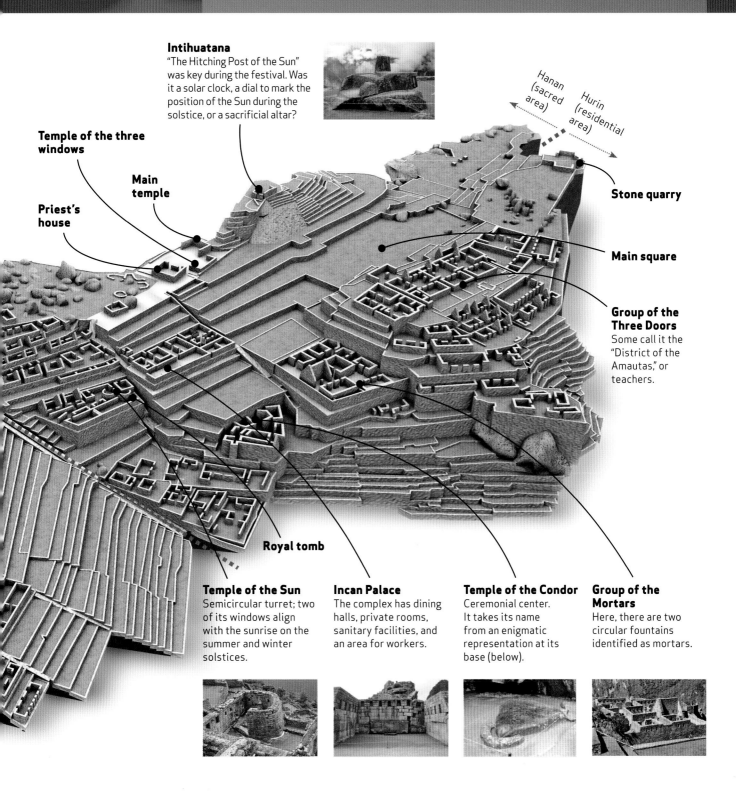

**Intihuatana**
"The Hitching Post of the Sun" was key during the festival. Was it a solar clock, a dial to mark the position of the Sun during the solstice, or a sacrificial altar?

**Temple of the three windows**

**Main temple**

**Priest's house**

Hanan (sacred area)

Hurin (residential area)

**Stone quarry**

**Main square**

**Group of the Three Doors**
Some call it the "District of the Amautas," or teachers.

**Royal tomb**

**Temple of the Sun**
Semicircular turret; two of its windows align with the sunrise on the summer and winter solstices.

**Incan Palace**
The complex has dining halls, private rooms, sanitary facilities, and an area for workers.

**Temple of the Condor**
Ceremonial center. It takes its name from an enigmatic representation at its base (below).

**Group of the Mortars**
Here, there are two circular fountains identified as mortars.

# Terraces and constructions

The urban area of Machu Picchu was designed with nobility in mind, and was home to several sacred temples and sites. Although the rural area was entirely dedicated to the plantations, all the evidence seems to suggest that Machu Picchu was not self-sufficient.

## Platforms

The rural area was made up of large terraces or platforms with crops located on the side of the mountain.

Rural sector

- Upper terraces
- Lower terraces
- Urban area

### BREAKDOWN OF A PLATFORM

Retaining Wall

Cropland

## Fill
Comprising large and small stones, gravel, clay, and fertile soil. It facilitated drainage, preventing water from collecting and compromising its structure.

Side of the mountain

## Function
The use of terraces enabled the Inca to cultivate crops on hillsides and avoid erosion caused by rainwater. It is believed that they also served for protection.

## Climate
As Machu Picchu is located in a mountainous area, the climate is warm during the day and cool at night. It rains frequently, especially between November and March.

75°
65°
50°
40°
32° F

Winter
Summer

Retaining wall

Steps of embedded rocks

## Irrigation
Cropland was nourished using rainwater. The channels that descended from the slopes were used by the urban area and the ceremonial fountains.

## How important were the crop terraces of the settlement?

Although the rural area occupied almost half the surface area of the settlement, it has been calculated that it was only capable of feeding 55 people, while the permanent population was at least 300 people. It is believed that it may have served as a crop experimentation area, which would then have been reproduced on a greater scale in other areas.

Urban sector

**Main building complex**

- Workshops, housing, and the city's gates
- Temple of the Sun, Royal Tomb
- Royal Residence
- Sacred Square (Temple of the Three Windows, Main Temple)
- Intihuatana
- Sacred Rock
- Group of the Three Doors
- Group of the Mortars
- Group of the Condor

Hanan

Hurin

N

0    50 m    100

## Architecture

When building, the Inca considered the position of the sun during the solstices.

**Roofs**

A wooden structure was erected on top of the stone; layers of straw were placed on top of this.

The significant amount of rain that fell in the region made it necessary for roofs to be slanted to prevent water from accumulating. This made it possible for rainwater to run off easily.

63°

**Walls**

Walls of stone were joined up by using mud mortar. All the material was sourced from the quarries of the complex.

**Lithic bolts**

The logs that made up the roof's frame were fastened using ropes tied to stone bolts.

## Distribution

In Hanan, there was a Royal Tomb, the district of the Amautas and the Mortars, the Royal Palace and the Intihuatana. In Hurin, the Group of Three Doors, the Temple of the Condor, the Turret (or Temple of the Sun) and the Acllahuasi can be found.

**Foundations**

Pilasters and dividing walls were sunk to make them sturdier.

Stone colonnade

# Incan treasures

Machu Picchu is an epic testament to Incan architecture. However, the refined artistry of this culture can also be seen in the production of textiles, ceramics, metalwork, and ornaments.

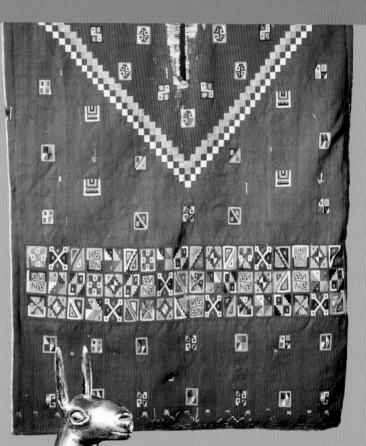

## Textile art

The Incas were expert weavers. For items of clothing, the Incas used horizontal and vertical looms, with sections comprising numerous strings, which facilitated the use of detailed designs. They used llama, alpaca, and vicuña wool, with the latter reserved for royalty. The Tokapu (square geometric designs with drawings inside), like the ones on the poncho to the right, may have represented a rudimentary form of writing. The combination of red and blue colors (a sign of royalty) and the stepped design of the neck opening suggest that this garment belonged to someone from the nobility.

### Silverware

Alpaca carved from a thin silver sheet, with a llama featuring a saddle decorated with geometric motifs. Camelids are often represented in Andean art.

### Ceremonial vases

The Kero (which means "wood," although they were also made from clay and metal) usually feature geometric and figurative decorations.

## Sacrificial knives

The Tumi is a ceremonial knife with a semicircular metallic blade and a handle featuring a figurative icon, usually a god. They were common throughout the entire Andean region and were used by cultures that preceded the Incas, such as the Sican culture. They were used for religious sacrifices and surgical procedures.

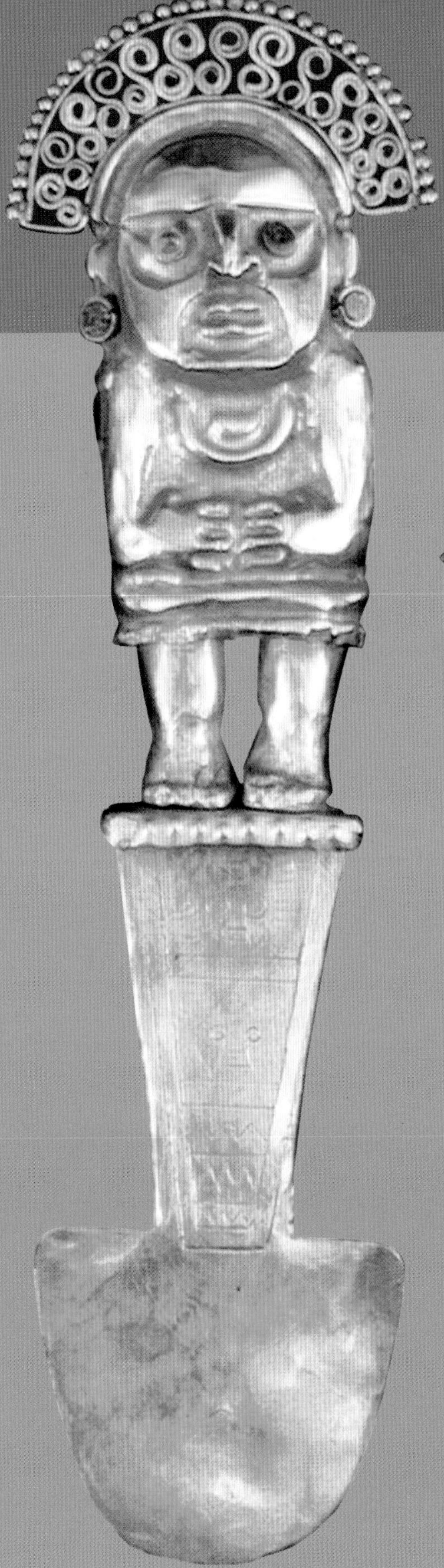

### Sacred plants

Representation in silver of a maize plant. Maize was a luxury crop for the Incas, given that the Andean terrain did not lend itself well to its production, which was limited to the valleys. Maize was used to make *chicha*, the alcoholic beverage used in rituals.

### Colorful feathers

A variety of textiles, ornaments, and figurines were decorated with colorful feathers from the Amazon region.

# The ceremony of the Sun

The shortest day of the year, June 21, was a sacred date in the Incan calendar on which the Festival of the Sun, dedicated to the god Inti, was held. The ceremony coincided with the start of the new farming cycle and involved rituals and celebrations.

## Natural cycles

As the Inca were an agrarian society, they needed to accurately track the cycles of nature. Therefore, it is not at all strange that the winter solstice, which takes place in the southern hemisphere on June 21 and is known as the Festival of the Sun, became the most important Incan celebration. The festival lasted days and included processions, dancing, singing, and animal sacrifices, all to ensure good harvests. This drawing reconstructs how the festival at Machu Picchu may have looked.

## The winter solstice

In Machu Picchu, during the winter solstice, the sun shone through the East Window of the Temple of the Sun. Sunlight shone on the sacred rock, which occupied almost the entire space. A cut on this rock, which framed the light that shone through the window, demonstrated that the temple was an astronomical observatory.

### KEY PLACES DURING THE FESTIVAL OF THE SUN

**① Entrance**
The llamas, loaded with a range of food and goods for festivalgoers, transported items though the main gate.

**② Intihuatana**
"The Hitching Post of the Sun" was key during the festival. A staircase with 78 steps connected it to the main square.

**③ Unfinished temple**
A religious site was left unfinished at the first stages of construction after the city was unexpectedly abandoned.

**④ Main square**
The only open space in the complex. Festivities took place here; it also provided a meeting space for Machu Picchu.

**⑤ Temple of the Sun**
Its use was restricted solely for royalty. The building's layout announced the arrival of the winter solstice.

# CHAPTER 14

# A Myth of Epic Proportions

Few historic legends have maintained such a power of fascination throughout the centuries as the one involving King Arthur. Yet the sparse amount of evidence on the existence of the Celtic monarch has not diminished his influence on European culture.

King Arthur is one of the great myths of European history. From his hazy origins as the British-Celtic military leader or monarch during the sixth century, his legend grew during the Middles Ages when he came to be known as the architypal rational, brave, and fair king and a national hero, especially during the twelfth and thirteenth centuries. But did he really exist?

The origins of the Arthurian myth are founded in a number of the oldest Welsh poems known to man. Arthur is mentioned in the "Elegy for Geraint", a text from the mid-sixth century in *The Book of Taliesin,* and in *Y Gododdin*, a compilation by the court poet Aneirin, dedicated to the warriors killed in battle against the Saxons. The manuscripts preserved from those works

date back to between the twelfth and fourteenth centuries, which casts doubt on their reliability. However, it is safe to say that the sheer number of references to Arthur in texts and legends from across Great Britain, especially in Scotland, Wales, and Cornwall, leads to the assumption that the Arthurian myth was already consolidated among the Celtic population when, in 1136, Geoffrey of Monmouth completed his monumental *History of the Kings of Britain* (*Historia Regum Britanniae*).

This work served as the basis for the Arthurian myth as it is known today. Although it is a historical text, Monmouth, a Welsh cleric who had studied at Oxford, recounts a great fantasy, mixing different periods of time, traditions, and places. He justified this by asserting that the

source of his work was "an ancient book in the British language" that Walter, Archdeacon of Oxford, had asked him to translate into Latin. Monmouth recalls the legendary birth of Arthur, his education away from the court, his accession to the throne, and the quests that led him to conquer Wales, England, Iceland, Norway, Brittany, and even to be crowned emperor by the Roman pope.

The almost instantaneous success of the book saw the Arthurian legend abandon its Celtic and Welsh origins to move first to Brittany, and then to the French courts.

Later redrafts of the myth expanded its literary nature and complicated the tracing of the real Arthur. In 1155, the poet Wace "created" the Round Table in his work *Roman de Brut*, perhaps at the request of the Norman House

**Arthur in bronze**
This statue of Arthur in his armor can be found in the Royal Chapel in Innsbruck, Austria. It was designed by Albrecht Dürer, and dates to 1513.

of Plantagenet, which reigned in England, as a way to legitimize the king as *primus inter pares* before his barons. Later, in 1180, Chrétien de Troyes, poet at the court of Marie of Champagne, linked Arthurian material with the search for the Holy Grail in *Perceval: the Story of the Grail*. Robert de Boron, a Burgundian poet from the end of the twelfth and beginning of the thirteenth century, followed this line in the trilogy *The Story of the Grail*, in which he identified the mythical island of Avalon (where Arthur rests until his return to the world of the living), with Glastonbury, the traditional headquarters of the first Christian church on English soil.

Around 1190, another monk and poet, Layamon, finished *Brut*, the first version of the King Arthur legends in English, which served to further popularize this literature. Finally, in 1485, William Caxton, the most famous printer in England, published *Morte d'Arthur*, written in prison by Sir Thomas Malory, who died in 1470, definitively setting in motion a cultural myth that would be taken up again at a later date. The success of the Arthurian myth, especially following its association with the search for the Holy Grail, has meant that even to the present day, there is a popular image of the hypothetical British king as a monarch dressed in shining armor, surrounded by other knights of exquisite manners and impeccable moral behavior, who led well-trained armies and lived in considerably fortified stone castles with halls designated for performing music and hosting balls.

Nothing could be farther from the truth. King Arthur's finery would have included linen jackets and leather waistcoats, tanned leather or linen trousers, woollen mantles worn as capes for added heat during winter, iron or animal-skin helmets, leather boots, and, as armor, a heavy iron sword, the same material from which the tip of his spear would have been made. This was the standard uniform for a Celtic warrior during the fifth and sixth centuries, the period during which this historic figure is believed to have lived.

### WHERE DID ARTHUR COME FROM?

Around 400 CE, beleaguered by the rise of the Barbarians, Rome decided to repatriate its legions to defend the metropolis that had declared itself helpless. According to tradition, extracted from the very few documents from and on the period, it was the usurper King Vortigern who, following Roman custom, called on the Saxons as a mercenary force to fight his other enemies. Gradually, the Saxons asked for more and more land in exchange for their support, until they rebelled against their old ally, pushing the modern-day Welsh people and other populations of Celtic origin eastward, toward Wales and Cornwall. It is in this context (of questionable historical accuracy) that the first mention of the figure of Arthur occurs, in a document, *Annales Cambriae*, written in Latin around 970 CE, which supports the theory of historic Arthur. It is alleged

### ↓Celtic Druids

The megalithic monument at Stonehenge is associated with the Celtic culture and the druids, with more than one researcher asserting that Merlin was a druid during the period.

## Magical Stonehenge

According to Geoffrey of Monmouth, it was the wizard Merlin who used his powers to transport the huge circle of stones (originally constructed by giants, according to Monmouth) from Ireland to England. He did this to fulfill the desires of Ambrosius Aurelianus, a Celtic-Roman leader during the fifth century, to erect a monument in honor of Britons killed in battle. Various others believe that King Arthur is merely a literary reflection of Ambrosius Aurelianus.

## Was South Cadbury Camelot?

Over time, the legendary court of Camelot has been attributed to different places. However, the most plausible option is Cadbury Castle, South Cadbury, in the English county of Somerset, close to Cornwall and where Glastonbury, associated with the tomb of King Arthur and the island of Avalon, is located. In reality, Cadbury Castle is not a castle, but a hill; the surrounding district was governed from its peak, a small plain 500 ft/150 m above sea level. Excavation work led by George Gray in 1913 demonstrated that the area had been occupied by settlers and warriors, who had sought refuge from their enemies here since the Middle Ages. The Romans pillaged the site and forced its inhabitants to move to the foot of the hill. In 1955, ceramic remains were found that were identified as similar to those found at Tintagel Castle, Cornwall (the legendary birthplace of King Arthur), and were dated back to the period in which Arthur is claimed to have lived. This would suggest that, between the fifth and sixth centuries, somebody important lived in Cadbury Castle who was rich enough to import luxury goods. Between 1966 and 1970, the Camelot Research Committee, an organization led by Leslie Alcock, carried out new excavations that confirmed that the Britons/Celts had fortified the hill on a number of occasions, making it a natural castle with embankments, stockades, and towers.

that its main sources were royal documents from the fifth, sixth, and seventh centuries. In these documents, Arthur is mentioned twice: in one, as the leader of the Britons who defeated the Saxons at the Battle of Mount Badon (around 519); in another, around 540 at the Battle of Camlann, Arthur is believed to have faced his son/nephew Mordred (Medraut in Welsh). Both lost their lives in the battle, although contemporary historians such as Gildas and the Venerable Bede make no mention of Arthur in their recollections of this event. However, it is stated in Chapter 56 of *History of the Britons*, written by Welsh monk Nennius during the ninth century: "Arthur, along with the kings of Britain, fought against them (the Saxons) in those days, although Arthur himself was the military commander."

### KING OR MILITARY LEADER?

This question is still cause for controversy: was Arthur a king, or merely a commander-in-chief of British troops? If he were just a military leader, his absence from the chronicles would be more understandable. Over the course of time, his battle ended up being in vain: Britannia, land of the Britons and Welsh, became England, land of the Angles and the Saxons. The lack of reliable documentation (many texts are dated to three or four centuries after the period of this historic figure) supports those who believe Arthur was merely a fictional hero. The problem is being able to separate historical accuracy from a cultural and literary myth that began over 1,500 years ago. The proliferation of Welsh and certain Scottish poems that mention the figure,

although after the sixth century, enhance the possibility that he may have existed. In 1191, the monks at Glastonbury Abbey claimed that they had discovered the tomb of Arthur and his wife, Queen Guinevere, during works carried out following the reconstruction of the building, which had been damaged by a serious fire in 1184. However, this claim is regarded with suspicion, as the consequent pilgrimages to "Arthur's tomb" saved the abbey from the economic disaster caused by the fire.

### A MYTH IN FLESH AND BONE

The chronicles recount that an ancient wooden tomb containing the skeletal remains of a man, considered large for the period, and a woman, were found beneath an iron cross: Arthur and Guinevere. In 1248, the remains were transferred to a marble pantheon, to allow pilgrims visiting Glastonbury to view them. The power of Arthur's spell dwindled over the centuries, until 1538, when Henry VIII, a fierce enemy of the Catholic Church, ordained the dissolution of all monasteries and abbeys in England. Thus, Glastonbury was abandoned and entered a period of deterioration. History has also granted some level of plausibility to the mythical island of Avalon, on which Arthur, following his battle to the death with Mordred, remained awaiting his victorious return to this world. Around 500 CE, Glastonbury occupied an area of marshland and swamps that were drained by man. However, the first traces of human settlements at the site are much older, dating back to around 150 BCE. Archaeology has been unable to confirm or refute the Arthurian myth with any level of certainty, although a number of findings have served

←**Cadbury Castle**
This hill, located in the county of Somerset, is one of several places considered to be the possible site of Camelot, the seat of King Arthur's court.

## Arthurs everywhere

One of the difficulties is the almost impossible association of Arthur with a single person. Sources vary, and the dates mentioned in documents have been unable to create a realistic profile of the figure. Therefore, with little basis in history, it is possible to attribute the identity of King Arthur to a number of figures. Geoffrey of Monmouth asserts that Arthur was the son of Uther Pendragon and grandson of Constantine II, the Roman emperor who declared himself Emperor of the West. Therefore, Arthur would have been a British king with Roman blood.

However, the name "Arthur" can also be traced back to other British regions. To the north, the Campbell Clan has traced its roots to Arthur ic Uibar, the legendary leader whose court was located in Cumbria. The existence of a King Arthwys has also been recorded; he is believed to have lived almost a generation before the orthodox Arthur and reigned in the northern Pennines. It is believed that Prince Artuir, son of Áedán mac Gabráin, lived on Scottish soil in the mid-sixth century.

The Welsh kingdom of Gwent and Glywysing also had a king named Arthur —Athrwys ap Meurig— believed to have lived during the seventh century and to have held his court in the town of Caerleon. In Powys, another Welsh county, there are two candidates: Owain Ddantgwyn, a prince from the end of the fifth century who belonged to the House of Cunedda; and his son, Cuneglas. Gildas affirmed that Owain, dubbed the "Bear" (*arth*, in Old Welsh), was defeated by his nephew and buried near a pond.

to underpin the legend slightly. In 1966, the Camelot Research Committee began excavations at Cadbury Castle, a small hill in Somerset with traces of a human presence since Neolithic times. Cadbury Castle had already been associated with King Arthur by John Leland who, in a letter dated to 1542, refers to an ancient tradition in the area that placed Camelot, the king's court, there. Cadbury Castle is not a castle, but a limestone hill that rises 500 ft/150 m above sea level, at the summit of which is a small plain. This natural defence had been fortified throughout the centuries with wooden stockades. During the excavations, ceramic fragments of Mediterranean origin were discovered. This would suggest that Cadbury Castle served as the residence of a local leader with the means to supply himself with luxury products such as jars and bowls from abroad.

Along with Cadbury Castle, the other great archaeological reference to Arthur is Tintagel, a castle that rises up on a steep hill on the Cornish coast; his legendary birth is believed to have taken place here, attributable to the magic arts of Merlin on behalf of Uther Pendragon. In 1998, a group of archaeologists from the University of Glasgow, led by Professor Chris Morris, found a slate among the ruins of the modern-day castle, erected in the thirteenth century, on which was an inscription referring to Artognou—Latin for Arthnou, or Arthur. This evidence may not be sufficient to confirm the existence of King Arthur. However, it keeps the door open to the possible accuracy of the enigma until further documentary or archaeological evidence is found that either supports or disproves the theory. And that is where information on the myth of King Arthur ends.

→**Ideal monarch**
In English literature, Arthur is described as an omnipotent king, both in war and in peace.

# The geography of King Arthur

In the time of King Arthur, Britain was inhabited by different Celtic tribes who had no political unity. Many distinct regions can be identified with important facts concerning the life of Arthur and his knights.

## Germanic invasions of the British Isles

From the fourth century, Roman England was invaded by the Angles, Jutes, and Saxons, who devastated the coastal communities of the East. Following the departure of the Roman legions, the Anglo-Saxon advance was stopped by the Britons at the Battle of Mount Badon. Later, Arthur was said to have led the Celtic people, giving impetus to his legend and that of his knights.

**❶**

### Ireland
The island was inhabited by different Gaelic Celtic peoples; among them were the Scots, who invaded Scotland in the fifth century.

**❷**

### Wales
In the time of the Roman invasion (first century CE), the country was divided between different Celtic tribes, the Deceangli, the Ordovices, the Demetae, and the Silures.

### Arthur's birthplace
Lady Igraine gave birth to Arthur at Tintagel Castle. At the base of the cliff where the ruins of the castle still stand is Merlin's Cave, where the magician and Uther Pendragon conspired to seduce Igraine.

**❸**

### Britannia
This was the name of the Roman province during their occupation between the first and fifth centuries. The island had been invaded by the Celtic Britons up to the 4th century BCE. Britons colonized Brittany in France around the fifth century.

### Cornwall
The sites with greater historical references associated with King Arthur are found in Cornwall in the southwest. Among the most important places is Tintagel, where the legend of King Arthur was born.

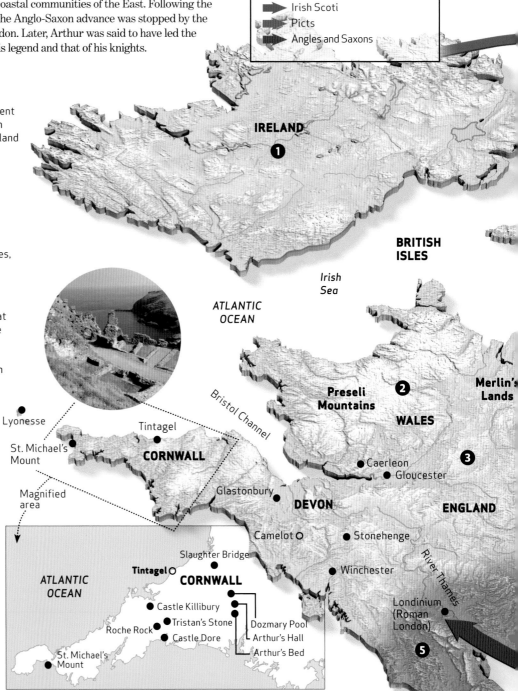

**British Isles c. 5th century**
- ➡ Irish Scoti
- Picts
- Angles and Saxons

IRELAND ❶

BRITISH ISLES

Irish Sea

ATLANTIC OCEAN

Preseli Mountains

Merlin's Lands

WALES

❷

❸

Caerleon
Gloucester

Bristol Channel

Lyonesse

Tintagel

St. Michael's Mount

CORNWALL

Glastonbury

DEVON

ENGLAND

Magnified area

Camelot ○

Stonehenge

Slaughter Bridge

Winchester

Tintagel ○

CORNWALL

ATLANTIC OCEAN

Castle Killibury

Tristan's Stone

Roche Rock

Castle Dore

Dozmary Pool

Arthur's Hall

Arthur's Bed

St. Michael's Mount

River Thames

Londinium (Roman London)

❺

## Does the so-called Arthur's stone have any relation to the mythical British King?

In 1998, "Arthur's stone" was discovered in Tintagel Castle in Cornwall, a piece of slate from the sixth century with an inscription believed to be the monogram of Christ. There was another piece of text, in Latin, which translates as: "Artognou, descendant of Paternus Colus, has made this." To Professor Chris Morris from Glasgow University, this text is nothing more than graffiti.

Magnified area

**SCOTLAND**

Antonine Wall

River Tweed

Hadrian's Wall

● Lancelot's Castle

● York

Saxons, Angles, and Jutes came from northern Germany and the Jutland peninsula (Denmark).

**4**

### Scotland
The Romans initially called the lands to the north of the wall, which they never conquered, Caledonia. The Picts or Caledonians lived there until the seventh century CE and after it was conquered by the Scots, it was renamed Scotland.

**5**

### Anglo-Saxons
Of Germanic origin, they included the Angles, Saxons, and Jutes. They invaded the southeast of Britain in the fifth century, escaping the savage invasions of the continent.

### Roman walls
In 120 CE, Hadrian ordered the construction of a wall measuring more than 70 miles/115 km long, to keep out the Caledonian tribes who lived in the south of Scotland. In 142 CE, Emperor Antoninus built a second wall.

### Germanic treasure
The funerary ship discovered at Sutton Hoo, Suffolk, is a valuable item that has increased our knowledge of the Germanic invasions.

### The death of King Arthur
Arthurian legends tell the story of a civil war started by Mordred, incestuous son of the king and Morgause. The first reference to Mordred (as Medraut) appears in the Annals of Wales. Arthur, mortally wounded, is carried to the island of Avalon, in expectation of his victorious return.

# King Arthur's Knights

The myth of the Knights of the Round Table took shape between the twelfth and thirteenth centuries. Book such as *Le Morte d'Arthur* by Sir Thomas Malory, were responsible for unifying the legend for posterity.

## The Knights of the Round Table

Although the Arthurian figures vary according to the different stories, the family ties of King Arthur and the main Knights of the Round Table can be traced.

**Igraine**
Became Uther Pendragon's wife after her first wedding to Gorlois, Duke of Cornwall.

**Uther Pendragon**
King of Britain, father of Arthur, he seduced Lady Igraine at Tintagel, after fighting against Gorlois in the Castle of Dimilioc.

**Morgause**
Queen of Orkney, Arthur's sister and wife of King Lot. In the *History of the Kings of Britain,* she was the mother of knights Gawain and Mordred.

**Guinevere**
Daughter of King Leodegrance of Cameliard, married to King Arthur. Her infidelity with Lancelot brought about the ruin of the Round Table.

**Morgan**
Arthur's sister. In early stories she was charitable, and took care of Arthur in Avalon. Later stories show her confronting Arthur, with whom she had Mordred.

**Mordred**
Arthur's incestuous son, the traitor in the legend. He corrupted and ruined King Arthur's court.

**Arthur**
In his youth he was renowned for being a brilliant idealist and infallible warrior. He was accepted as king thanks to Merlin's magic. He repelled the Anglo-Saxon invasions.

**Merlin**
Welsh magician, central to the Arthurian legend. Adviser to Uther and Arthur, he ended his days in the Forest of Brocéliande with his companion, Viviane.

**The Lady of The Lake**
Viviane, daughter of the King of Northumberland, educated Lancelot and gave Excalibur to Arthur. In some accounts she seduced Merlin, from whom she robbed his magic secrets.

## Chronology of Arthurian Literature

The main works referring to King Arthur are presented as historical treatises. The others are stories of knights.

| 830 | 1138 | 1155 |
|---|---|---|
| **History of the Britons** | **Historia Regum Britanniae** | **Roman de Brut** |
| *Nennius* | *Geoffrey of Monmouth* | *Wace* |
| Relates the early history of England and Wales. First mention of Arthur as a historical figure. | Pseudo-historical work. Based on the *History of the Britons.* First mention of the sword Excalibur. | Anglo-Norman poet. Wrote on the origins of England in French. First mention of the Round Table. |

## Where is "King Arthur's cross" that marked the location of his tomb at Glastonbury?

In 1191, the monks of Glastonbury Abbey discovered a tomb and a cross with this inscription: *"Hic iacet sepultus inclitus rex Arturus in insula Avalonia"* ("Here lies the famous King Arthur, on the island of Avalon"). The cross disappeared in the eighteeth century and only a reproduction, made by historian William Camden in 1607, remains.

**Galahad**
The most noble Knight of the Round Table, descendant of Joseph of Arimathea. Son of Lancelot and Elaine.

**Perceval**
Main hero in the first stories of the Grail. Known as the "Perfect Fool."

**Pellinore**
King, loyal to King Arthur and father of Perceval. He killed King Lot and misfortune befell him.

**Lionel**
Brother of Sir Bors and cousin of Lancelot. He supported his cousin against Arthur.

## Arthur's legacy

In 1485, Henry VII became the first Tudor King. He came from a Welsh noble family and used his origin as heir to Arthur to claim the throne. Prior to this, the Norman Plantagenet dynasty had used the Arthurian legend to unite the subjects of Celtic origin against the Saxons, whom William of Normandy defeated in 1066.

**Bedivere**
Sheriff of Logres and Arthur's companion. He was born in Normandy and buried in Bayeux.

**Lancelot**
Adopted by the Lady of the Lake, whom he presented to Arthur. He embodied the strength and weakness of the Round Table.

**Gawain**
The oldest of the sons of King Lot of Orkney, and friend of Lancelot.

**Bors**
Son of King Bohort. The only knight who returned to Camelot after seeing the Grail.

**Tristan**
By tradition, his tomb is located near Fowey, Cornwall. Nephew of King Mark of Cornwall.

**Kay**
One of the first of King Arthur's knights. He was the seneschal and adoptive brother of Arthur.

| c. 1170 | 1191 | c. 1200 | c. 1210 | 1215/1235 | 1485 |
|---------|------|---------|---------|-----------|------|
| **Lancelot, Knight of the Cart** | **Perceval, the Story of the Holy Grail** | **Joseph of Arimathea** | **Parzival** | **The Vulgate Cycle** | *Le Morte d'Arthur* |
| *Chrétien de Troyes* | *Chrétien de Troyes* | *Robert de Boron* | *Wolfram von Eschenbach* | *Anonymous* | *Sir Thomas Malory* |
| First mention of Lanzarote and Camelot, King Arthur's Court. | First mentions the Holy Grail—the cup that Christ used at the Last Supper. | In these two poetic works written in French, the Grail has an explicitly Christian value. | Completes the unfinished work of Troyes, with new contributions on the origin of the Holy Grail. | Five works that present the first cohesive structure of the legend. | Links the different traditions of the Arthurian cycle. The most influential version in later times. |

# The many faces of King Arthur

There are no reliable descriptions of the Knights of the Round Table. It was medieval literature that shaped their features. The iconography of Arthur varies between that of a skilled warrior and an old and venerable monarch.

## Attributes of an Emperor

In the picture to the right, from the original manuscript of the work, *Abbreviatio Chronicorum Angliae*, King Arthur sits on a folding campaign chair, an allusion to his warring and conquering nature. The crowns surrounding him symbolize the kingdoms he ruled (the number of which vary, although it is usually three, which could be Wales, England, and Scotland). The depiction of Arthur as both imperial and ruthless is shown in the image, where his feet are resting on the head of an enemy.

**Warrior**
Arthur in combat, in an illustration from the fifteenth century with his typical coat of arms—a shield with a blue background and three gold crowns.

## Youth

Arthur is usually depicted at two moments in his life: in and around the time when he was crowned and after many years on the throne. Here the images of him as a youth show him as clean-shaven, inexperienced, and with almost feminine features, both in the Middle Ages (illustration right, from the early fourteenth century) and in the nineteenth century (far right, ceramic panel by William Morris).

## The death of the king

There was a rise in Arthurian legends in the nineteenth century with the rise of Romanticism. The death of Arthur was one of the favorite themes of the artists of the period, as shown in this oil painting from 1860 by James Archer, based on a poem by Alfred, Lord Tennyson.

## The coronation

During this period of change (for Arthur as well as for Great Britain), medieval manuscripts show King Arthur as a young man and as a mature bearded man.

## Idealized

With the passing of time, illustrations of the "Matter of Britain" became increasingly idealized and romantic. An example is the painting (above) by John H. Bacon, depicting the wedding between Arthur and Guinevere, from the beginning of the twentieth century.

## Old age

Characteristically, the depictions of Arthur in old age (as he loses prominence in the legends) show him as a venerable and respected, yet static and inactive figure. The long beard and the crown, well-established attributes, are repeated in these images: a stained glass window in Bath Abbey (right) and a drawing by Gustave Doré (far right).

# The Round Table

The fellowship of the Knights of the Round Table has inspired artists from all historical periods. The legend continues to live, although it is likely that it has little to do with the reality of Arthur's life between the fifth and sixth centuries.

## Legacy

The Arthurian legends, which began in the twelfth century, depict the court at Camelot with typical characteristics of the time: armor, maces, solid castles of stone, and warriors who follow a strict code of chivalry. They are anachronisms in respect of the possible history of King Arthur, but it is the way that the legend has been passed down.

## No leadership

There was no place of privilege at the Round Table. Therefore, it was assumed that each knight had equal value for the king.

## Dangerous chair

The first mention of a "danger seat" is found in the work of Robert de Boron (around 1200). It describes an unoccupied chair at the Round Table, reserved for the knight destined to find the Holy Grail. Whoever sits there without due right shall die. In de Boron's work, the hero of the Grail is Perceval.

### Numbers

The number of knights that sat at the Round Table varied depending on the author: between 25 to 50, 150, and up to 1,600 in different stories. Robert de Boron lists 13 knights—an explicit allusion to Jesus and the 12 Apostles.

# Body and Spirit of the Crusades

The Order of the Temple continues to be a fascinating story in European history 700 years after its dissolution in 1312. The saga of these soldier-monks symbolizes the continuing conflict between political and religious power.

In the eleventh century, signs of demographic, economic, and cultural recovery could be seen in the Christian West, although devastation in the form of epidemics, wars, and feudal pressure continued to threaten the majority of people. The Catholic Church was gaining prestige and influence in social and political life. It legislated rules and customs, collected taxes, and became increasingly more active in political matters. It was a period in which pilgrimages to Rome, Jerusalem (by Arab agreement), and Santiago de Compostela gained increasing importance.

However, the situation changed when the Seljuq Turks came onto the scene and conquered the Holy City in 1071. At the Council of Clermont, France, in 1095, Pope Urban II proclaimed the need to recover the Holy Land, for which he appealed to the Christian sentiments of the main French and German noblemen of Europe. Spain and Portugal had already been fighting against the Muslims for centuries in the Reconquest, so by decree of the Pope, the Christian West united and turned against the Muslims to regain access to Jerusalem. And so the Crusades came about, which also served to channel the growing aggression of the elite European military groups.

### THE CONQUEST OF JERUSALEM

The First Crusade was successful: in 1099 the expedition body under the command of Godfrey de Bouillon conquered Jerusalem, of course with blood and fire. The Crusaders established a Latin kingdom in Jerusalem, but pilgrims continued to be accosted by bandits or local chiefs, particularly along the main road linking the port of Jaffa to the Holy City.

Around 1115, French knight Hugues de Payens found himself in the Holy Land. Together with eight companions, he mooted the idea of creating a monastic order that would guarantee the defense of the pilgrims by forming a small and stable military force; so around 1118 or 1119, the Order of the Poor Knights of Christ was created. They were subject to the authority of the patriarch of Jerusalem, before whom the knights swore the three vows of obedience, poverty, and chastity. These knights used their weapons to fight while wearing the habit, even against the infidels, which was a genuine revolution because this was completely prohibited under the rules

**Defense**
The Order of the Temple was the main defender of Christianity in the Holy Land. The illustration shows the Knights Templar in around 1150.

of the Church. Baldwin II, king of Jerusalem (1118–31), gave them a permanent seat in the defensive compound of the Holy Sepulcher, which today is the location of the mosque of Al-Aqsa, on the terrace that occupied the ancient Temple of Solomon. This location paved the way for the brotherhood to be known as the "Order of the Temple," and its members as the "Knights Templar." In 1127, following renewed strength and the gaining of territory by the Muslims, Hugues de Payens, aware that the new order needed more resources to ensure its survival (according to Michael the Syrian, Monophysite Patriarch of Antioch and historian, there were around 30 knights and several hundred assistants) returned to Europe together with several of his companions, carrying letters of introduction from King Baldwin II to the major monarchs.

De Payens had the enthusiastic collaboration of Bernard of Clairvaux, the future St. Bernard. Considered the greatest theological authority of his time, he was a close friend of Hugh, Count of Champagne, who in 1125 left his possessions and family to become a Knight Templar. Bernard of Clairvaux organized a council at Troyes at the beginning of 1128 to consecrate the new Rule of the Temple. In 1130, he wrote a *Tribute to the New Templar Military*, which stated that killing an enemy of the true faith in the name of God followed the strict moral Templar code and was not a sin. The soldier-monks of the Temple were also likened to Christian martyrs. The mission was so successful that hundreds of men decided to join the military, while others were granted land, castles, and weapons.

With this rapid growth, the Order of the Temple came to be a real army that, in combat, showed signs of preparation and discipline that contrasted with the rest of the Christian forces. It was a hierarchical militia: Master (the term Grand Master was only used in the presence of provincial or local masters), seneschal (lieutenant), marshal (military leader), sergeants, auxiliaries, and mercenary troops. Among the last were the Turcopoles (a military force of Byzantine origin with mounted archers, used by the Romans in the East), as well as Armenian and Syrian Christians, who were the majority of the population and an important part of the local nobility. Another Templar figure was that of gonfalone (standardbearer), key in regrouping troops in combat.

### DEFEAT AT HATTIN

The cost of maintaining the fortifications and a permanent army in the Holy Land was enormous. The money came from the hundreds of plots or fiefdoms, where farms owned by the Order in Europe, especially France, were developed. In 1139, Pope Innocent II granted the Templars the power to have their own chaplains and build their own churches. This represented the removal of the authority of bishops, placing it under the sole dependence of the Supreme Pontiff of the order. Despite

the increasing powers, finance, and strength of the protective forces, territory was slowly being lost to the resurgent Muslim armies, and resources were spread relatively thinly. After a failed second crusade in 1147, the Knights suffered a heavy defeat in 1187, when Sultan Saladin united the Muslim kingdoms and reconquered Jerusalem after destroying the Christian forces in the Battle of the Horns of Hattin. Some 140 Templars died, although Saladin spared the life of Master Gerard de Ridefort, one of the culprits of the disaster. The Third Crusade, despite having the king of England, Richard the Lionheart behind it, achieved no more than a truce to allow pilgrims access to the Holy City. It was not until 1229, when the King of Jerusalem, Frederick II of Hohenstaufen (r. 1225–1243), reached a new agreement, that it was declared an "open city." In 1244, the Turks led the Muslim reconquest of Jerusalem and in 1291, with the fall of St. John d'Acre, the Christian kingdoms of the Holy Land finally disappeared.

The Knights Templar were forced to take refuge in Cyprus. Without pilgrims to protect, without any real chance of reconquering Jerusalem, with Venice and Genoa already trading with the Muslims, and the European kings being more concerned with organizing their national monarchies, the Order of the Temple lost its raison d'être. In Europe, the bishops were wary of monks who could collect tithes without asking their permission. Some of the kings and princes began

to realize that the Order of the Temple was becoming a kind of independent state. And with Jerusalem in the hands of the infidel, why did they need so much money? This appears to be the question asked by Philip IV (Philip the Fair), the French monarch, who paradoxically, when struggling with his finances, had to turn to the banking services of the order after a popular revolt as a result of an increase in prices. It should be noted that the powerful Templars managed various plots of land throughout France, had the largest food distribution center in Paris, had a fleet that transported goods and pilgrims between Europe and the Holy Land, and, if that wasn't enough, had the largest and most efficient banking service of the time, comparable with those of the Jews and Venetians, and from which everyone from lowly pilgrims to whole kingdoms, such as France, benefited.

### THE END OF THE TEMPLARS
The treasurer of the Order of the Temple in Paris belonged to the Royal Council and, from 1303, the Royal Treasure was kept in the Temple. In 1305, unhappy with the Templars' financial strength, Philip IV was given the opportunity he had been waiting for: a Frenchman Esquiu de Floyran, following a lack of interest in his account from King James II of Aragon, went to Paris and exposed some terrible accusations from a former Templar whom he had met in prison. With this

## The fortunes of the Knights Templar

The main source of documented wealth of the Temple was the administration of hundreds of plots of land, farms on which the Templars showed their skill for economics. Any surpluses generated were sold in provincial markets and the property on the land generated rental income.

However, the most prominent economic facet of the Order was its transformation into the most important bank of its time. Documents certified by the Order of the Temple had the same validity in Paris, London, Tyre, and Jerusalem. There was no need to carry money or jewels; it was enough to have a certificate of income in any "branch" of the Order of the Temple, which could be converted into cash on arrival in the Holy Land.

From kings to pilgrims, thousands of people left their wealth with the Order with the certainty that it would be intact on their return. Treasurers of the Order, together with the Lombard, Florentine, and Jewish bankers, helped create the bill of exchange, or check. The Temple managed guarantees, loans, and refunds without charging commissions. They obtained benefits from the authority granted to them by the powerful people using their services, beginning with the kings of France, who entrusted them with the royal treasury.

information, without regard for its reliability, along with his chancellor, William of Nogaret, right hand of the monarch in his confrontations with the Church, Philip prepared the fall of the Temple, organizing a popular smear campaign against the Templars on charges of apostasy, sodomy, obscene rites, idolatry, and rejection of the cross and Jesus Christ.

Anxious about the pope's reluctance to follow in his footsteps, Philip IV drafted a warrant for the arrest of the Templars on September 14, 1307. Starting on Friday October 13, 1307, royal officials entered the manors and castles of the Knights in France with no resistance. As soon as the Templars were under arrest, Philip IV was merciless. He demanded confessions, and his officers obtained them with the use of torture. Just 12 days later, the tortured Grand Master, Jacques de Molay, confessed to the truth of the allegations. In November, Pope Clement V, overtaken by events, also ordered the arrest of the Templars. The situation then swung in the Knights' favor in 1310: the Templars had spent three years in France as prisoners. Some 54 had been burned at the stake to speed up the process of destroying the Order, but in Aragon, Castile, and Portugal they had been cleared by the different national councils. This left Philip IV alone in his persecution.

The pope called a council in Vienne, France, in 1311 to find a solution, and began to consider the idea of confronting the French monarch. However, on March 20, 1312, ignoring ecclesiastical authority, Philip went with part of his army to Vienne to make his intentions clear. Shortly after, Clement V ordered the Temple assets to pass to the Order of the Hospitallers. Annoyed by this decision, Philip IV claimed huge amounts of money in return for keeping the knights captive and instructed his officials to sell their

assets and land. More than 70 years would pass in Castile before the crown recognized the papal bull. The Templars, now each individually absolved, integrated themselves into other orders, decided to hang up their habits, or simply died from natural causes, thus preventing the reorganization of the Order.

A few years later, on March 18, 1314, Jacques de Molay and his companions were sentenced to life imprisonment for their relapses (repeating a sin that had been renounced). The Grand Master protested and abnegated his first confession, made as a result of torture. Philip IV again acted ahead of the pope and made royal officials take de Molay and 36 Templars over to a small island in the Seine, where they were burned at the stake for heresy, without respecting the judgment. So why didn't the Templars, a military and economic force protected by the pope, resist their persecution and eventual downfall?

Prior to Philip's personal conquest, in August 1307, de Molay had asked Clement V to open an investigation concerning rumors against the Order, certain that it would come out unscathed. It is also logical to think that many Templars were aware of what was going on politically through their family connections with the royal and ecclesiastical officials. But they incorrectly trusted that their autonomy in terms of royal power would be respected, that the pope would come to their aid and would play fair with them, and that their relations with Philip IV were cordial. Interestingly, those most resistant were the Templars from the Iberian Peninsula kingdoms, who benefited from eventual absolution. In the end, everything capitulated and adapted to the demands of a new generation of kings who were laying the foundations for future European nation-states.

## Aragon and the Order

In 1311, King Alfonso I of Aragon appointed the Order of the Temple, the Order of the Holy Sepulcher, and the Order of the Hospitals as heirs to his kingdom. The Aragon nobles opposed this and proclaimed his brother Ramiro as king. Ramiro promised to deliver the kingdom to these orders, respecting the will of Alfonso I, if the new royal dynasty ended. He conceded to the Templars castles, a tithe of their income, exemption from paying a fifth of the spoils of war to the king, authorization to build forts, and a fifth of the land taken from the Muslims.

**↓ Maritime Power**
Around the thirteenth century, the Templar boats left the French ports and headed to the Holy Land, loaded with military equipment. They also carried goods and pilgrims between Europe and Palestine.

**↑ Temple enclosure**
From the thirteenth century, work began on the Temple Enclosure in Paris. This walled space included a church, lodgings, stables, and the stronghold of the Temple.

## Did they hide their treasure?

Royal officials who assumed control of the plots of land, abbeys, and castles of the Templars in 1307 did not find significant amounts of money or valuable relics. Nevertheless for many, not finding their mythical treasure was proof that it had been concealed. One of the more bizarre explanations is the suggestion that a group of Templars managed, ahead of Philip IV's actions, to move the treasure from Paris in time. Some believe it ended up in Scotland, and others that it was hidden in a castle or even taken to America. Others argue that it ended up in Switzerland, where the Templars eventually formed rural communities in what is now the most famous banking society in the world.

# The era of the Crusades

Starting in the eleventh century, the Western Christian kingdoms embarked upon a series of military campaigns in the Near East to reclaim the Holy Land from Islam. The Order of the Temple was created against this backdrop of military and religious fervor.

## The Eight Crusades

The Christians organized eight crusades to the Holy Land. The Order of the Knights Templar was created in 1118–19, following the foundation of the kingdom of Jerusalem, conquered in 1099 during the First Crusade.

### References

- Cities
- ◎ Capitals
- Islam
- Western Christianity
  End of the 13th century
- Eastern Christianity
  End of the 13th century
- ✕ Battles, by year

### The Crusades

- ⇨ 1st Crusade (1096–99)
- → 2nd Crusade (1147–49)
- → 3rd Crusade (1189–92)
- → 4th Crusade (1199–1204)
- → 5th Crusade (1217–21)
- → 6th Crusade (1228–29)
- → 7th Crusade (1248–54)
- → 8th Crusade (1270)

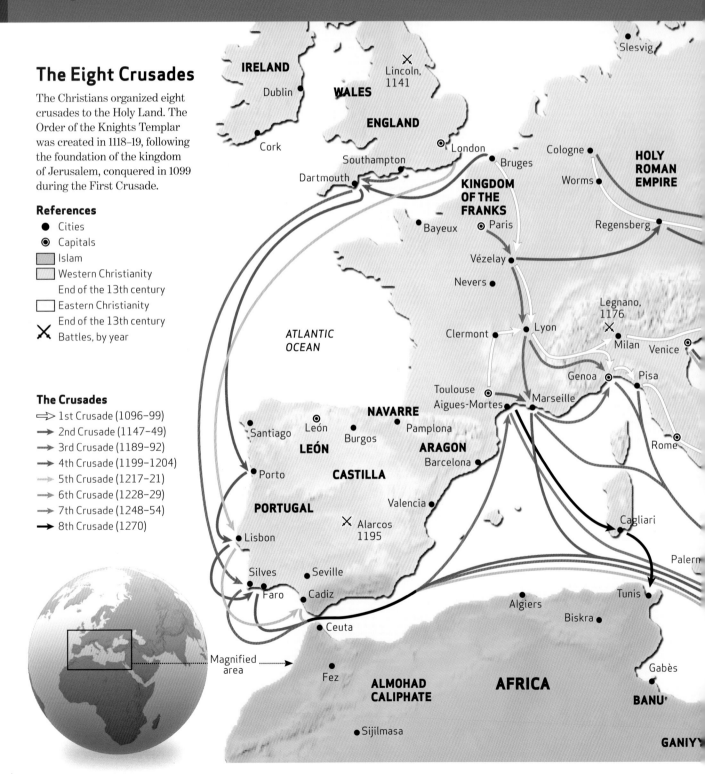

IRELAND
Dublin
Cork
WALES
ENGLAND
Southampton
Dartmouth
London
Bruges
Bayeux
KINGDOM OF THE FRANKS
Paris
Vézelay
Nevers
Clermont
Lyon
Toulouse
Aigues-Mortes
Marseille
Genoa
Pisa
Milan
Venice
Rome
Cologne
Worms
Regensberg
HOLY ROMAN EMPIRE
Slesvig
Lincoln, 1141 ✕
Legnano, 1176
✕
ATLANTIC OCEAN
Santiago
León
Burgos
Pamplona
NAVARRE
ARAGON
Barcelona
Valencia
CASTILLA
LEÓN
Porto
PORTUGAL
Lisbon
Silves
Faro
Seville
Cadiz
Ceuta
✕ Alarcos 1195
Cagliari
Palerm
Tunis
Algiers
Biskra
Gabès
Fez
ALMOHAD CALIPHATE
AFRICA
BANU'
GANIY'
Sijilmasa

Magnified area

## What did Pope Urban II say at the Council of Clermont, held in 1095?

"God wills it!" This was how Pope Urban II closed his speech given at the Council of Clermont before a congregation of clergymen and laymen on November 27, 1095, to free the Holy Land from the grasp of the infidels. "God wills it!" would become the motto of the First Crusade.

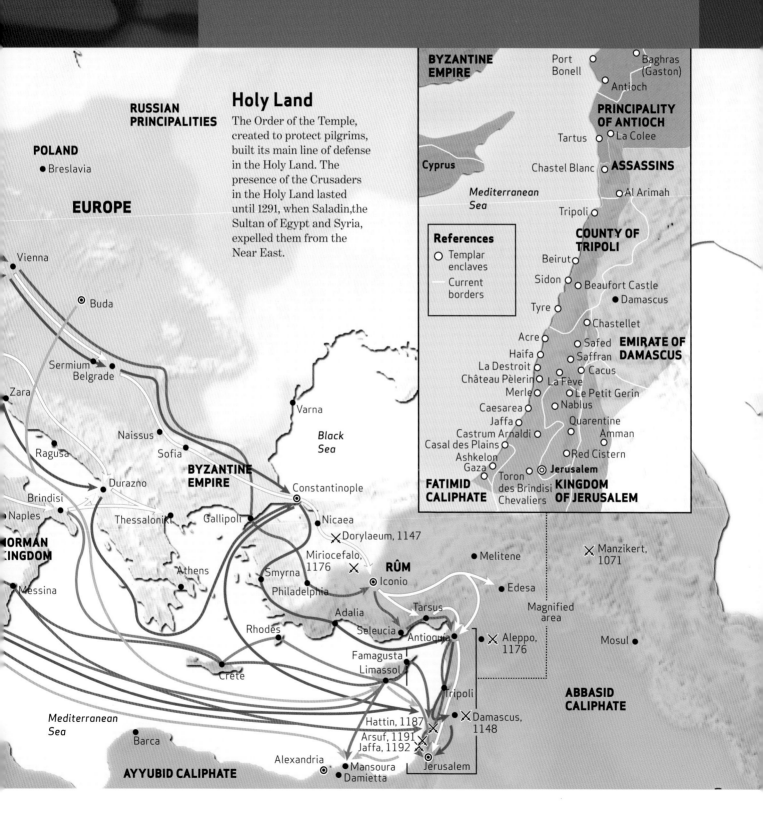

### Holy Land

The Order of the Temple, created to protect pilgrims, built its main line of defense in the Holy Land. The presence of the Crusaders in the Holy Land lasted until 1291, when Saladin, the Sultan of Egypt and Syria, expelled them from the Near East.

RUSSIAN PRINCIPALITIES

POLAND
● Breslavia

EUROPE

Vienna

● Buda

Sermium
Belgrade

Zara

Naissus

Ragusa

Sofia

Durazno

BYZANTINE EMPIRE

Brindisi

Naples

NORMAN KINGDOM

Thessaloniki

Gallipoli

Messina

Athens

Smyrna

Philadelphia

Rhodes

Adalia

Seleucia

Crete

Famagusta
Limassol

Mediterranean Sea

Barca

Alexandria

Mansoura
Damietta

AYYUBID CALIPHATE

Varna

Black Sea

Constantinople

Nicaea

✕ Dorylaeum, 1147

Miriocefalo, 1176 ✕

RÛM
◎ Iconio

Tarsus

Antioquia

Hattin, 1187

Arsuf, 1191
Jaffa, 1192

Jerusalem

✕ Aleppo, 1176

✕ Damascus, 1148

Tripoli

✕ Melitene

● Edesa

Magnified area

✕ Manzikert, 1071

Mosul ●

ABBASID CALIPHATE

#### References
○ Templar enclaves
— Current borders

BYZANTINE EMPIRE

Port Bonell ◉

Baghras (Gaston)

Antioch

PRINCIPALITY OF ANTIOCH

Tartus ○   ○ La Colee

Cyprus

Chastel Blanc ○  ASSASSINS

Mediterranean Sea

○ Al Arimah

Tripoli ○

COUNTY OF TRIPOLI

Beirut ○

Sidon ○  ○ Beaufort Castle
● Damascus

Tyre ○

○ Chastellet

Acre ○  ○ Safed   EMIRATE OF DAMASCUS
Haifa ○  ○ Saffran
La Destroit ○  ○ Cacus
Château Pèlerin ○  ○ La Fève
Merle ○  ○ Le Petit Gerin
Caesarea ○  ○ Nablus
Jaffa ○  Quarentine
Castrum Arnaldi ○  ○  Amman
Casal des Plains ○
Ashkelon ○  ○ Red Cistern
Gaza ○  Toron des Brindisi  ◎ Jerusalem
Chevaliers

FATIMID CALIPHATE

KINGDOM OF JERUSALEM

# The Order of the Temple

Over just two centuries, the Order of the Poor Knights of Christ went from being a small military body to an extremely rich, powerful, and influential organization with a significant presence across Europe and the Near East.

## Knights, sergeants, and priests

Regardless of their role and duties, members of the Order were divided into four large groups, depending on their social origins and whether they were warriors.

**Turcopoles**
They did not belong to the Order. They were mercenary soldiers of Byzantine origin.

**Artisans and squires**
Responsible for manual tasks and maintenance of the knights' weaponry.

**Priests**
Combined religious matters and the Order's administrative tasks.

**Sargeants**
Warriors of noble origins. The roles they occupied were of limited responsibility.

**Knights**
Of noble origins, only the knights were permitted to use the white cape and mantle with the red cross.

## Territorial organization

The main administrative unit was the trust (fief), that was grouped into bailiwicks, which in turn were grouped into provinces.

**Bailiwick**
A section of land on which several trusts were located.

**Trust**
There were both rural and urban trusts. Generally, a trust comprised a castle, a chapel and different households.

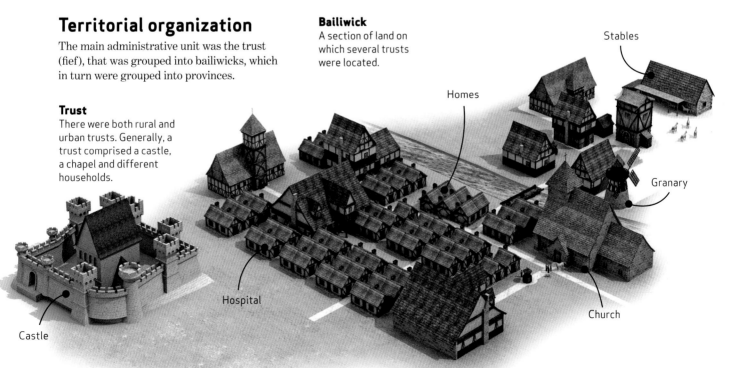

Stables

Homes

Granary

Castle

Hospital

Church

# Did the Knights Templar manage to hide their sacred relics?

There are those who assert that, before the reprisals they suffered during the Inquisition, the Templars were able to destroy part of their records and hide some of their treasures, among them the Shroud of Turin. However, who warned them of the imminent inquisitorial danger? Where were the treasures stored? These questions remain unanswered.

Image of a typical daily scene: two Templars playing chess.

**Grand Master**
Leader of the Order. His power was only limited by the Chapter.

**Seneschal**
The Grand Master's right-hand man.

**Marshal**
Military head of the Order and battle strategist.

**Draper**
Responsible for uniform.

**Commander of the Kingdom of Jerusalem**
Treasurer of the Order.
**Commander of the City of Jerusalem**
Protector of the pilgrims and the relic of the True Cross.
**Provincial commander**
Responsible for a given province.

## THE POSITIONS

**Local commander**
In charge of a trust.

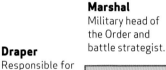

## CHAPTERS
Collegiate bodies that exercised the effective power of the Order. There were three types:

**General Chapter**
Presided over by the Grand Master and comprising the main leaders, it was responsible for making the Order's key decisions.

**Provincial Chapters**
Provincial authorities dealt with local matters.

**Ordinary Chapters**
The authorities of each trust would meet once a week to deal with domestic issues.

## PROVINCIAL HOUSES
The bailiwicks were governed by provincial houses, with several of these houses together comprising the province. There were nine provinces (see map).

## THE HEADQUARTERS

**A** **Jerusalem (1120–87)**
Home to the Templar headquarters until the city was lost to Saladin.

**B** **Acre (1191–1291)**
To the north of Israel, reconquered by the Christians during the Third Crusade.

**C** **Cyprus (1291–1311)**
The headquarters were located on this Mediterranean island until the dissolution of the Order.

England, Scotland, and Ireland

**WEST**

France and Auvergne

Germany and Hungary

Italy

Portugal

Aragon and Catalonia

Castile, León, and Majorca

Apulia and Sicily

Cyprus

**EAST**

Edessa

Antioch

Tripoli

Jerusalem

# Templar symbolism

The symbols of the Templars—the white mantle, the black and white battle standard, and the cross—were added to over the years by a range of apocryphal iconography, products of the imagination, or misguided misconceptions.

## Agnus Dei

Some Templar seals bore the Agnus Dei (Latin for "Lamb of God"), the image of the lamb that intertwines one of its legs with the flagstaff or cross. Although its meaning is unclear, it is believed to allude to the sacrifice of Christ on the cross; other researchers have suggested that the image symbolizes pagan rituals. Other experts, however, have associated the Agnus Dei with John the Baptist, who is usually represented as being dressed in lambskin, with a staff and a scroll that reads "Ecce Agnus Dei" ("Behold the Lamb of God"). Although each trust had its own seal, there were two types of seal that were used throughout the Order; with the same obverse face, the Temple of Solomon. On one, the reverse face featured the Templar cross and on the other a horse mounted by two Knights Templar.

### Greek cross

Cross with crossbeams of equal length. The Greek cross plan is typical of Byzantine architecture; it also features in buildings that the Templars constructed in Spain and Portugal. On many seals, the Greek cross appears surrounded by astronomical symbols (moons, suns, and stars), the layout of which tends to follow the same order.

### Abrasax

Anthropomorphic figure with the head of a rooster and snakelike legs. It was attributed with special powers and used as a talisman.

## Patriarchal cross

Unlike most crosses, the patriarchal cross has two horizontal crossbeams rather than one. The upper, and smaller, represents the inscription that Pilate ordered to be affixed to the cross (INRI). The lower is the crossbeam on which the upper limbs were nailed. This cross was the standard of Godfrey of Bouillon during the First Crusade.

### Green Man
A pagan symbol; a male head, from which leaves and branches grow that frame the face. It is believed to represent ancient deities and appears to be related to reincarnation and the different cycles of nature.

### Baphomet
Deity with a bearded face with horns, which the Templars started to use having been influenced by the Saracens of the Holy Land. In their worship of it, they were accused of heresy by the Church.

### Cross *pattée*
The word *pattée* is French, and is used to refer to an animal's leg. This cross started to form part of the seal and the habit worn by Templar monks from 1146, at the request of Bernard of Clairvaux.

# Freemasonry, a Permanent Mystery

Although they have exercised considerable worldwide influence for three centuries and generated strong positive and negative opinions, the Freemasons still remain a mystery. Few are able to define their real objective.

Few times has a topic, about which so little is known, been discussed so frequently. Freemasonry is a controversial subject about which everything has been said, though not always backed up by strong evidence. It is known that the Freemasons decisively influenced the French Revolution and the American War of Independence. Many of the biggest leaders in world history were Freemasons, including 16 presidents of the United States and several kings and emperors of England, France, and Germany, in addition to many leaders in South America.

A select list of famous Freemasons would include names like Simón Bolívar and José de San Martín; a wide range of authors and philosophers from different eras, such as Goethe, Voltaire, Oscar Wilde, Rudyard Kipling, and Tolstoy; musicians including Mozart, Schubert, Puccini ,and Louis Armstrong; military men and heads of state, such as Giuseppe Garibaldi, Winston Churchill, Salvador Allende, and Martin Luther King; scientists like Alexander Fleming and Enrico Fermi; the founders of Ford, Citroën, and Chrysler; the magician, Houdini, the astronaut Buzz Aldrin, Buffalo Bill, Cantinflas, Clark Gable, John Wayne; and even fictional characters like Sherlock Holmes and Corto Maltese.

Today, more than five million people across the globe are involved in Freemasonry and the movement has been capable of standing against the Catholic Church and all the fascist and communist regimes of the twentieth century. Since the official birth of modern Freemasonry, at the beginning of the eighteenth century, the intellectual and economic weight of many of its members, combined with the secrecy of its activities (referred to by the organization as simple discretion), have incited governments of many countries to fight against institutions outside their control. Although the creation of the United Grand Lodge of England in 1717 is often cited as the founding charter of Freemasonry, both in initiate and philanthropic societies, the organization's roots date back to the early Middle Ages. At the time, economic activity ("trades and craftsmanship") was dependent on guilds, professional brotherhood organizations, that made full use of slogans and codes to make labor infiltration more difficult.

**Spotless**
The smock and white gloves worn by Freemasons symbolize honor, innocence, and purity. They endeavor always to preserve them intact.

In the era of cathedral building, it is understandable that one of the most prestigious guilds was the masons' guild, whose meeting places were close to the great works. In these spaces, known as "lodges," the masons (*maçons* in French) worked, rested and even ruled on conflicts between members, with no opportunity for appeal, in order to maintain the level of discipline required to complete works to the highest standards.

### HIERARCHIES AND CEREMONIES
Construction of a church, palace, or public building could last for many decades; during this time, masons were able to establish solid friendships with their brethren. Each local guild subjugated its members to the authority of a Grand Master, found in the upper echelons of a solid hierarchical scale. The brotherhood was equally willing to accept stonemasons who converted raw stone into ashlar; artists who carved sculptures; and architects who designed the building.

Candidates for acceptance into the brotherhood had to demonstrate that their lives adhered to principles of virtue and good practice, being faithful to their wives and fulfilling their religious duties. Following admission to the society by a ritual ceremony, the candidate became an apprentice who was offered guidance by a master who showed him the secrets of the profession (based on geometry and arithmetic, shielded behind mystical symbolism) until he was considered ready to

be a fellow—the intermediate level in the lodge's hierarchy. During the rite of passage from apprentice to fellow, the candidate was provided with a symbol, which he would use thereafter as a type of signature, chiseled into a discreet place in all his works. This symbol was associated with a word that served as a key to enter the lodge and as a form of protection against unfair competition from those who avoided the costly apprenticeship in the guild. As part of the same ritual, the new member was also assigned a greeting and touch or gesture to identify himself before his brethren.

During the initiation ceremony, the candidate swore never to divulge any knowledge, codes, words, or greetings learned at the lodge, pledging so "under no less penalty than to have my throat cut across, my tongue torn out by the roots, and my body buried in the rough sands of the sea." After several years as a fellow, the medieval Freemason aspired to become a master, a non-permanent position: a decision was made among the brethren to elect one member to perform the role of master on the completion of any given work. In the lodge, the master was responsible for preserving the society's books and for rendering judgment on brethren who had breached the law of the guild. Professionally, the master was the builder who had reached a maximum creative capacity—the ability to design huge buildings, a talent that gave him proximity to divine works. In fact, in the eighteenth century, Freemasons started

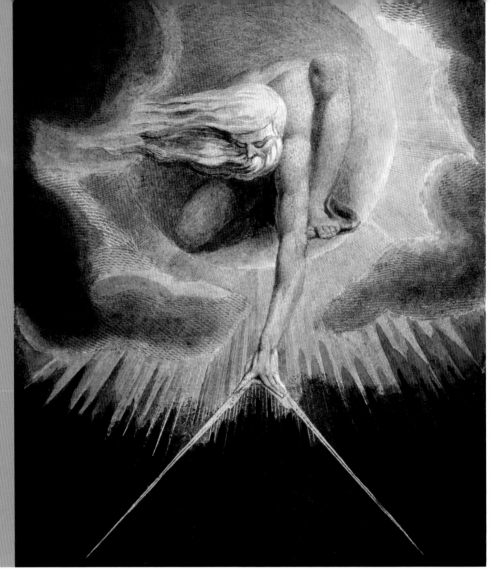

**← St. Paul's**
This cathedral in London was built between 1676 and 1710 on the ruins of the old cathedral that was destroyed by the Great Fire of 1666. The architect Christopher Wren, a well-known Freemason, led the reconstruction.

**→ *The Ancient of Days***
William Blake painted this image to accompany his poem *Europe, a Prophecy*. In it, he uses the image of God, the Great Architect of the Universe, with the compass—a common feature of Freemasonry.

to call God the Great Architect of the Universe (a concept taken from medieval Christianity), with a large compass coming to symbolize Him, an image that has survived to this day.

### THE DECLINE OF THE GUILDS
With the end of the Middle Ages, the era of great cathedrals ended and guilds went into decline. The Enlightenment saw the creation of the first academies and faculties of architecture, teachings that made the antiquated guild education system redundant. Masonic lodges, despite maintaining their great social status, were rendered corporately and professionally useless. Under these circumstances, a large number of noblemen, lawyers, businessmen, doctors, and even religious people, many of whom were rich sponsors of great architectural works, were admitted to the secret meetings of the lodges under the title "accepted Freemasons." As time passed, especially toward the late seventeenth and early eighteenth century, accepted Freemasons started to push their traditional brethren aside, assuming control of the lodge. This would see the emergence of the so-called speculative masonry, an initiate society that preserves the spirit, organization, and symbolism of medieval or operative masonry, but that abandoned the teaching of architecture and the cooperative, guild-led nature of the lodges. While medieval Freemasons built majestic cathedrals, modern Freemasons tried to perfect themselves as individuals who would be useful in building the ideal symbolic temple: humanity. Stripped of its practical usefulness, thereafter Freemasonry became a philanthropic society that served an ethical purpose: defending the dignity, solidarity, and brotherhood established with one another. These objectives were embodied for the first time in 1723, with the creation of the so-called "Anderson's Constitutions," drafted to govern the functionality of the United Grand Lodge of England. During his years at the lodge, the Freemason had to polish his morality with the help of his most experienced brethren. Construction tools and architectural terms belonging to operative masonry lost their practical purpose and acquired a more symbolic meaning: the smock, an allegory for work, had to be white, representing virtue; the square served to measure actions; the compass, to keep oneself within the organization's limits; the gloves, to avoid the stain of evil; and so on.

### DEFENDERS OF HUMANISM
In an era marked with the blood and fire of religious wars between Catholics and Protestants, the lodges attracted men who, heavily influenced by the ideals of the Enlightenment, sought a return to universal humanism, tolerance, and brotherhood against fascism and ignorance. The revolutionary expression, "Liberty, equality, fraternity" has Masonic connotations, and is visible today on the walls of many lodges.

**↓Freemasons in the United States**
Although many American Freemasons remained faithful to the king of England, at least ten of the 56 people who signed the United States Declaration of Independence belonged to one of the lodges founded in the North American colonies—one of whom was Benjamin Franklin.

## Revolutionary inspiration?

Incapable of accepting that the French Revolution was the logical reaction of the least fortunate sections of the Ancien Régime, the monarchy, nobility, and clergy responded by feeding the myth that the Freemasons had conspired to cause the revolution.

Ever since the foundation of the first French lodge in 1738, the Freemasons had been subject to a complete lack of trust among the powerful echelons of society, given their egalitarian roots and abstract theism. Many Freemasons featured among the most important figures of the Revolution: moderates such as the Marquis de Lafayette, who had fought with George Washington

to secure American independence, alongside radicals like Jean-Paul Marat and Georges Jacques Danton.

However, it is also true to say that many Freemasons fought on behalf of the royalists, and dozens met their fate at the guillotines. It is worth remembering that at the time, most Freemasons were aristocrats. In fact, Freemasonry was accused of being monarchic and many lodges were closed as a result.

However, it was only explicitly used by Freemasonry after the French Revolution. Anderson's Constitutions induced Freemasons to exercise virtue as a sense of duty; Freemasonry was defined as a gathering of men who believe in a single god —Christian, Muslim, Jewish or other minority monotheistic religions—who wish to work together, despite the differences in their social origin or political and religious beliefs. Over half a century before the Revolution, at the peak of the Absolutist period, these universal ideals were highly innovative and, in the opinion of some monarchies that were completely polarized by the Reformation and the Counter-Reformation, most troubling.

### EXPANSION AND DIVERGENCE
Throughout the eighteenth and nineteenth centuries, the success and expansion of Freemasonry throughout Europe and America, and the liberal nature of the lodges, resulted in growing discrepancies between different societies. It was religion in particular that caused the greatest division between Freemasons: in 1877, the Grand Orient de France, which was the country's largest federation of lodges, decided to remove the obligation of believing in God, the use of vows, and references to the Great Architect of the Universe as prerequisites for admission to Freemasonry. The English and United States lodges, heavily influenced by the theism that was core to the United Grand Lodge of England, believed they were obliged to cut ties with the Grand Orient, creating a schism between regular Freemasonry (of Anglo-Saxon and Nordic practice) and liberal Freemasonry (the secularist nature of which spread, especially throughout the Latin world). This separation has been a feature of the organization

throughout the twentieth century and is still active today. However, the totalitarian governments that came to power in the twentieth century were not interested in these subtle internal divisions: regardless of affiliation, Freemasonry as a whole has been persecuted and banned by different regimes—such as under Vichy's French Republic, fascist Italy, Stalin's Soviet Union, Nazi Germany, and Franco's Spain—always accused of conspiring against the established power, a charge supported by the secretive nature that characterizes Masonic activities.

Today, Freemasons are organized in local lodges, where meetings promote social activities, offer charity assistance, and carry out standard business required by all institutions. Thus, they have been able to build up what sociologists refer to as "social capital." Belonging to a lodge entails teaching the customs required to form part of the group and forming the links of trust required in order for people to work together in social, political, and commercial organizations. In recent decades, despite promoting humanistic values, tolerance, and universal brotherhood, lodges have experienced a period of crisis. The difference between secularists and theists is now facing a serious anachronism: in the twenty-first century, many lodges still prohibit the admission of women. The publication of the successful novel written by American author Dan Brown, *The Lost Symbol*, has generated palpable (though somewhat ill-informed) publicity. However, the evolution of modern-day society, much more materialistic and individualistic than during the Enlightenment, has once again put the organization (which feels like the relic of a bygone era, given its nature, objectives, and secrecy) to the test.

## → The pelican, the rose, and the cross

These are the main symbols of the Rosicrucian Order, created by the Protestants as a counter to the Society of Jesus of the Catholic Church.

## The Rosicrucians

Created in the seventeenth century and inheriting the esoteric order founded by German traveler Christian Rosenkreuz (an allegorical name, his identity and even existence are debated to this day) in the fourteenth century, the Rosicrucians used parascientific disciplines (alchemy, kabbalah, hermeticism) to achieve inner peace. While the Freemasons assert that the Rosicrucians were inspired by their organization (they call their meeting places "lodges," have established a similar hierarchical structure, and also employ the smock as their symbolic garment), the Rosicrucians maintain that Freemasonry is a branch of the Order of the Rose-Croix, stating that the main Masonic rites call one level of brotherhood the "Sovereign Prince Rose-Croix," which serves to prove its influence. Spread throughout Latin America, following a "rebirth" in the nineteenth century, this secret society is divided into several organizations. The biggest is the Ancient and Mystical Order Rosæ Crucis, famous for delivering self-help courses that employ new age techniques.

## The Illuminati

Also known as the Perfectibilists, or the Bavarian Order of the Illuminati, the Illuminati is a secret society, founded in 1776, with the objective of toppling governments and kingdoms, suppressing religion and private property, and creating what they refer to as a "New World Order." The expression appears on one dollar bills and has been repeated hundreds of times by U.S. presidents, from Woodrow Wilson to Barack Obama himself. Made popular by their appearance in Dan Brown's novel *Angels and Demons*, it is believed that the Illuminati are still in existence, working to promote globalization, a substitute for a New World Order. At the end of the eighteenth century, the Illuminati were successful in infiltrating several European lodges. During this period, both they and the Freemasons were accused of preparing the ground for the French Revolution, which was on the verge of not happening.

### → The all-seeing eye

The truncated pyramid with the all-seeing eye and the motto *"Novus Ordo Seclorum"* on the Great Seal of the United States, is considered a symbol of the Illuminati.

# Levels of Freemasonry

Apprentice, Fellow, and Master are the first three levels of Freemasonry; the Degrees of Freemasonry. The appearance of the first Grand Lodge in England catalyzed Freemasonry in Europe and the so-called "Upper Degrees" were created.

## The Degrees of Freemasonry

Through rituals and readings, the Freemasons obtain the tools and knowledge that equip them with virtues (the Degrees of Freemasonry) and go forth in their quest to achieve perfection by means of searching for the truth.

## The first Freemason

Hiram Abiff, architect of the Temple of Solomon (tenth century BCE) organized his members into three groups (apprentices, fellows, and masters). Certain initiation rituals of the first three degrees are connected with the construction of this temple.

### Scottish Rite

It has 33 degrees and is the most common in Europe and Latin America. It is derived from a system that was practiced in France during the eighteenth century.

**Council of Princes of the Royal Secret**

Sovereign Grand Inspector General

**Council of Princes of the Royal Secret**
- Sublime Prince of the Royal Secret
- Inspector Inquisitor Commander
- Knight Kadosh
- Grand Scottish Knight of St. Andrew — 29th
- Knight of the Sun — 28th
- Knight Commander of the Temple — 27th
- Prince of Mercy — 26th
- Knight of the Brazen Serpent — 25th
- Prince of the Tabernacle — 24th
- Chief of the Tabernacle — 23rd
- Knight of the Royal Ax — 22nd
- Noachite, or Prussian Knight — 21th
- Master of Symbolic Lodges — 20th
- Grand Pontiff — 19th

**Chapter Council**
- Knight of the Rose-Croix — 18th
- Knight of the East and West — 17th
- Prince of Jerusalem — 16th
- Knight of the East — 15th

14th
13th
12th
11th
10th
9th
8th
7th
6th
5th
4th

**Lodge of Perfection**
- Grand Elect
- Knight of the Ninth Arch
- Master Architect
- Sublime Knight Master Elect
- Illustrious Elect of the 15
- Elected Knight of the Nine
- Intendant of the Building
- Provost and Judge
- Intimate Secretary
- Perfect Master
- Confidential Secretary

**Grand Lodge**
- Master Mason — 3rd
- Fellowcraft — 2nd
- Entered Apprentice — 1st

## Do the "blood oaths" between Freemasons really exist?

Freemasons promise always to assist the brethren of the lodge, even to the point of committing perjury. It is well known that punishments were in place for revealing the secrets of eighteenth-century societies and among the guild of medieval Freemasons.

### York Rite

It has only 13 degrees, and is the most followed in North America. Its origins can be attributed to the British "Upper Degrees," which were later encoded in the U.S.A. The rite then extended across Europe.

13th Order of the Knights Templar

12th Order of St. John of Malta

33rd
32nd
31st
30th

11th Illustrious Order of the Red Cross

10th Super Excellent Master

9th Select Master

8th Royal Master

7th Supreme Order of the Holy Royal Arch

6th Most Excellent Master

5th Virtual Past Master

Although there are differences between the two rites, both respect the first three degrees—apprentices, fellows, and masters.

4th Degree Mark Master

3rd Master mason
2nd Fellowcraft
1st Apprentice

## Two large branches

In Freemasonry, there are two large branches: the regular, more dogmatic branch; and the liberal, less dogmatic branch.

APPROVED BY U.G.L.E.

### Regular branch

Governed by the United Grand Lodge of England. Its members have to hold some kind of religious belief. It does not admit women, nor have contact with lodges that do admit them. Discussions about politics and religion are strictly forbidden.

### Liberal branch

Governed by the Grand Orient de France, the existence of mixed lodges, the presence of women, and discussions on politics and religion are permitted. No religious belief is required in order to become a member.

## Other groups

Although Freemasonry is traditionally associated with adult men, there are also lodges for specific groups.

### Women

The more liberal branches accept mixed and female lodges. For certain "regular" branches, lodges that accept a female presence are "irregular."

### Children

There are a number of "Youth Masonic" lodges for youths aged between 13 and 21, which are active in a number of countries. There are even youth lodges that accept young women.

### Ethnicity

The B'nai B'rith (Jews) and Prince Hall (the black community), among others, are types of freemasonry specific to certain ethnic groups.

# The temple's symbolism

Masonic lodges or temples represent the universe. Each brick and piece of furniture, each inscription or decoration on clothing, every gesture of the participants at meetings and ceremonial rites have a meaning.

## A miniature universe

Order and symbolism are distinguished inside the Masonic temple. Each building is an attempt to synthesize the universe, and faces east, where the sun rises.

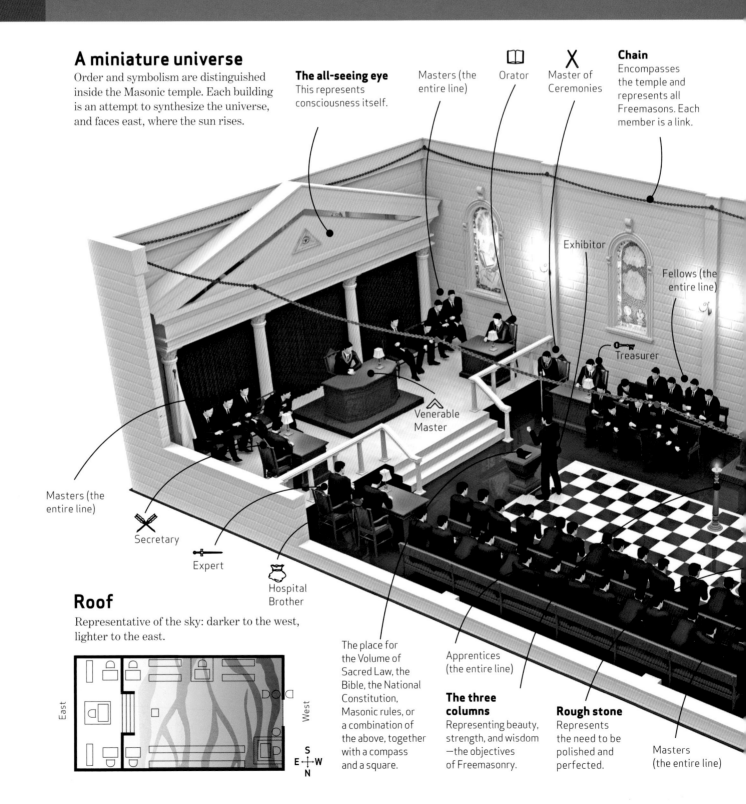

**The all-seeing eye**
This represents consciousness itself.

Masters (the entire line)

Orator

Master of Ceremonies

**Chain**
Encompasses the temple and represents all Freemasons. Each member is a link.

Exhibitor

Fellows (the entire line)

Treasurer

Venerable Master

Masters (the entire line)

Secretary

Expert

Hospital Brother

## Roof

Representative of the sky: darker to the west, lighter to the east.

East

West

S
E + W
N

The place for the Volume of Sacred Law, the Bible, the National Constitution, Masonic rules, or a combination of the above, together with a compass and a square.

Apprentices (the entire line)

**The three columns**
Representing beauty, strength, and wisdom —the objectives of Freemasonry.

**Rough stone**
Represents the need to be polished and perfected.

Masters (the entire line)

## Does part of Masonic symbolism come from the Pythagorean school of philosophy?

Although geometric and numerical symbolism are undeniably inherited from Pythagorean tradition, it has not been demonstrated that Freemasonry is an adaptation of Pythagoreanism. In Masonic legend, Pythagoras, the "Gnostic teacher," appears with Hermes, "the great initiator," as one of the founders of the Order.

### MAIN SYMBOL

The Great Architect of the Universe—a compass, a square, and the "G" of Gnosticism. In more liberal branches, each member interprets it individually; for example, as the "God" of a known religion or one of the "Guiding" principles of the universe.

### THE EAST SECTIONS

This is the elevated part of the temple, where the highest levels of authority are seated. It is separated from the Valley by three steps.

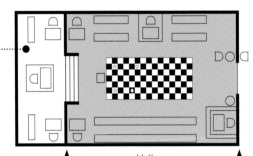

Valley

Here is where apprentices and fellows, along with other authorities, are seated..

## Clothing

During meetings, members are obliged to wear a dark suit, white shirt, black tie, and the medallion of their lodge. Their collars and smock identify their degree within the Order.

### The collar

This is interlinked with the smock. Each member may add his own decoration.

### The smock

The smocks of the apprentice and fellow are white, although the latter's upper triangle is featured inside the square. The seams of the master's smock are embellished with a ribbon, red in the Scottish Rite and blue in the York Rite. It also bears the image of the compass and the square, with the letters "M" and "B" to the sides.

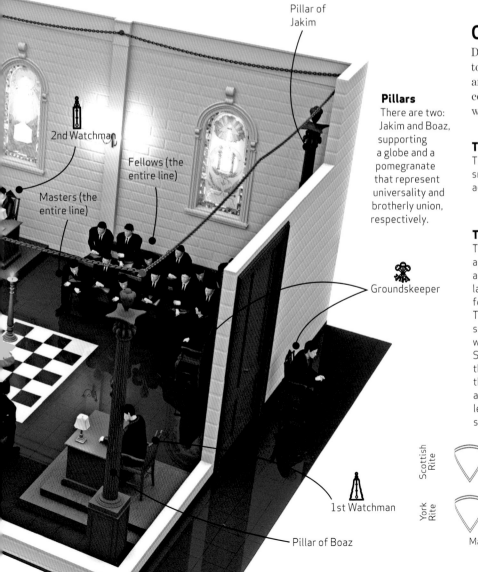

Pillar of Jakim

### Pillars

There are two: Jakim and Boaz, supporting a globe and a pomegranate that represent universality and brotherly union, respectively.

2nd Watchman

Fellows (the entire line)

Masters (the entire line)

Groundskeeper

1st Watchman

Pillar of Boaz

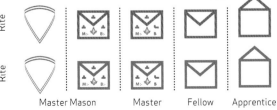

Scottish Rite

York Rite

Master Mason

Master

Fellow

Apprentice

# Masonic symbols

Numbers, geometric shapes, tools ... these symbols represent the vehicle for moral teachings and the obtainment of metaphysical knowledge.

## The compass

In traditional Masonry, the compass is one of the three key symbols, together with the square and the Volume of Sacred Law. In speculative Masonry, it symbolizes wisdom. Its relationship with one of the basic geometric forms—the circle—is clear. The center of the circumference is the image of the Beginning, while the circumference itself expresses the diversity of expressions generated by the irradiation of this Beginning. This remains unchangeable while everything around it changes. Thus, the compass symbolizes the creative activity of the Great Architect, whose most important work is the Cosmos and represents the metaphysical plane. It is also one of the tools associated with the Master.

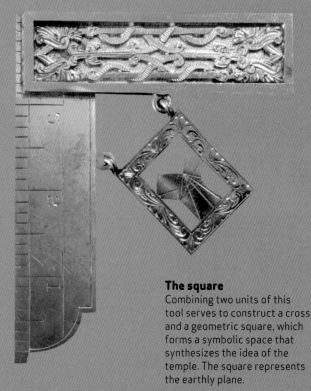

### The square
Combining two units of this tool serves to construct a cross and a geometric square, which forms a symbolic space that synthesizes the idea of the temple. The square represents the earthly plane.

### Wooden gavel
Since ancient times, the gavel has been a symbol of supreme authority. It is used by masters to open and close most ceremonies, in addition to establishing the rhythm at which Masonic rites progress.

## The smock

The smock, or apron, is a symbol of work; it is the only distinguishing feature that allows Freemasons to enter temples and participate in meetings at the lodges. All members, even senior dignitaries, are required to wear this garment. This example (left) contains the symbolic emblem of the First Degree.

## Candelabra

The golden candelabra represents enlightened understanding. It has seven arms, which is the number of the Jubilee. There are also the seven eyes of God, the book with seven seals, and the seven months (of construction) of the tabernacle. Easter is celebrated seven times, seven days before the gift of His Law. These are, traditionally, some examples of the most perfect numbers that appear in the Bible.

### Mallet and chisel
Respectively, these tools represent willpower and the faculty of intelligence, or intellectual rigor at work.

### Flaming sword
The sword symbolizes power and strength in all cultures. In speculative Masonry, the so-called flaming sword is used, the curved blade of which represents a flame. It is employed by the Venerable Master to open and close proceedings at the lodge, and during initiation ceremonies.

# Secrets of World War II

It was a deadly and terrifying time. The war engulfed the five continents and took the lives of between 50 and 70 million people. In addition, thousands of "unknown" events occurred during this time, many of which remain unresolved.

Author Henry Miller said: "Each war is the destruction of the human spirit." In fact, a mammoth number of lives, consciences, and dignities were broken throughout the bloody and traumatic period of the 1930s and 40s, which began with the militarist and destructive madness of Adolf Hitler and culminated in the dropping of atomic bombs over Hiroshima and Nagasaki. The enormous scale of the military struggle is indisputable.

Whereas in World War I, 28 countries participated in the bloodshed, between 1939 and 1945 a total of 71 countries fell into the clutches of hate and violence. World War II was particularly chilling as, for the first time in history, science and technology were used for criminal ends: the Third Reich, in search of the

pure race, invoked scientific calculations and rational methods to exterminate six million Jews and other "undesirables." Civilians were the main losers of the second main struggle of the twentieth century.

While between 1914 and 1918, civilians accounted for 5 percent of all fatalities, between 1939 and 1945 this rose to 66 percent. Thus, in countries like the Soviet Union, Poland, Hungary, and France, more civilians died than soldiers. Conscious of the terrifying balance of the conflict, after 1945, world leaders created institutions such as the United Nations and judicial and legal frameworks in an attempt to prevent the planet ever becoming a mammoth battlefield again. And beyond official history, certain enigmas remain to be resolved.

**DOUBTS ABOUT PEARL HARBOR**

On December 7, 1941, a fleet of 183 Japanese planes surprisingly stormed the skies over Hawaii. In just a few hours, the attack destroyed the main U.S. naval facilities in the Pacific, and left thousands dead and injured. On top of this, the heavy bombers that the United States had stationed in the Philippines, which served as an important deterrent in the area, were also destroyed by Japanese bombs ten hours after the Pearl Harbor attack. This left the United States very vulnerable to further Japanese attacks.

Before the bombardment at Pearl Harbor, public opinion in the U.S.A. had been strongly against becoming involved in the new war that was unfolding in Europe. However, the attack by Japanese planes,

**Nazi parade**
Three young girls watch a Nazi parade in the free city of Danzig, where World War II erupted.

without a declaration of war having been signed, unleashed national fury and ended American isolationism. The following day, President Roosevelt obtained the declaration of war against Japan from Congress. Three days later, thanks to the declaration of war that Hitler had signed on December 11, the U.S.A. finally found itself at war against the European Axis alliance.

Some historians maintain that Roosevelt knew about the Japanese attack on the naval base in Hawaii beforehand, but did nothing to stop it. They mention a diplomatic intrigue that could have deliberately provoked the Japanese to attack the United States, to use it as an excuse to enter the war. Defenders of this theory argue it was sheer "coincidence" that all U.S. aircraft carriers were at sea at the time of the attack and that, while the Atlantic Charter was being drafted in Terra Nova, under which the United States and Great Britain promised to mutually respect one another, Roosevelt had mentioned to Churchill that "everything possible had been done to provoke an incident that would lead the United States to war." Speculation aside, Roosevelt's team had received very clear information on the willingness of Japan to attack U.S. bases.

On December 1, four documents reached the White House that had been produced by intercepting messages sent from Tokyo to the embassy in Berlin. One of them was from Japanese Prime Minister, Hideki Tojo, who affirmed that "the risk of war breaking out between the Anglo-Saxon nation and Japan would begin before anybody could imagine." Roosevelt remained doubtful as to whether the U.S.A. would participate in the war or not, and decided to use diplomacy once again while the secret service investigated the threat in-depth. However, the call for peace sent to Emperor Hirohito was to no purpose. Other sources maintain that the threat of a Japanese attack was never taken seriously. On the one hand, it was believed that if attacking a target in the Pacific, Japan would opt for the Dutch East Indies, given that the area had significant oilfields that would have been essential for maintaining the Japanese war machine. On the other, the strategic capacity of the Japanese was always underestimated.

Statements made by a number of witnesses to the bombing of Hawaii confirm that the United States attached little importance to the threat of an attack, despite the high number of Japanese planes detected on the radar at 7 a.m. First, it was believed that the radar had broken; then precious time was lost trying to find a technician who could fix it. Finally, it was found that the radar was working correctly and it was believed that the fleet detected was a B-17 squadron heading toward California. The result of such high levels of incompetence was that senior officials were

unaware of the attack until the first bombs started to fall. Despite there being no conclusive evidence to show that the president was certain that the Japanese would attack Pearl Harbor, suspicions about Roosevelt have never dissipated. Evidence of this can be seen in the 1999 annulment, granted by the U.S. Senate, of the punishment previously handed down to senior officials in Hawaii, as it was deemed that they had not received available information from Washington that would have helped to repel the attack.

### HITLER'S NUCLEAR AMBITIONS

The dropping of the first atomic bomb over Hiroshima on August 6, 1945 ended a mad race against time started in 1938 with the discovery of the nuclear fission process by German chemist Otto Hahn. Hitler would never witness the destructive power of the bomb (he committed suicide in his Berlin bunker in April 1945), but he had always dreamed of possessing "the definitive instrument of destruction" to wipe his enemies off the map. Despite the advances made by Nazi scientists, an accumulation of errors would put an end to the nuclear ambitions of the Führer. The first, and undoubtedly one of the most important, was the exile of many Jewish German scientists, such as Albert Einstein, Otto Frisch, and Rudolf Peierls, persecuted by anti-Semitic Nazi laws. Concern among the Jewish community about the creation of a weapon

of such never-before-known destructive proportions by the Third Reich emerged in 1939, following a study completed by Lise Meitner, one of Hahn's assistants, who was also exiled because of her Jewish roots, about the repercussions of the discovery of the nuclear fission process. Hahn's experiment was repeated in a variety of United States laboratories, as well as in Warsaw, Saint Petersburg, and Paris. The conclusions were stunning: the possibility of the Nazis manufacturing a nuclear bomb was no longer a pipe dream. It was just a matter of time.

Meanwhile in Washington and London, scientists endeavored to prevent Hitler from obtaining the bomb before them. In Germany, three different teams were working on the project under the supervision of German nuclear physicist, Werner Heisenberg. Having the biggest uranium field in Europe, located in Czechoslovakia, was a huge advantage for Nazi Germany, as was control of Norsk Hydro, the first factory to manufacture "heavy water" for commercial purposes, in Norway. Heavy water, in which the two hydrogen atoms that are joined to the oxygen atom are replaced by two deuterium atoms, was used at the time as a moderator in nuclear fission processes. Today, normal water and graphite are used. In April 1940, the Norwegian resistance informed Great Britain that the Germans had increased their production of heavy water, and London

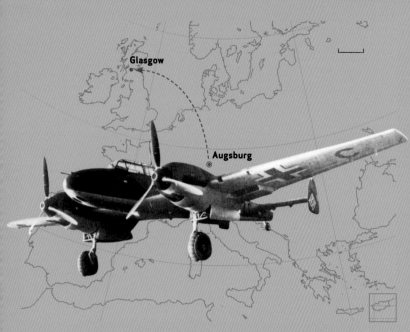

**↑Hess, the pilot**
Hess was an incredibly skilled pilot; this was confirmed by his nocturnal solitary flight of over 750 miles/1,200 km, most of which unfolded over the sea and escaped the scrutiny of surveillance systems.

## The strange journey of Rudolf Hess

On May 10, 1941, Rudolf Hess, the former number two in the Nazi party and a close ally of Hitler, took off from Augsburg airfield in southern Germany. His objective was to land on the estate of the Duke of Hamilton in Scotland where, theoretically, a runway had been prepared and fuel was to be made available for his return trip to Germany. As fate would have it, he never found the runway, he ran out of gasoline and had to eject from his plane using a parachute. A farmer found him, injured during the fall, and took him to a military detachment, where he confessed his identity and asserted that he was carrying a message from Hitler with a view to reaching a peace agreement with Great Britain. While Churchill failed to believe the explanation given by the Duke of Hamilton, in Berlin, the news infuriated Hitler, who issued a statement asserting that Hess was "the victim of pacifist hallucinations and that he suffered mental disorders."

Hess's real objective was never discovered, but many theories were discussed. The most convenient theory for the British government was that Hess had deserted Hitler, having realized that Germany was going to lose the war. Others suggested that Hitler may have sent him as he did not want to come into conflict with the British Empire.

However, the most plausible theory is that his objective was to contact pro-Nazi leaders in Great Britain, overthrow Churchill, and form a puppet government, subject to German control.

tried three times to destroy the facilities, without ever actually fully achieving its goal. The failed English attacks on Norwegian soil caused concern in Berlin, where the decision was made to transfer all the heavy water obtained to German soil. Fortunately, the tanks never reached their destination: the boat transporting them sank in Lake Tinn following an attack by the resistance.

### A MATTER OF LUCK?
Some historians have suggested that it was sheer luck that the Nazis had not obtained the atomic bomb before. One of them, Rainer Karlsch, maintained in his work, *Hitler's Bomb*, that the scientists reporting to the Führer had experimented with small prototypes. According to the author, the Nazis carried out at least three nuclear tests: the first on October 12, 1944 on the Baltic island of Rügen; the other two in March 1945, at a military base in Thuringia close to the Buchenwald concentration camp. According to Karlsch, the Germans tested a type of "atomic grenade" (a device very different from the destructive capacity of the bombs dropped over Japan), made of a core of radioactive material wrapped in large quantities of conventional explosives. Those responsible for manufacturing them were the scientists Erich Schumann, Kurt Diebner, and Walter Gerlach, who were directly linked to the army. In the tests at Thuringia, 700 human guinea pigs were used from the Ohrdruf and Buchenwald concentration camps. Karlsch also states that the first functional German nuclear reactor was built on the outskirts of Berlin, and that by 1941 plans were already in place for a project to build a plutonium bomb.

However, other historians have highlighted that the Nazi propaganda machine, headed by Joseph Goebbels, was responsible for making the Allies believe that the atomic project was almost complete. It was Goebbels, in fact, who coined the term *Wunderwaffe* ("wonder-weapon") to refer to all the weapons invented by the Nazis during the war. These ranged from tanks, planes, submarines, missiles, rockets, and incendiary devices to nerve gas and toxins. Other more implausible inventions were also mentioned, such as a flying saucer or a parabolic mirror sent into orbit in order to aim the sun's light at the Earth. In addition, it has been demonstrated that the scientists who worked on Hitler's project were never in fact capable of building a nuclear reactor. They were also unable to calculate the critical mass of a bomb, nor did they have sufficient information on the properties of plutonium. At least this is what is contained in a report from August 1945, which was released by the British government, based on recordings made of captured Nazi scientists housed on a farm close to Cambridge, in order to discover the scope of their research.

At the time, none of them believed that the bomb dropped over Hiroshima represented atomic ingenuity. In addition to the Nazi scientists' lack of knowledge, other less important factors must also be considered. On the one hand, the regime's complex bureaucratic and hierarchical system. On the other, the significant development of the German arms industry during the war, which led to Hitler himself pushing his "wonder-weapon" plan into the background, convinced of the superiority of the Aryan race and his eventual victory.

**↓Richard Sorge , aka "Ramsay"**
Prejudice toward Sorge dissuaded Stalin from paying attention to the accurate information provided by the spy about the date of the German attack on the U.S.S.R.

**↓Joan Pujol García "Garbo"/"Arabel"**
Double agent who managed to deceive the Nazi secret services, and was even decorated at the request of Hitler himself.

## Spies and allies

At the end of World War II, accusations of spying became generalized and frivolous on all sides, and suspicions affected famous people such as Errol Flynn and Coco Chanel, although they were not the only ones.

Flynn was accused of spying on behalf of the Germans and the Japanese, although the evidence presented was not watertight. The misunderstanding was caused by the appearance of a photograph of the actor at a European seminar, held in Spain in 1937, with a battalion of German soldiers; the caption did not specify which side he was on.

In the case of Coco Chanel, there was evidence of her relationship with the Nazis, as stated in the biography of her written by Hal W. Vaughan. He maintains that the designer undertook missions in Madrid and Berlin. Suspicions arose as a result of Chanel's relationship with an SS officer.

Far from the image of glamorous spies, the role of professional agents was key. Among them, Richard Sorge, considered by many as the greatest spy of the struggle, is worth particular mention. Although his father was German, Sorge spied for Stalin, disguising himself as a Nazi journalist. From Tokyo, he informed Moscow of the date scheduled for Operation Barbarossa, the Nazi invasion of the U.S.S.R., and contributed to the Soviet victory by convincing a distrustful Stalin that the Japanese would not attack the U.S.S.R. Spanish spy Joan Pujol García, also known as "Garbo" and "Arabel," was a double agent who provided the Nazis with incorrect information about the date and location of the Normandy landings. He worked for the British, and convinced the Germans that the allied invasion would take place in Pas de Calais.

**←Errol Flynn**
The British also investigated the actor, especially after his 1937 meeting in Lisbon with Sean Russell, the commissioner of the I.R.A. It would appear that Flynn tried to convince the Irish to end their Soviet alliance and take up the German cause.

**←Coco Chanel "Westminster"**
According to documents discovered by Hal Vaughan, the French fashion designer was on the payroll of the *Abwehr* (German military intelligence organization )from 1941, and was attributed agent number 7124.

# The war in Europe

The beginning of the end for Nazi Germany began with the defeat of the Axis troops in Stalingrad and in North Africa. From that moment, the Allied offensive was unstoppable, until the total defeat of the Third Reich in May 1945.

## The defeat of Germany

In 1943, the war changed direction. The Allies invaded Italy and, a year later, landed in Normandy. Meanwhile, the Red Army was unstoppable, advancing on the Eastern Front. In May 1945, Berlin fell and Germany surrendered unconditionally.

**The Allied offensive**

- Axis powers and satellite countries
- Occupied by the Axis, March 1943
- Controlled by the Allies in March 1943
- Neutral countries
- Allied offensives (1942–45)
- Major battle fronts
- Front line, December 1943
- Front line, August 1944
- Front line, December 1944
- Front line, April 1945
- Siege

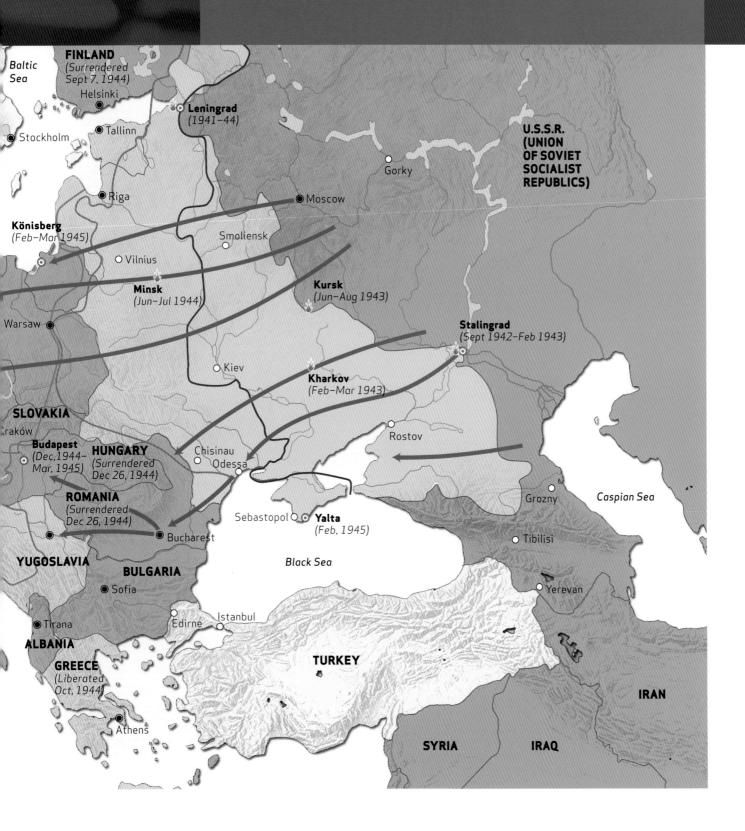

## Where are the treasures of the Amber Room, looted by the Nazis?

Much of the wealth stolen by the Nazis was recovered. But gold, silver, and other treasures looted from the Amber Room of the Catherine Palace in Saint Petersburg has never reappeared. The Amber Room was a gift from Frederick I of Prussia to Peter the Great.

*Baltic Sea*

**FINLAND**
*(Surrendered Sept 7, 1944)*
Helsinki

**Leningrad**
*(1941–44)*

Stockholm

Tallinn

**U.S.S.R.
(UNION
OF SOVIET
SOCIALIST
REPUBLICS)**

Gorky

Riga

Moscow

**Könisberg**
*(Feb–Mar 1945)*

Smoliensk

Vilnius

**Minsk**
*(Jun–Jul 1944)*

**Kursk**
*(Jun–Aug 1943)*

Warsaw

**Stalingrad**
*(Sept 1942–Feb 1943)*

Kiev

**Kharkov**
*(Feb–Mar 1943)*

**SLOVAKIA**

raków

Rostov

**Budapest**
*(Dec, 1944–
Mar, 1945)*

**HUNGARY**
*(Surrendered
Dec 26, 1944)*

Chisinau

Odessa

*Caspian Sea*

Grozny

**ROMANIA**
*(Surrendered
Dec 26, 1944)*

Sebastopol

**Yalta**
*(Feb, 1945)*

Tibilisi

Bucharest

**YUGOSLAVIA**

**BULGARIA**

*Black Sea*

Yerevan

Sofia

Tirana

Edirne

Istanbul

**ALBANIA**

**GREECE**
*(Liberated
Oct, 1944)*

**TURKEY**

**IRAN**

Athens

**SYRIA**

**IRAQ**

# The attack on Pearl Harbor

The Japanese surprise attack on the United States naval base in the Pacific accelerated the U.S.A.'s entry into World War II—a fact that would ultimately mean the defeat of the Axis powers.

## Surprise Attack

On the morning of December 7, 1941, without any previous declaration of war, Japan attacked the U.S. naval base at Pearl Harbor in the Hawaiian Islands. The Japanese aircraft sank most of the U.S. Pacific Fleet, severely damaged its air power, and caused thousands of casualties. But they found no aircraft carriers, the main target of the attack, among the ships docked in Hawaii.

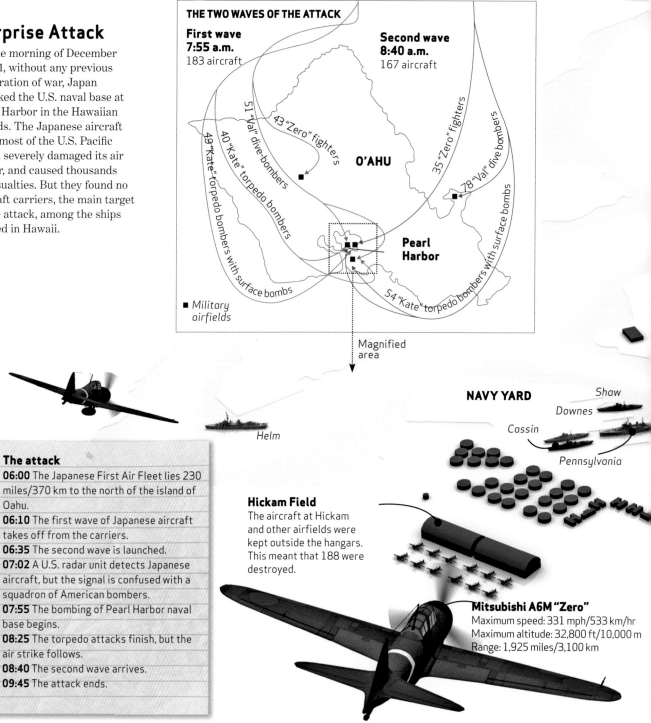

**THE TWO WAVES OF THE ATTACK**

**First wave**
**7:55 a.m.**
183 aircraft

**Second wave**
**8:40 a.m.**
167 aircraft

51 "Val" dive-bombers

43 "Zero" fighters

49 "Kate" torpedo bombers with surface bombs

40 "Kate" torpedo bombers

O'AHU

35 "Zero" fighters

78 "Val" dive bombers

Pearl Harbor

54 "Kate" torpedo bombers with surface bombs

■ Military airfields

Magnified area

**NAVY YARD**

Shaw
Downes
Cassin
Pennsylvania

Helm

### Hickam Field
The aircraft at Hickam and other airfields were kept outside the hangars. This meant that 188 were destroyed.

**Mitsubishi A6M "Zero"**
Maximum speed: 331 mph/533 km/hr
Maximum altitude: 32,800 ft/10,000 m
Range: 1,925 miles/3,100 km

### The attack
**06:00** The Japanese First Air Fleet lies 230 miles/370 km to the north of the island of Oahu.
**06:10** The first wave of Japanese aircraft takes off from the carriers.
**06:35** The second wave is launched.
**07:02** A U.S. radar unit detects Japanese aircraft, but the signal is confused with a squadron of American bombers.
**07:55** The bombing of Pearl Harbor naval base begins.
**08:25** The torpedo attacks finish, but the air strike follows.
**08:40** The second wave arrives.
**09:45** The attack ends.

# Why did Nagumo decide not to launch a third attack on the U.S. base?

It could have been a fatal blow, but the commander of the operation, the Japanese admiral Chuichi Nagumo, preferred caution after confirming that most of the objectives had been met. The absence of U.S. aircraft carriers in Pearl Harbor aroused his suspicion and he feared a counterattack.

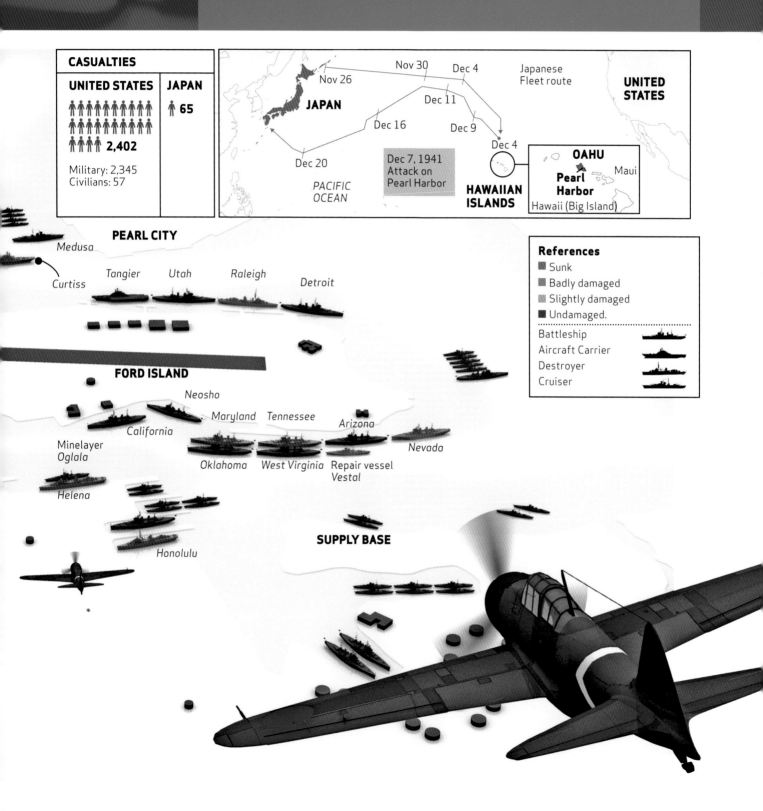

## CASUALTIES

| UNITED STATES | JAPAN |
|---|---|
| 2,402 | 65 |

Military: 2,345
Civilians: 57

Nov 26
Nov 30
Dec 4
Japanese Fleet route
JAPAN
Dec 11
Dec 16
Dec 9
Dec 4
Dec 20
PACIFIC OCEAN
Dec 7, 1941 Attack on Pearl Harbor
HAWAIIAN ISLANDS
UNITED STATES
OAHU
Pearl Harbor
Maui
Hawaii (Big Island)

**PEARL CITY**

Medusa
Curtiss
Tangier
Utah
Raleigh
Detroit

**FORD ISLAND**

Neosho
Maryland
Tennessee
Arizona
California
Nevada
Minelayer Oglala
Oklahoma
West Virginia
Repair vessel Vestal
Helena
Honolulu

**SUPPLY BASE**

### References
- Sunk
- Badly damaged
- Slightly damaged
- Undamaged.

Battleship
Aircraft Carrier
Destroyer
Cruiser

# Roswell: the Beginning of the UFO Era

The discovery of a spacecraft, presumably piloted by alien beings, in the desert of New Mexico in 1947 started the "flying saucer" phenomenon. Between myth and reality, UFO sightings continue to this day.

Early in July 1947, a storm battered the state of New Mexico. About 75 miles/120 km north of the town of Roswell, a rancher, Mac Brazel and his son found a series of scattered fragments of something unrecognizable. They later described this to a local newspaper as "bright objects, formed by rubber strips and something similar to aluminum foil, but almost indestructible."

Between July 6 and 7, Brazel called the local sheriff to inform him that he had found some remains and the sheriff then informed Roswell Air Base about the incident. Hours later, accompanied by Brazel, Major Jesse Marcel and an unnamed man dressed in plain clothes recovered fragments spread across the ground. It is possible that the rumor of a flying saucer crash had already reached town. The people of Roswell must have been mindful of news of the strange craft witnessed just a week earlier, on June 24, by Kenneth Arnold, while he flew close to Mount Rainier, in Washington state. The civilian pilot reportedly saw nine craft in perfect formation, whose spasmodic movements he compared to "saucers skipping across water."

The journalist who interviewed him, taking note of the description of the way in which the shapes moved, baptized them "flying saucers." Rumors must have been so widespread that, in the first statement made by the Air Force, they limited themselves to "confirming" that a flying saucer had crashed on the outskirts of Roswell. This was the first statement, but another would follow. As quickly as the news spread across the majority of newsrooms in the United States and abroad, an order was received to transfer the remains of the object to Fort Worth, in Texas.

At the base, General Roger M. Ramey completely changed the terms of the first statement, apologizing for the error, and asserting that in reality, the enigmatic remains belonged to a weather balloon. Perhaps the military believed that in doing so, they would be able to brush under the carpet a topic that required many more explanations than were offered at the time. Unknowingly, it would open a 60-year-old question that still plagues the world to this day.

### THE SCULLY EVIDENCE

Alien fever spread, and the sightings that originated from the events in the United States started to be repeated worldwide. Three years after Roswell, in 1950, an entertainment critic, Frank Scully, published the book, *Behind the Flying Saucers*, which pulled together evidence of dozens of craft.

Although Scully did not mention the Roswell case, he was able to get a witness to describe the crash of three flying saucers in the New Mexico region and the features of the 37 bodies found in these accidents. The sources named by Scully were Silas Newton and a scientist named "Doctor Gee," who reported that in the area outside Aztec, New Mexico, a flying saucer had crashed in 1948. The structure of the craft had not suffered significant damage, although its crew—beings measuring 3 ft 6 in/1.1 m—died on impact.

Apparently, when entering the Earth's atmosphere, the heat had incinerated them. On the control panels, only buttons with a previously unseen writing style were found. An interesting piece of information offered by Doctor Gee was the discovery that there was no toilet on the craft, leading researchers to believe that the creatures only undertook short journeys. It was then that they hazarded a guess that the aliens had come from Venus. The simple style used by Scully in his book, his naive explanations about magnetism, and the fact that he did not review the arguments put forward by his witnesses, allowed him to sell books, although they were not particularly well-received among critics.

To make matters worse, two years later, a reporter called J.P. Cahn decided to demonstrate that every "scientific" definition used by the amateur investigator was, in fact, nonsense. Cahn revealed that the two people

**Flying saucer**
This is how the first UFO observed in Roswell was described. Sightings would later multiply.

who were shielded by the names Silas Newton and Doctor Gee were two pranksters with an extensive history. In the footnote, the journalist cast doubt on Scully, but eventually admitted that the author had been deceived. Despite everything, years later Scully's book would serve to revive the Roswell case and convert it into the indisputable architype of alien contact. This reappearance cleared Scully's name and was also the grounds on which, as a tribute, his surname was used for one of the characters of the *X Files*, skeptical Dr. Dana Scully.

### THE GREAT CONSPIRACY
In 1950, former naval aviator and science-fiction author Donald Keyhoe started to ask for explanations from the Air Force about the lights that lit up the North American sky. Offended by the lack of official response, and without taking into consideration the ongoing Cold War between the U.S.A. and the Soviet Union, Keyhoe concluded that his government had a secret pact with aliens that explained the silence. This belief in an infinite chain of deceit, discredited truths, and accentuated lies saw the birth of one of the most frequent UFO-related topics: conspiracy theories.

From these hypotheses, subthemes of UFO culture were born, such as the "Men in Black," alien abductions, and the evil actions of "gray" aliens, all of which have been expanded upon in one way or another in cinema and television. The idea that other beings, this time peaceful beings, visited us from the far reaches of the cosmos to compensate the balance between good and evil would also emerge soon thereafter. At the beginning of the 1970s, two very clear positions about UFOs clashed: on the one hand, the scientific presence of Josef Allen Hynek and Jacques Vallée, two scientists who tried to explain the phenomenon from a scientific standpoint. On the other, a Swiss author who had previously popularized the idea of an alien presence, Erich von Däniken. His books *Chariots of the Gods?*, *Return to the Stars*, and *The Gold of the Gods* and his entire saga dedicated to past contact and alien influence managed to bury "serious" ufology. Eventually, Hynek and Vallée would abandon the realm of ufology.

The book that revitalized Roswell and perhaps gave meaning to the case, appeared in 1980. That year, *The Roswell Incident* was published by Charles Berlitz and William Moore. The latter, with ufologist Stanton Friedman, interviewed the survivors or relatives of those who had participated in the Roswell case thirty years after the incident, and they were surprised to find that most witnesses were resolute that they had seen a UFO. With that material, and the involvement of author Charles Berlitz, known at the time for books like *The Mystery of Atlantis* and the highly successful *Philadelphia Experiment*, they finished building the Roswell case. Berlitz collected witness statements while taking a fresh look at the book by Frank Scully. The

fact that Scully had not mentioned Roswell in his account was attributable, according to Berlitz, to the rush in publishing the revelations that divided public opinion. Equally, Berlitz felt his fear of censorship may have been the reason why Scully did not overtly state that what he was describing actually took place in Roswell. As regards the suspicious identity of Scully's sources—Mr Silas Newton and Doctor Gee—Berlitz and his co-author asserted that this was attributable to an operation carried out by the U.S. government to discredit the witnesses.

## BETWEEN THE PAST AND THE FUTURE
The Roswell case is important given the suspicion it created, but it also resulted in the birth of a certain type of investigator, dedicated to studying an object that apparently refused to be seen. These researchers would only be granted the title of "ufologists" in the 1960s, when the UFO acronym was made popular by fighter pilots (using the initials of Unidentified Flying Object). Even at the time of the first sightings, the theories that explained what had been seen, and their tendency to hide themselves, were already starting to multiply. However, as the object of study was only a fleeting presence, ufologists realized there was a place that they could trace their presence without chasing after both inconsistent and disputable lights or evidence. That place was the past. In this vast space, frozen in time, it was not difficult to find cultures and civilizations

that had believed in a magical and sacred relationship with the skies. Furthermore, their monumental works were the best proof of a superior presence in the stars that quickly came to be considered the creator of our human past. Question marks about the construction of the Egyptian pyramids, the huge Nazca lines, and the call to the heavens common among all cultures were seen as conclusive evidence of visits from outer space. This research was given a name: "Extraterrestrial creationism."

Not even the verses of the Bible are exempt from interpretation from an extraterrestrial viewpoint: the cloud that guided Moses through the desert and that was always over the Tabernacle, was a UFO; the angels that advised Lot to flee from Sodom, were in reality extraterrestrials. Furthermore, from this perspective, it was not difficult to identify the object that descended from the sky before the prophet Ezekiel as a spacecraft. From these ideas to the creation of religions there was one step—this is how UFO sects were born that generally believe in the return of Christ, but this time on a UFO.

## CONTINUATION
During the 1980s, the UFO phenomenon continued to encompass the entire planet. New forms of contact were created, and many people attempted to communicate with beings from outer space by means of trance sessions or

# Pursued aircraft

Numerous military, civilian, and commercial airline pilots have reported unidentified flying objects in the air. Among these are reports from commercial airline pilots that are most noteworthy. The "Manises incident" occurred in 1979 and took place over Spain. On November 11, around 11 p.m., a UFO measuring 650 ft/200 m in diameter with bright red lights, forced an aircraft traveling from Majorca to Tenerife to make an emergency landing in Valencia. Shortly after, a Mirage F-1 plane of the Spanish Air Force took off in search of the craft although, despite reaching supersonic speeds, it was unable to trace it. The minister stated that "it was not possible to establish the origins of the lights." Another plane, this time a Japan Airlines cargo plane, was chased by a mother ship on November 17, 1986 while it flew over Alaska; science has since been unable to explain what happened.

On July 31, 1995, an Aerolíneas Argentinas pilot complained about persistent lights during his descent into Bariloche airport. His account was supported by the rest of the crew, while a plane from the Air Force that was flying in the area confirmed the UFO sighting. However, when people explained the sighting as nothing more than the outline of a mountain, the pilot resigned from his job.

**Chased in the air**
Graphic representation of one of the incidents.

automatic writing ("psychography"). Something even more terrifying would also become more common: alien abductions, and "bedroom visitations": the possibility that aliens were installing small appliances with which they monitored human beings. Finally, in 1989, the Berlin Wall came down and the Cold War was at an end. This resulted in the Pentagon releasing a huge amount of secret material and, at last, the truth about Roswell was made public.

In January 1994, the U.S. Air Force confessed that in 1947, what crashed was neither a weather balloon nor a UFO. In reality, it was an experimental device comprising a series of balloons raised to great heights for the purposes of spying, by using the sound waves of the atmosphere to monitor Soviet atomic testing. As a result of the thirst for accurate information, it was asserted at the time that the Roswell incident corresponded to the launching of balloon number 4. So was that the end of the mystery? No, recently a new range of explanations have come to light that even involved the Nazis. Thus, the theory was born that asserted that flying saucers had been mechanical devices created by Hitler's Germany, used by senior members of the Third Reich to flee to a heated base in the frozen Atlantic.

### THE END?

What nobody expected was that, in 1995, an almost unknown British television producer, Ray Santilli, would announce to the world that he possessed a film of the autopsy performed by the Air Force on one of the aliens inside the UFO that crashed in July 1947 during the well-known Roswell incident. With the exception of a few hardened believers, almost nobody doubted that it was a hoax, of terrible quality. The camera work is shaky and it loses focus; it is very evident that the "alien" is, in fact, a rubber dummy. The doctors' clothing, their way of using the scalpel, the filming environment, everything is more reminiscent of a B film than pathologists in the operating room of a military base. Santilli's explanation of how he came into possession of the film material did little to clarify the matter. He had purchased it from the very cameraman responsible for the filming, Jack Barnett, who was apparently willing to sell this valuable material as he needed money. Shortly after, rumors started to spread: Santilli's version was actually a recreation of the "real" film that captured the genuine autopsy.

What was the truth? In 2006, a British-German film, entitled *Alien Autopsy*, depicted what happened in a comical way: in 1992, Santilli traveled to the USA to purchase material on Elvis Presley. The same man who sold him that showed him yards of film of the autopsy, in which President Truman appeared, and asked him for a sum of money that Santilli did not have; he therefore returned to England and obtained the money, a loan from a demented, UFO-obsessed member of the Mafia. On his return to the United States, Santilli purchased the film. However, on arrival back in England, Santilli discovered that the film had deteriorated. His outlook was bleak: the head case who had loaned him the money would kill him before he had a chance to explain. So he decided to "reconstruct" the film to show it to the lender and save his own life. In 2006, Santilli asserted that he had restored part of the original film. It would seem that the end of the controversy is yet to be reached.

# Manmade UFOs?

It has recently come to light that the Nazis may have built disk-shaped craft that, after the war, the United States and the Soviet Union perfected in order to spy on one another. Would this be the explanation that would settle the phenomenon? From the first descriptions obtained from sightings, UFOs appeared more like "flying wings" than the popular image of two superimposed circular plates. In fact, the first prototype of the flying wing was built by U.S. engineer John K. Northrop in 1930. However, it is argued that the craft may have been of Nazi origin. Recently, designs of discoidal craft were made public that may have been built by the Germans. Of this recent "discovery," only a few designs, and a number of blurry photos, have been found. The first of these craft, the RFZ-1, was built in 1934 and then adapted on a number of occasions until in 1939 the *Haunebu I* was created. This discoidal craft measured 85 ft/26 m in diameter and 30 ft/9 m in height, and was capable of carrying a crew of eight men. It was supposedly capable of reaching speeds of almost 3,100 mph/5,000 km/h. This device evolved into the *Haunebu III*, measuring 233 ft/71 m in diameter and capable of carrying 31 people at a supposed top speed of around 25,000 mph/40,000 km/h. Where are these craft now? It is claimed that senior Nazi leaders fled to an unknown location with them, while others mantain that they may have been perfected by the USA, or the former USSR, for the purposes of spying.

Alleged photocopy of SS plans for a Haunebu I b 1939. From the German book *Die Dunkle Seite Des Side of the Moon)* by Brad Harris (1996, Pandora B

Alleged photocopy of SS plans for a Ha 1945. From the German book *Die Dunkle Side of the Moon)* by Brad Harris (1996,

hotocopy of SS plans for a Haunebu II being designed in the German book *Die Dunkle Seite Des Mondes (The Dark Moon)* by Brad Harris (1996, Pandora Books, Germany).

**→Strange craft**
Images of experimental planes and the alleged Nazi designs of the Haunebu.

## What type of fuel would they use?

The origin of these circular craft was not earthly, given that the technology involved would have been obtained by mental contact with esoteric societies: Thule and Vril, from Aldebaran. When the Nazis came to power, legend has it that Thule became part of Himmler's SS, while Vril continued its scientific research. In 1934, this may have resulted in the production of the RFZ-1, a craft that operated on gravitational energy. In 1938, Vril made a huge step toward mastering electro-gravitational levitation, in addition to ion-drive propulsion, which are forms of cosmic-telluric-terrestrial power. Neither the United States nor the Soviet Union have given credit to similar crafts or technology.

# UFOs worldwide

Following the Roswell incident the world started looking to the skies, and not surprisingly, alleged sightings of alien spacecraft began to increase. This is a chronicle of the main cases registered in each continent.

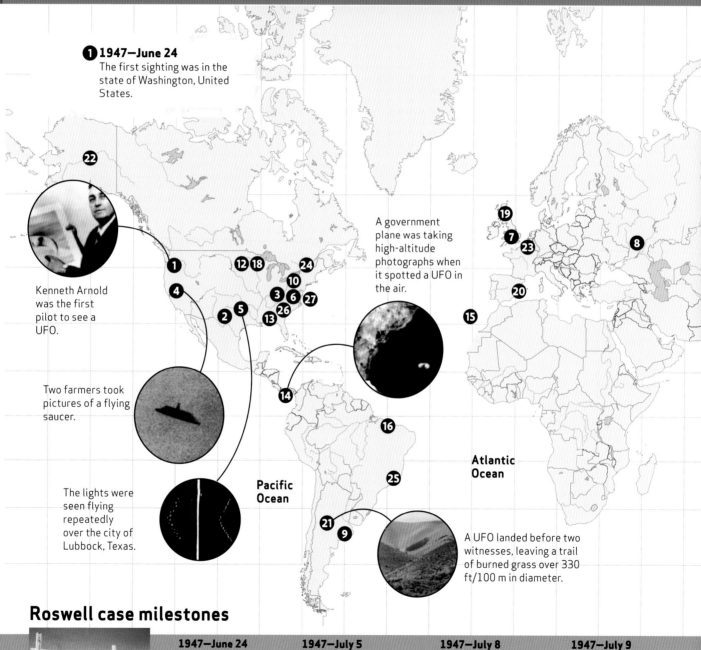

**❶ 1947—June 24**
The first sighting was in the state of Washington, United States.

Kenneth Arnold was the first pilot to see a UFO.

Two farmers took pictures of a flying saucer.

The lights were seen flying repeatedly over the city of Lubbock, Texas.

**Pacific Ocean**

A government plane was taking high-altitude photographs when it spotted a UFO in the air.

**Atlantic Ocean**

A UFO landed before two witnesses, leaving a trail of burned grass over 330 ft/100 m in diameter.

## Roswell case milestones

| 1947—June 24 | 1947—July 5 | 1947—July 8 | 1947—July 9 |
|---|---|---|---|
| First sighting by pilot Arnold. The first idea of "flying saucers." | Farmer Mac Brazel found wreckage in his field, which was removed by the U.S. Air Force to its base at Roswell, New Mexico. | First Lieutenant Walter Haut, public information officer for the base, announced that a flying saucer had crashed. | A general at the military base in Fort Worth (Texas) denied it was a spaceship. |

## How do you classify encounters with alien vehicles and beings?

In 1972, astronomer and ufologist Josef Allen Haynek classified sightings into three categories: encounters of the first kind are sightings more than 500 ft/150 m away; the second, where there are traces or remnants of the ship; and the third kind refers to a direct contact between the human witness and the ship or its occupants.

| Date | Place | Date | Place |
|---|---|---|---|
| **2 1947** July 8 | Roswell, New Mexico, United States | **16 1977** Sept. | Colares Island, Pará, Brazil |
| **3 1948** January 7 | Kentucky, United States | **17 1978** Dec. 21 | Kaikoura, South Island, New Zealand |
| **4 1950** May 11 | McMinnville, Oregon, United States | **18 1979** August 27 | Minnesota, United States |
| **5 1951** August 28 | Lubbock, Texas, United States | **19 1979** Nov. 9 | Livingston, Scotland, United Kingdom |
| **6 1955** August 21 | Kentucky, United States | **20 1979** Nov. 11 | Valencia, Spain |
| **7 1957** 20 May | East Anglia, United Kingdom | **21 1986** January 9 | Capilla Del Monte, Cordoba, Argentina |
| **8 1959** February | Vizhai, U.S.S.R. | **22 1986** Nov. 17 | Alaska, United States |
| **9 1965** Nov. 14 | San Miguel, Buenos Aires, Argentina | **23 1990** March 30 | Wallonia, Belgium |
| **10 1965** Dec. 9 | Kecksburg, Pennsylvania, United States | **24 1990** Nov. 7 | Montreal, Quebec, Canada |
| **11 1966** April 6 | Clayton South, Victoria, Australia | **25 1996** January 20 | Varginha, Minas Gerais, Brazil |
| **12 1966** August 25 | North Dakota, United States | **26 2002** January 14 | Paintsville, Kentucky, United States |
| **13 1969** October | Leary, Georgia, United States | **27 2005** April 27 | Washington, D.C., United States |
| **14 1971** Sept. 4 | Arenal, Alajuela, Costa Rica | **28 2007** March 3 | New Delhi, India |
| **15 1976** June 22 | Canary Islands, Spain | **29 2007** March 7 | New Delhi, India |

Pacific Ocean

Indian Ocean

| 1950 | 1980 | 1994 | 1995 | 1998 | 2006 |
|---|---|---|---|---|---|
| *After the Flying Saucers* by Frank Scully was published, with mention of several alien corpses. | *The Roswell Incident* was published, supporting the idea of the ship and the aliens. | The U.S. Air Force stated publicly that it was an experimental balloon to spy on the Soviets. | Film producer Ray Santilli unveiled the movie *Roswell Alien Autopsy*. | There was talk of another film about the autopsy and the possibility that the one released could have been a reconstruction. | The film, *Alien Autopsy*, confirmed that the famous movie was a reconstruction of the alleged previous autopsy, of which only fragments remained. |

# Anatomy of a UFO

Popularly termed "Flying Saucers" for their supposed disk shape, a number of variants have developed over the years. The air force term "UFO," used to indicate an unidentified aircraft, is now used to describe these alien craft.

## The Roswell craft

Here is a fictional recreation of a ship for five crew modeled on the "Adamski" type. Many accounts of events have been considered that so far remain unproven, among which is the Roswell incident of 1947.

### COCKPIT

The ships would have little flight autonomy, leaving the mother ship with precise targets. In the upper part are the crew, below the energy systems.

1. Commander's Chair
2. Pilot's Chair
3. Flight Engineer's Chair
4. Spacesuits
5. Controls
6. Monitors

### Strange crystals

According to some abductees, there are transparent crystals like vertical TV screens, except that the images can be seen from both sides.

### Engine room

There are countless theories about the propulsion and energy source for these ships. They make no noise and at high speed they become invisible.

## Types of UFOs

Of the innumerable forms reported, these are the five most observed by witnesses:

### Foo Fighter

The presence of these small objects was observed by airmen during World War II.

### Adamski type

Photographed by George Adamski in the desert of Colorado, United States, December 13, 1952.

### Pleiadian

In 1975, the Swiss Billy Meier began taking photographs of astonishing clarity showing a type of ship that he says comes from the Pleiades.

# Do we know where in the universe the Roswell aliens came from?

According to Stanton Friedman, the aliens came from a planet near the binary star, Zeta Reticuli. According to ufologists, they belong to the same class of aliens which in 1961 kidnapped the married couple, Betty and Barney Hill, in what was the first documented case of abduction. Friedman believed that it was the dreaded "gray," a type of alien that has shown a high degree of violence toward humans.

## MOTHER SHIP
The area of 20 football fields, and the size of an aircraft carrier, the motherships have hangars for the scouts that come down to the planet.

## Observation screens
It has never been reported that the ships have portholes or any kind of direct visual access to the outside. They may have screens to see out.

## Getting in and out
In the center of the cabin, a glass tube provides access to the ship. The ETs enter or leave by levitation.

## Structure
The different parts of the ship seem not to be physically assembled, but to be held together by some mysterious force.

## Saturn type
Observed by Kenneth Arnold in June 1947. A central body surrounded by a circle that rotated at high speed.

## Triangular craft
This type was seen in the "Belgian UFO wave" of 1989–90. In the angles there are changing colored lights.

# CHAPTER 19

# Disappearances in the Bermuda Triangle

Also known as the "Devil's Triangle," many ships and aircraft have disappeared in this Atlantic region located between Florida, Puerto Rico, and Bermuda. Few phenomena have created so much intrigue and filled so many pages as this one.

Some 70 percent of the Earth's surface is covered in water, and within the oceans of the planet lies another world that still holds many mysteries for mankind. Just as on land there are extensive highlands 16,500 ft/5,000 m up and mountain ranges more than 26,000 ft/8,000 m high, under the sea there is a world with prairies 16,500 ft down and trenches 36,000 ft/11,000 m deep—deeper than Everest is high.

The deep ocean also comprises some of the most extreme living conditions: no light, little food, freezing temperatures, and pressure that can crush the hull of even the strongest submarine. In short, it is a hostile environment that is home to strange creatures, the appearance of which has fueled the imagination of many generations. Fortunately, in the last few decades, scientific and technological advances have allowed us to use our lungs and eyes in this hostile territory, opening the doors to a whole new world. With the help of sonar and the modern bathyscaphe, we have mapped the deep sea and met creatures such as the sea spider, which can measure more than 5 ft/1.5 m long, the terrifying dragonfish, and the legendary giant squid, which really exists and can reach a length of 65 ft/20 m.

However, our knowledge of the marine environment is only just beginning. It is not surprising, then, that there is a high accident rate for boats and planes in some ocean regions of the planet, the cause of which, because of the many hostile conditions that may arise, is sometimes very difficult to ascertain.

**DANGEROUS COCKTAIL**
One of these areas is known as the Bermuda Triangle, which almost forms an equilateral triangle. The points are in Miami, the largest city in Florida, San Juan in Puerto Rico, in the Antilles, and Bermuda, a small archipelago located in the North Atlantic, more than 620 miles/1,000 km from the coast of the United States.

This ocean region of more than 62,000 sq miles/1 million km², has a mountainous and unstable seabed on which a very high number of ships and aircraft lie as testimony to a history rich in conflict and confrontation, and, above all, a changing and dangerous climate. The physical phenomenon that

**Shipwreck in the Bahamas**
The high volume of traffic in the Triangle's waters, together with a variable climate, results in a high number of shipwrecks in the region.

most influences this region is probably the Gulf Stream. This huge current within the Atlantic, measuring 620 miles/1,000 km wide and 330 ft/ 100 m deep, carries the warm waters from the Gulf of Mexico to the coasts of northern Europe. This makes the climate warmer, saving the eastern coast of America and the Antilles from becoming arid and determining the circulation of the prevailing winds of the region.

### A SHIP GRAVEYARD

The Gulf Stream flows north opposite the eastern coast of the United States and Canada and marks the western and northern limits of the Sargasso Sea—the only sea in the world that has no coast. This sea has a surface area equivalent to two-thirds the size of the U.S.A. and is completely enclosed by a belt of oceanic currents that move in a clockwise direction. Since the time of Christopher Columbus, the Sargasso Sea, at the center of which is Bermuda, has gained notoriety for being a true sailing ship graveyard, as it occupies a vast region characterized by long periods of calm that terrorized sailors in the age before steam. It is precisely these periods of complete absence of wind that cause the surface of this sea to accumulate forests of algae—sargassum—the density of which can make it difficult to navigate and even creates the illusion of having reached dry land. To the south of this sea, however, there is

a completely opposite type of danger. The North Equatorial Current, returning to the Caribbean from the coast of Africa, heats up as it moves west. The moisture from the ocean winds, coupled with the caloric effect of the current, is the main cause of hurricanes that lash the Gulf of Mexico every year. This complex geographical factor is one of the main arguments used by scientists opposed to the supernatural explanations of the numerous incidents involving ships and aircraft that have occurred in the Bermuda Triangle and surrounding areas.

The majority of these incidents, they say, are related to climatic phenomena common to the region, such as hurricanes, tropical storms, tornadoes, and waterspouts, although many of the accidents still have no confirmed scientific explanation. This is the case of the U.S. brig, the *Mary Celeste*, which has become one of the greatest enigmas in the history of navigation. The story, which is constantly discussed in theories about the Triangle, despite the fact that the boat was discovered between the Azores and Portugal, more than 3,000 miles/5,000 km east of Bermuda. Measuring 100 ft/30 m long, the *Mary Celeste* set sail from New York on November 5, 1872, carrying 1,700 barrels of alcohol. One month later it was discovered drifting by another boat, the *Dei Gratia*, with no one on board. There was no sign of the captain, his wife, or the eight crew members. The lifeboat

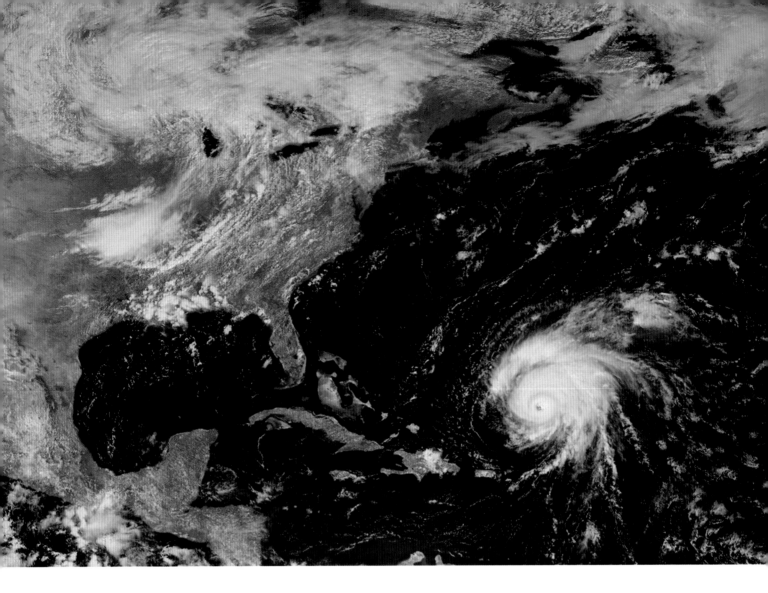

was missing, but the cargo was intact. Also, many personal items were found and there were provisions on board for six months. The court that heard the case covered several hypotheses: a mutiny by the crew against the captain, an act of piracy by the alleged discoverers of the abandoned ship, and fear of an explosion of the cargo following alcohol leaks in the hold. The investigations were concluded without determining what happened with any certainty.

Years later, on December 5, 1945, a squadron of five torpedo bombers, Grumman TBM Avengers, left the U.S. military base in Fort Lauderdale, north of Miami, to carry out a routine two-hour exercise in which the aircraft would travel 300 miles/500 km before returning to base. Some 20 minutes after takeoff, heading east, the squadron, known as Flight 19, carried out the required bombing practice over a group of small islands, after which the planes were to head north and then west to complete their mission. However, at 15:45, the time they were due to land, base received the first worrying message from the squadron leader Lieutenant Charles Taylor: "Emergency. We seem to be off course. We cannot see land." In response to the suggestion of the control tower to turn west, the Lieutenant responded, "We can't find west. Everything is wrong. Everything looks strange. Even the ocean." A short while after 16:20, nothing more was heard from the planes of Flight 19, although it is thought they flew

for more than four hours until they ran out of fuel and ditched into the sea. A rescue operation was soon launched, involving hundreds of ships and aircraft, which lasted for three days and covered nearly 200,000 sq miles/0.5 million km² of the Atlantic Ocean and Gulf of Mexico. The result? No trace of the five Avengers was ever found. Their tragic fate was amplified when, on the same day, one of the rescue planes, a Martin Mariner seaplane, exploded in the air shortly after takeoff. An expert in paranormal phenomena told the *Miami Daily News* that the crew of Flight 19 "were still there, but in a different dimension." An inquiry was opened to find a scientific cause of the incident. It found that there was a series of errors and adverse circumstances, including Taylor's compasses malfunctioning, failures in radio communications, the sudden bad weather, nightfall, and so on.

## HYPOTHESES

These, and other mysteries, allowed a series of American researchers, from the middle of the twentieth century, to link together a collection of hypotheses far removed from possible meteorological or human causes. Writer Vincent Gaddis (1913-97), was the first person to use the expression "Bermuda Triangle," in 1964, to identify the region of the Atlantic in which many ships had sunk and many aircraft had disappeared.

## The Bimini Road

In 1968, Joseph Manson Valentine (1902–94), zoologist, amateur archaeologist, and specialist in paranormal matters, discovered a singular rocky underwater formation to the west of the island of North Bimini, in the Bahamas. The Bimini Road is a series of rectangular limestone blocks, about 2,600 ft/800 m long and about 18 ft/5.5 m deep, that looks as if it has been created by the hand of man. In addition, there are another two shorter, narrower, and rougher roads, although there appears to be no connection between the three. For many people, this "road" could, in one go, resolve two great mysteries: Atlantis and the Bermuda Triangle. The stones, nicknamed Bimini Road, are square blocks measuring between 6 and 13 ft/2 and 4 m wide that seem to fit together, like the city walls built by the Incas. Dozens of scientists headed to the waters of Bimini to analyze the discovery, but they found no evidence for the use of tools to carve the blocks. Although they also examined the bedrock without finding any traces of excavations, many researchers argued that erosion would have erased any traces of visible human tools.

← **Natural formation**
Despite the evidence, many people refuse to believe in a natural explanation for the Bimini stones.

The magazine *Argosy* opened with a question that over the years has received many different answers: "What is there in that particular part of the planet that has destroyed hundreds of ships and planes without a trace?" Ten years later, in 1974, another writer Charles Berlitz launched his book *The Bermuda Triangle*, which sold several million copies and became a bestseller. This allowed the mystery surrounding the Bermuda Triangle to escape the small esoteric circles and reach the mainstream public. What reasons did Gaddis, Berlitz, and other subsequent researchers, all of them convinced that there was more to the area than hurricanes, pirates, and mutinies, offer?

### THE SINKING OF ATLANTIS?

One of the causes put forward is connected to one of the greatest enigmas of humanity—the sinking of Atlantis. Quoting specialist Edgar Cayce, Berlitz speculates that at the bottom of the ocean, probably close to the coast of the Bahamas, there are extremely powerful force crystals, that according to Cayce used to provide energy for the lost continent and, in more recent times, exert a gravitational force that is responsible for the major disturbances in ships and aircraft compasses. Another cause often given by experts is the presence of extraterrestrials, which abduct entire ships but, sometimes, just their crews. The high number of mysterious disappearances in the Triangle has caught the attention of scientific organizations as stringent as the National Geographic Society, which mentions the phenomenon in its prestigious *World Atlas*, and the U.S. Coast Guard. However, investigations by these organizations and many others refute the theories of Berlitz and others. Many believe that if you drew a triangle of the same dimensions in any other area of the world's oceans, the number of incidents and disappearances would be similar. In fact, the records of Lloyd's insurance company, traditionally specializing in navigation, have demonstrated an accident rate for the Bermuda Triangle similar to any other area. And of course, Lloyd's does not charge a risk premium for frequenting this area. Despite this, many of the causes that official investigations have determined for these accidents may, in the eyes of some, appear as confused as those who defend the champions of the supernatural.

In addition to causes such as weather phenomena, piracy, mutinies, human error, acts of war or conflict consequences, abandoned mines and bombs, disease, or explosions of dangerous cargoes, there are also among the findings a little-known-condition—ergotism or St. Anthony's Fire—caused by a fungus that develops on rye bread; the so-called clear air turbulence, the whirlwinds generated in blue holes common in the Bahamas; or methane bubbles released from the ocean subsurface that were capable of sinking the BP oil platform in the Gulf of Mexico. The truth is that because of the widespread use of technologies such as sonar and GPS in sailing and aviation, the number of unexplained accidents has declined significantly, but there is always a proportion of accidents, the investigations into which are closed without conclusion, and are thus added to the mysteries of that great unknown—the sea.

## Dangerous Regions

In the 1972 edition of the magazine *Saga*, Scottish specialist Ivan T. Sanderson published an article, *The Twelve Tombs of the Devil in the World*, in which he spelt out his theory of malignant vortices. Twelve areas, positioned equidistantly over the tropics of Cancer and Capricorn with the final two over the polar ice caps, produce mysterious phenomena that explain the disappearances of aircraft and ships and other paranormal events. Included within these vortices are the Bermuda Triangle, the Devil's Sea, and other ocean areas, such as Easter Island, the Mozambique Channel, and other sectors of the Indian, Atlantic, and Pacific oceans. Surprisingly, it also includes regions on land, such as the Indus Valley, the center of the Sahara and Antarctica.

## The legend of Lake Ontario

The surface area of the Great Lakes is almost 96,500 sq miles/250,000 km² and is one of the largest areas of fresh water on the planet. Because of their size, the lakes have weather patterns similar to those of seas, including storms that have caused a high number of disappearances. Some researchers say that many of these events are not the result of weather conditions and have identified three mysterious areas: the so-called Marysburgh Vortex, in the northeast of Lake Ontario, which accounts for two-thirds of all disappearances; the Sophiasburgh Triangle, just 55 miles/90 km tnwest, in which an alleged variation of the magnetic field changes the way that compasses work and causes serious accidents in times of storm and fog; and the Lake Michigan Triangle (above), known after two disappearances: that of a large coal cargo ship in 1937, and a Northwest Orient Airlines flight in 1950, with 58 people on board, which vanished without a trace.

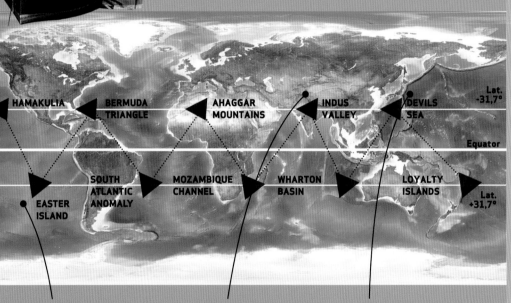

HAMAKULIA — BERMUDA TRIANGLE — AHAGGAR MOUNTAINS — INDUS VALLEY — DEVILS SEA — Lat. -31,7°

EASTER ISLAND — SOUTH ATLANTIC ANOMALY — MOZAMBIQUE CHANNEL — WHARTON BASIN — LOYALTY ISLANDS — Lat. +31,7°

Equator

### ↓Easter Island
More than 600 Easter Island statues carved from volcanic rock provide the face for this enigmatic island situated in the southeast of the Pacific, 2,174 miles/3,600 km off the coast of Chile.

### ↓Mohenjo-daro
Located in the center of a valley in Pakistan, the ancient ruins of Mohenjo-daro demonstrate the level of civilization that its residents reached.

### ↓Miyake Island
Visible from Tokyo and located in the center of the Dragon Triangle, Miyake Island is actually a volcanic cone, which last erupted in 1983.

# The geography of the Triangle

The ocean region bounded by the Bermuda Triangle and the land and water surrounding it has seen many accidents: from the sandbanks of the Bahamas to the Puerto Rico Trench, at a depth of 28,000 ft/8,600 m.

## The Bermuda Triangle

The area covered by the Bermuda Triangle is subject to a number of very powerful geographical and climatic factors that strongly influence flight and navigation in the area.

### Sargasso Sea

This North Atlantic ocean region, which coincides with part of the Bermuda Triangle, is the only sea on the planet that has no coastlines, and is characterized by the dense layer of seaweed (called "sargasso") that covers it and by the calm that slows the navigation of vessels crossing it.

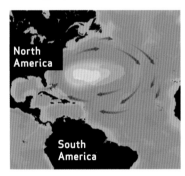

### The Tongue of the Ocean

With hundreds of small islands, the Bahamas archipelago forms a shallow platform, penetrated by a large deep area called the"Tongue of the Ocean" that separates the islands of Andros and New Providence, reaching a depth of 5,900 ft/1,800 m.

**Gulf Stream**
A huge mass of water crossing the North Atlantic from the Gulf of Mexico to Europe. It allows Europe to have a milder climate than its latitude would suggest.

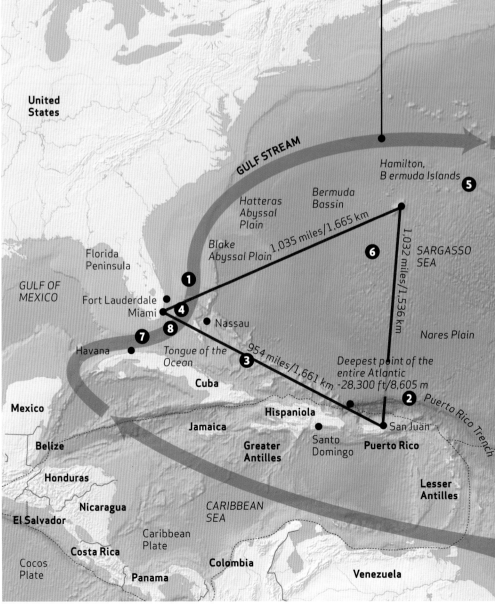

United States

GULF STREAM

Hamilton, Bermuda Islands **5**

Hatteras Abyssal Plain

Bermuda Bassin

Florida Peninsula

Blake Abyssal Plain

1,035 miles/1,665 km

**6**

1,032 miles/1,536 km

SARGASSO SEA

GULF OF MEXICO

Fort Lauderdale
Miami **4**

**1**

Nassau

Nares Plain

**7**

**8**

Havana

Tongue of the Ocean

**3**

954 miles/1,661 km

Deepest point of the entire Atlantic -28,300 ft/8,605 m

**2**

Puerto Rico Trench

Cuba

Mexico

Hispaniola

San Juan

Jamaica

Greater Antilles

Santo Domingo

Puerto Rico

Belize

Honduras

Nicaragua

CARIBBEAN SEA

Lesser Antilles

El Salvador

Caribbean Plate

Cocos Plate

Costa Rica

Colombia

Venezuela

Panama

## Could tsunamis have caused some of the disappearances in the Triangle?

There is no record that any tsunami has been a cause of disappearances in the Bermuda Triangle, although the Puerto Rico Trench is the deepest point of the fault between the tectonic plates of North America and the Caribbean, so it's a very unstable area.

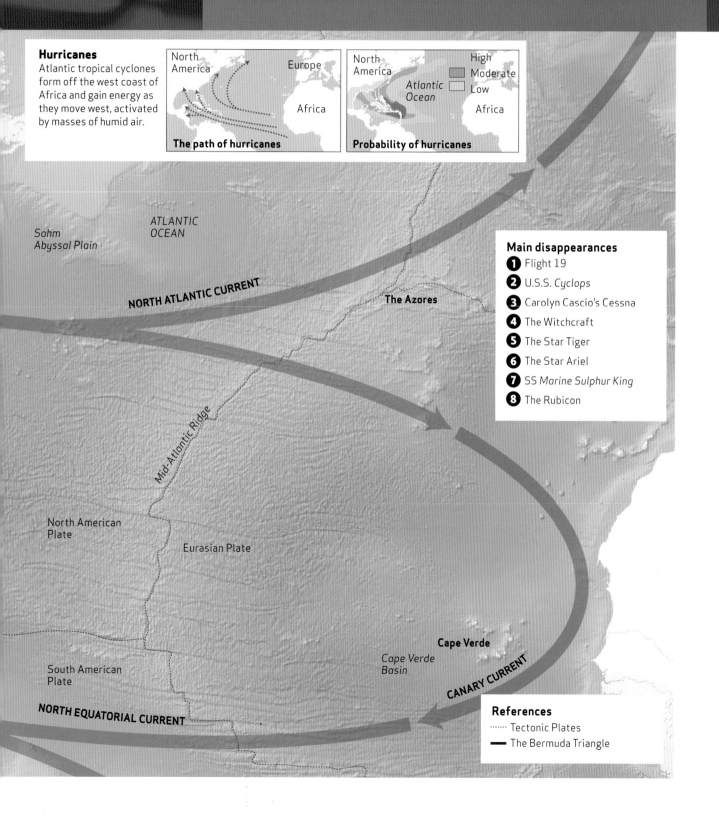

**Hurricanes**

Atlantic tropical cyclones form off the west coast of Africa and gain energy as they move west, activated by masses of humid air.

North America — Europe — Africa

**The path of hurricanes**

North America — Atlantic Ocean — Africa

High / Moderate / Low

**Probability of hurricanes**

ATLANTIC OCEAN

Sahm Abyssal Plain

NORTH ATLANTIC CURRENT

The Azores

Mid Atlantic Ridge

North American Plate

Eurasian Plate

South American Plate

NORTH EQUATORIAL CURRENT

Cape Verde

Cape Verde Basin

CANARY CURRENT

**Main disappearances**

1. Flight 19
2. U.S.S. *Cyclops*
3. Carolyn Cascio's Cessna
4. The Witchcraft
5. The Star Tiger
6. The Star Ariel
7. SS *Marine Sulphur King*
8. The Rubicon

**References**

······· Tectonic Plates

—— The Bermuda Triangle

# A flight of no return

The history of the Bermuda Triangle is full of accidents and mysterious disappearances. The 1945 disappearance of Flight 19, a squadron of five Grumman TBM Avenger aircraft, is one of the most famous.

## The disappearance of Flight 19

The Grumman TBM Avenger was a torpedo plane used by the U.S. Air Force and Navy from 1942. A pilot, a gunner, and a radio operator made up the crew. Flight 19 was led by Lieutenant Charles Taylor.

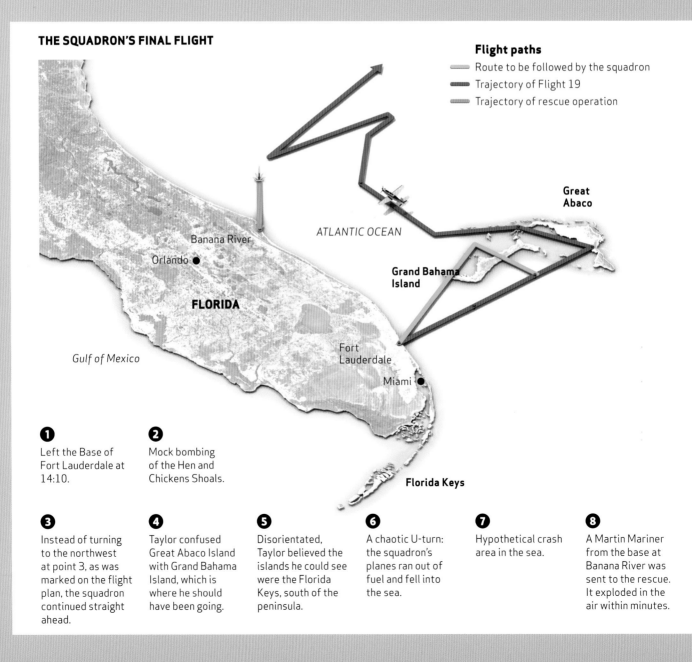

**THE SQUADRON'S FINAL FLIGHT**

**Flight paths**
— Route to be followed by the squadron
— Trajectory of Flight 19
— Trajectory of rescue operation

Great Abaco

ATLANTIC OCEAN

Banana River

Orlando

Grand Bahama Island

**FLORIDA**

Gulf of Mexico

Fort Lauderdale

Miami

Florida Keys

**❶**
Left the Base of Fort Lauderdale at 14:10.

**❷**
Mock bombing of the Hen and Chickens Shoals.

**❸**
Instead of turning to the northwest at point 3, as was marked on the flight plan, the squadron continued straight ahead.

**❹**
Taylor confused Great Abaco Island with Grand Bahama Island, which is where he should have been going.

**❺**
Disorientated, Taylor believed the islands he could see were the Florida Keys, south of the peninsula.

**❻**
A chaotic U-turn: the squadron's planes ran out of fuel and fell into the sea.

**❼**
Hypothetical crash area in the sea.

**❽**
A Martin Mariner from the base at Banana River was sent to the rescue. It exploded in the air within minutes.

# What caused the disorientation of Lieutenant Taylor, leader of Flight 19?

The disorientation of Lieutenant Taylor can only be attributed to nervousness or some outside influence that put all the aircraft's instruments out of action. The Avengers had gyroscopes, a kind of precision compass, and up to three location instruments with sophisticated mechanisms.

## CABIN OF THE AVENGER

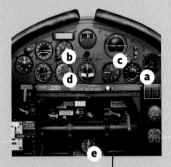

**a**
**Radio altimeter**
Shows the altitude of the aircraft above the ground.

**b**
**Altimeter**
Marks the altitude above sea level.

**c**
**Inclinometer**
Measures the inclination of the wings in relation to the Earth's surface.

**d**
**Anemometer**
Measures the speed of the aircraft relative to the air moving around it.

**e**
**Directional gyro**
Shows the direction that the plane is heading. It did not work on Flight 19.

**Grumman TBM Avenger**
It was tough, stable, easy to maneuver, had an excellent radio and remarkable endurance.

## Technical Specifications

| | |
|---|---|
| Empty Weight | 4,851 kg |
| Crew | 3 people |
| Fuel tank | 1,267 l |
| Range (empty) | 1,954 |
| Maximum speed | 434 km/h |
| Maximum altitude | 7,132 m |

## OTHER NOTABLE DISAPPEARANCES

**Star Tiger (Jan. 1948) and Star Ariel (Jan. 1949)**
The Star Tiger airliner disappeared without a trace. A year later the same thing happened to Star Ariel.

**SS *Marine Sulphur Queen* (Feb. 1963)**
This merchant ship disappeared in the Florida Keys, with a crew of 39 people and a load of molten sulfur.

**USS *Cyclops* (Mar. 1918)**
One of the world's largest freighters sank with 308 people and a cargo of manganese. The Navy called it "disconcerting."

**The Cessna 172 of Carolyn Cascio (Jun. 1964)**
Cascio's last words: "This should be Grand Turk, but there's nothing down there, no airport, no houses... nothing."

# Navigation instruments

Techniques have greatly developed over the centuries, from the simple observation of the sun, moon, and stars by the first navigators of the past, to the current GPS system, which provides almost pinpoint accuracy in sea crossings.

## Safer

Triangle researchers often look back to the nineteenth century, or even to antiquity, to evoke mysterious disappearances of ships and legends related to certain sea areas. However, one cannot analyze a shipwreck from the early nineteenth and twenty-first centuries on the same terms, because the knowledge we have today of the marine environment is far superior to that of the navigators at the time of the first steamships. Current technology allows a much greater mastery of ships and their dangerous environment on the high seas, making navigation safer and making it more difficult for disappearances to occur without a clear cause.

### Sextant
This appeared in the eighteenth century to replace the astrolabe and measure angles between the sun, the North Star, and the horizon. If you knew the time, you could determine latitude with some precision.

### Old compass
The traditional compass indicates magnetic north with a magnetic needle. The fact that it did not indicate the geographic pole, located several degrees to the east, induced errors.

### Modern compass
Incorporating electronic technology has made it possible to correct the traditional error between magnetic and geographic north and increase the accuracy of measurements.

### Nautical chart
Portolans, the medieval charts used to recognize coastlines became charts in the fifteenth century, when sailors set out across the open sea. This chart from the late sixteenth century shows the Triangle area, the Caribbean, and the Gulf of Mexico.

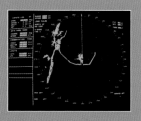

### Radar
Radar is an electronic system that emits electromagnetic waves to measure distances, directions, and speeds of fixed and mobile objects, such as ships and aircraft. It is fundamental for air and sea traffic control and meteorology.

## The Foucault gyroscope

Invented in 1852 by French physicist Jean-Bernard Léon Foucault to demonstrate the rotation of the Earth, the gyroscope was not originally a guidance tool, but Foucault himself realized that it could be used to indicate the north if movements of the support were fixed, since the device then aligns itself with the meridian.

### Quadrant
This was used from the fifteenth century to find the latitude by measuring the distance between the horizon and the sun or the North Star, but needed two people to operate it.

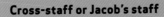

### Astrolabe
Created by Greek astronomers in the second century BCE, the astrolabe, a circle that lets you locate the stars and measure latitude from the time or vice versa, was widely used until the invention of the sextant.

### Cross-staff or Jacob's staff
Developed in the fourteenth century to make astronomical measurements, the cross-staff was a strip of wood that slid on a transverse stick. To measure the latitude, you had to point the device at the sun or the Pole Star and then move the transverse bar to coincide with the horizon.

### GPS
Available commercially from the 1990s, it has meant a jump in navigation as decisive as the compass or sextant in their time. The system uses a complex structure of satellites to give the position with an error of less than 10 ft/3m.

# The Enigma of Unexplained Healing

When all hope is lost, only a miracle remains. Believers think that healing without explanation is the work of divine intervention. However, the Catholic Church turns to science to help explain the unexplainable.

St. Teresa levitated while she prayed and her body had the wounds of Jesus Christ, something that also happened to St. Francis of Assisi. Catherine of Siena mysteriously survived the severe mystical fasts and her body, like that of other saints, remained preserved for centuries. But in addition, many of these chosen ones, and others that have reproduced similar circumstances, have been able to heal the terminally ill immediately and inexplicably.

For a long time, believers had no doubt that such strange phenomena as these were the manifestation of God. Today, many still believe it is true, but many others, both believers and nonbelievers, have their doubts. Millions of people who have not been able to find an answer in conventional medicine need to think that there is hope for them and they ask for help in places where rational science does not apply—in places where it is said that a miracle is possible. If the real world denies them an opportunity, they search for one in a mystical land where the impossible seems possible. And it is interesting to see to what extent the rituals required are based on tradition.

### SHRINES FOR ALL TIMES

Each year, some six million Catholics visit the shrine at Lourdes in France, while the shrine of Fátima in Portugal, another major world center for miraculous cures, receives about four million pilgrims annually. The numbers are very high. Nineteenth-century French psychiatrist, Jean-Martin Charcot, explains in his article, *The Faith that Cures* (1897), how little the shrines have changed over time. In the text, the doctor compares the French site with the Asclepion in Athens, according to Charcot the "direct son of the shrines of ancient Egypt." All of them, he says, had a miraculous statue, inherited from healing gods such as the Egyptian Serapis.

In Greece, as in the modern shrines, there were also healer-priests and mediators, "those who in different cities surrender themselves to God to beg for his protection on behalf of their clients." The petitioners deposited valuable offerings at the altar and immersed themselves in the cleansing fountain, such as the one at Lourdes. The walls are also covered with votive offerings in the form of arms, legs, and any other part that was cured.

**Devotion**
Open-air mass at the shrine
of Krastova Gora, in Bulgaria,
famous for its cures.

Today, in Lourdes, apart from the possibility of praying to the rosary live from the website, from where one can also see the grotto live, this layout has changed little. The reasons people come to places like this, with a firm faith in having their health restored, have changed even less. For Charcot, one of the keys to producing the healing phenomenon is spending the night near the temple. "Thus begins the incubation, a propitiatory novena, in which the 'faith in healing' is increased by self-suggestion, by participation, by a kind of unconscious force, and then the miracle occurs … if it occurs." If the environment provides a sense of normality for miracles, patients improve their condition to receive them.

### HEALERS OR CHARLATANS

Instead of going to shrines, some people turn to shamans, shrine caretakers, healers or mediums who rely on assistance from beyond, or televangelists who claim they can heal those who believe in them. Often these "miracle workers" are simple charlatans who trick their vulnerable victims, but sometimes they are sincere people who really believe in their power—which puts science to the test. Contrary to what some people may think, a belief in miracles is not a belief restricted to the working classes or uneducated gullible people, who may be easy to deceive.

The belief in miracles is not as indisputable as it was two or three centuries ago. Some 15 years before the philosopher David Hume published his essay, *On Superstition and Religion* (which paved the way for secular thought), in 1699 a young student from Edinburgh was hanged for saying that religion was an absurdity. Until then, doctors and priests debated whether a patient with seizures was having an epileptic attack or was possessed by a demon.

But this situation has continued to change over time. With the eighteenth century came the Age of Enlightenment, a movement that spread the idea that everything could be explained with reason, thus dispensing with divine influence. The Catholic Church also found itself immersed in this development. It had taken important steps to seek, as far as possible, scientific justification for inexplicable events that until recently had been attributed to divine action, no questions asked. Perhaps for this reason, because it felt that it was losing ground to science and was trying to recover it, the Church designed new rituals designed to catalog miracles.

### VERIFYING HEALING

To make the official recognition of the healing miracles at Lourdes more stringent, in 1905, Pope Pius X ordered all unexplained healings at the site to be reviewed by the Office of Medical Findings. The report, if favorable, ends up at the

Lourdes International Medical Committee. The members of this permanent body, of which there are more than 20, mainly consist of European doctors who meet each autumn to study about 50 cases, five of them in depth. Their criteria are strict, and since these controls have been carried out, only 60 cases have been designated as miracles (seven more were approved between 1859 and 1862, before this process was followed). The last, in 2005, concerned an Italian, Anna Santaniello, who regained mobility in her legs and re-established her lung capacity after being immersed in water. There was a 68th cure recognized in March 2011, which actually took place in 2002, involving Frenchman Serge François, who was suddenly healed of a crippling sciatica on leaving the shrine of Lourdes, after having prayed in the grotto and drunk from its waters. In reality, the success rate for passing the screening committee is not very high when taking into account that thousands of sick people, and many others who ask for the Virgin's intervention, visit the site each year.

The Vatican medical board analyzes cases from around the world with similar rigor, especially in some of the processes of beatification and canonization. The Medical Committee of the Congregation for the Causes of Saints, which issues a kind of health certificate to continue the path toward holiness, consists of more than 50 medical experts (all of them Italian, men, and Roman Catholics according to Kenneth L.

Woodward, the specialist journalist in religious matters for *Newsweek* magazine) and examines around 40 cases a year. Only 15 go on to the next stage. Science subjects religion to ongoing scrutiny. Experts have already demonstrated that they can make an image cry tears of blood by applying a liquid that oxidizes on contact with air and suddenly turns red. They have also described the phenomenon of collective suggestion, the natural process that prevents the deterioration of bodies, as well as a range of dramatic effects that often accompany apparitions, miraculous cures, and many other events deemed miracles. It is true, however, that some phenomena remain difficult to explain.

### THE GOD GENE

Dean Hamer, a Harvard-trained scientist and director of the Genetic Structure Regulation Unit at the National Cancer Institute, has arrived at the conclusion that belief in God is determined by a tiny gene called VMAT2. Hamer has confirmed that Buddha, Muhammed, and Jesus all share a series of mystical experiences or changes of consciousness, probably conditioned by VMAT2. His book, *The God Gene: How Faith is Hardwired into our Genes*, has greatly concerned Catholic circles. It has even been questioned by some of his colleagues trying to reconcile their faith in God with their white coats.

# And if there are no miracles ... ?

The idea that our emotions are intimately connected to our body has been established and is now commonly accepted. Today, we know that many diseases are aggravated (some say even caused) by the influence of negative moods. Of course, this also occurs in reverse. A positive mood or a sign of hope could eventually cure. Sigmund Freud spoke of the concept of "conversion," a mechanism that converts psychic energy into physical symptoms. His follower and colleague, Wilhelm Steckel, later coined the term "somatization," which is understood to be a psychological disorder that causes bodily disorders. Other psychiatrists introduced the term "psychosomatic" to refer to physical problems that do exist, but can be influenced by psychological factors. It is therefore understood that if the mind can cause an illness, it can also make it disappear, and therefore wouldn't be viewed as a miracle. In addition, behind some supposed miracles there could be misdiagnosis.

Medicine is not infallible, and some physicians may fail to interpret the symptoms, so if the disease follows an unexpected course when compared to the initial diagnosis, it is easy to confuse it with supernatural healing. Nevertheless, when the Church certifies a miracle as such, it is well established. And it is irrelevant whether or not science discovers how it happened.

**↑In full catharsis**
Participants in a ceremony held by Korean evangelist preacher, Jaerock Lee, who claims to have healing powers, in Jerusalem, in 2009.

The geneticist Francis S Collins, responsible for sequencing the human genome, considered himself an atheist until the age of 27, when the spirituality of some of his sickest patients made him think. His life changed after reading *Mere Christianity*, by C S Lewis, the religious companion of the literary club of JRR Tolkien and author of the children's saga, *Chronicles of Narnia*. Collins was the driving force behind the BioLogos Foundation, which brings together a number of scientists who believe in God and who try to demonstrate that natural laws dictated by science do not conflict with theology. For Collins, the human genome is 'the language of God' (the title of one of his most celebrated books), and miracles are a real possibility. 'If you need Divine intelligence to create everything, this intelligence is also required to select and order all the genetic information to produce a variety of species which work together as a natural system', he said. On the alleged discovery of a 'God gene' Collins says simply that it is an exaggeration. This gene, he says, is only present in 1 per cent of individuals and is not as important as will.

### FAITH OR BUSINESS?

Generally, today's world is less willing to believe in miracles than the world of just a hundred years ago, although it cannot be said that the door has been closed on them definitively. Pilgrimages to ask a divinity for favours or cures became a massive phenomenon in the fourteenth century - a period in which travelling was neither comfortable nor easy – and this practice still continues today, with pilgrimages to miraculous places made by millions although it must be recognized that the journeys are now much easier and that the visits to sanctuaries or healers can be, for many, a form of tourism. Psychiatrist Sigmund Freud said that religion was a human construction, an instinct that individuals use to respond to real-world situations to which they cannot adapt and which cause them distress. According to Freud, disease can be a disguise for this discomfort. When the cause of the disease is organic, many try to get away from reality by going in search of a miracle and taking refuge in a social environment that is confident they will find one. It is the opposite of what is usually said. In this case, believing is seeing. The problems are relatively minor when faith becomes a way of healing, when it is a mental switch that makes the body suddenly begin to operate normally.

The dark side of these supposed miracles arises when some patients stop taking their medication and die. Less dangerous, although just as sad, is the business that often operates behind the alleged Marian apparitions or the healers with paranormal powers. These are people who make a lucrative business selling magic talismans, or water with alleged extraordinary powers or who, gaining the trust of patients, often in very delicate emotional states, charge for 'medical' consultations at exorbitant prices.

Anthropologist Claude Lévi-Strauss said that 'the great sorcerer is not a great sorcerer because he cures, but he cures because he is a great sorcerer'. The charisma, which undoubtedly some people possess and which sometimes can even miraculously cure the sick, can also be used to benefit financially from an easy target. No miracle there.

## Do healers exist?

At the beginning of the twentieth century, in the area around Vancouver, in Canada, anthropologist Franz Boas heard the story of a man who did not believe in healers and was determined to expose them. To do this, he posed as one of them, but his convictions began to falter as he realized that he had cured some people. In the end, the fictional healer concluded that there really were healers who had the ability to cure others. Also, anthropologist Claude Lévi-Strauss believed that in order to produce a miracle cure, the following situation must exist: the healer must believe in their ability to heal. In practice this is not always the case, as the patient must fully believe that they will be cured. This must be supported by a social community that supports the power of healing. This community is what adds a sense of normality to the healing practices and paves the way for producing the healing process.

**↑Preserved body**
In the chapel of Our Lady of the Miraculous Medal in Paris, is the body of clairvoyant and saint, Catherine Labouré.

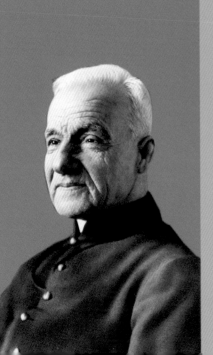

**←Alfred Bessette**
Born in Canada in 1845, he was a religious visionary, mystic, and miracle-worker, whose miraculous cures became famous throughout the world, to the point that he was recognized by the Church. He was canonized in 2010 with the name of St. André Bessette.

## Can the dead cure?

There is a belief that incorruptible saints have healing powers. The devotion given to them dates back to the Middle Ages and it is said that their bodies give off a pleasant fragrance. The nun, Catherine of Bologna, was never famous during her lifetime, although on occasion she revealed that the Virgin Mary had appeared to her. When she died in 1463, she was buried without a coffin. It was said that a sweet scent spread around the town and a large number of sick people gathered near the convent, in the hope that the deceased nun would heal them. After 18 days, the nuns decided to dig up their companion and saw that her skin was soft, her cheeks pink, and her muscles flexible, so she was exhibited. A century later, at the Council of Trent (1545-63), the Catholic Church ruled that this preservation was a sign of divine intervention that should be revered. So in 1712, Catherine of Bologna was canonized. Like her, the bodies of St. John of the Cross, Catherine Labouré, Pope John XXIII, and many others, remain preserved. Over centuries, for many believers these preserved saints have been able to cure any disease. However when, in the 1980s, the Church decided to entrust the study of these venerable bodies to scientists, the magic began to disappear. In most cases, it was found that there had been a process of natural mummification.

# Miraculous shrines

*"Turismus religiosus"*: this is the expression used by the Vatican to define travel to a sacred place. In some of these places they say that a miracle has occurred. Most of them, though not all, are shrines to the Virgin Mary.

**Type of miracle reported**

- Apparition of the Virgin
- Healing
- Salvation
- Prophecy
- Victory in War
- Image of the Virgin
- Image of Christ
- Miracle relic

Mexico

Mexico City **5**

PACIFIC OCEAN

Dominican Republic

Cuba

El Cobre **16**

**9** Higüey

El Salvador **15** Honduras

Nicaragua

San Miguel **14** **6** El Viejo

Caribbean Sea

**2** Cartago

Costa Rica

**7** Cartago Guanare

Venezuela

**3** Chiquinquirá

**LATIN AMERICA**

Pilgrimages to miraculous shrines are very popular in Latin America. Features of local identity are added to the evangelism of the Spanish. Sanctuaries like the Virgin of Guadalupe or the Virgin of Carmen de Maipú are visited each year by thousands of pilgrims.

**13** Quito

Ecuador

Peru

**10** Lima

Brazil

**4** Copacabana

Bolivia

**1** Caacupé

**8** Aparecida

Chile

**12** Maipú

**11** Luján

Argentina

Our Lady of Aparecida, Brazil

Our Lady of Luján, Argentina

**Miraculous shrines**

1. Basilica of Caacupé
2. Basilica of Our Lady of the Angels
3. Basilica of Our Lady of the Rosary of Chiquinquirá
4. Basilica of Our Lady of Copacabana
5. Basilica de Santa Maria de Guadalupe
6. Basilica of the Immaculate Conception of Mary
7. National Shrine of Our Lady of Coromoto
8. Basilica of Our Lady of Aparecida
9. Basilica of Our Lady of Altagracia
10. National Shrine and Monastery of the Nazarene
11. Basilica of Our Lady of Luján
12. National Shrine of Maipú
13. Shrine of Our Lady of Quinche
14. Church of San Miguel
15. Shrine of Our Lady of Suyapa
16. Basilica of Our Lady of Charity

## Does the Virgin really appear or are they episodes of mass hysteria?

Fact or suggestion? Science says that the apparitions of the Virgin are simple episodes of hysteria that cause a trance state. The Church, which has recorded 22,000 apparitions of Mary—such as Fátima, and Lourdes—in the history of Christianity, argues otherwise.

ATLANTIC OCEAN

### EUROPE
The European Marian Network, created in 2003, makes it possible to cross the continent via 20 shrines in as many countries—the same number as the mysteries of the rosary. These shrines are usually famous for the apparitions of the Virgin, for the miracles they have inspired, or for the devotion they have awakened.

Knock **9**
Ireland
United Kingdom
Walsingham **18**

Lithuania
**17** Vilna

Poland
Belgium **2** Banneux
Germany
**5** Czestochowa
**20** Ternopil

France
Altötting
**1**
Slovakia
**10** Levoca
Ukraine

Einsiedeln **6**
Switzerland
Austria
**15** Mariazell
**14** Máriapócs

Brezje **3**
Slovenia
**16** Marija Bistrica
Hungary
Croatia
**4** Csiksomlyó
Romania

Portugal
**12** Lourdes

**7** Fátima
Zaragoza **19**
Spain
Loreto **11**
Italy

Black Sea

**8**
Gibraltar
Mediterranean Sea

Malta **13**
Malta

### European Marian Network

1. Altötting Sanctuary
2. Sanctuary of the Virgin of the Poor
3. Basilica of the Virgin Mary
4. Sanctuary of Our Lady of Csiksomlyó
5. Shrine of Jasna Góra
6. Monastery of Einsiedeln
7. Sanctuary of Fátima
8. Our Lady of Europe
9. Knock Shrine
10. Levoca Sanctuary
11. Sanctuary of Loreto
12. Our Lady of Lourdes
13. Our Lady of Mellieha
14. Máriapócs Sanctuary
15. Basilica of the Birth of the Virgin Mary
16. National Shrine of Marija Bistrica
17. Shrine of Our Lady of the Gate of Dawn
18. Shrine of Our Lady of Walsingham
19. Basilica of Pilar of Zaragoza
20. Shrine of the Mother of God of Zarvanytzia

Our Lady of Fátima, Portugal

# The Sanctuary of Lourdes

Located in a small town in the French Pyrenees, this shrine is one of the most visited in the world. Millions of pilgrims flock to it every year to take its miraculous waters and receive hope and comfort.

## The miracle of apparitions

Between February 11 and June 16, 1858, the Virgin Mary appeared 18 times to a girl, Bernadette Soubirous, in a cave near Lourdes. On March 25, the Virgin gave her name, "I am the Immaculate Conception." The authenticity of the apparitions was recognized by the church in 1862.

### The miraculous numbers

| | |
|---|---|
| Appearances | 18 |
| Official miraculous healings | 67 |
| Inexplicable cures | 7,000 |

### The Sanctuary in figures

| | |
|---|---|
| Area | 128.5 acres/52 ha |
| Places of worship | 22 |
| Visitors | 6,000,000 a year |
| Volunteers | 100,000 pilgrims 7,000 resident helpers |
| Permanent religious staff | 30 chaplains 5 female communities |
| Employees | 400 |
| Annual budget | 30 million euros/year |

### The formalization of miracles

Since 1905, the Office of Medical Findings has reviewed the declarations of people who claim to have been miraculously healed at Lourdes. If a case is successful, it is passed on to the Lourdes Medical Bureau and then to the International Medical Bureau.

### Basilica of Our Lady of the Rosary

A global symbol of brotherhood among people for its architecture, the basilica was built between 1883 and 1889. In the front esplanade the blessing of the sick takes place.

### Shelters for patients

Lourdes receives more than 6,000,000 visitors each year. Many are ill or disabled. The sanctuary offers hope for a cure and is prepared for and receives those traveling alone or in groups, and those who have health problems or low incomes.

## Why does the Virgin Mary almost always appear to children and teenagers?

Believers maintain she only appears to the most pure of people, and for this reason the majority of witnesses are young. Bernadette Soubirous was ten when the Virgin of Lourdes appeared to her, as was Lucía de Jesus dos Santos, the oldest of the three seers of Fátima. Mariette Beco, the seer of the Virgin of the Poor in Banneux, Belgium, was 11.

**The Temple**
Bernadette explained that the Virgin asked her to find the chaplains and tell them to build a chapel. The Basilica of the Immaculate Conception was built over the grotto by Monsignor Laurence, in 1872.

**The Rock**
The pilgrims touch the rock of the cave where the Virgin appeared to try to capture its energy.

**The grotto and the statue**
The grotto consists of three chambers. In the largest, mass is held and it also houses the image of the Virgin, just where it is said that she appeared.

**Springs**
Our Lady instructed Bernadette to wash her hands and drink the water of the grotto, which immediately became famous for its miraculous power.

**The sanctuary**
🏛 Site of the Apparition
▲ Basilica
† Chapel
✚ Reception Center for the sick

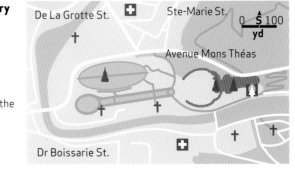

De La Grotte St.  Ste-Marie St.

0 — 100 yd

Avenue Mons Théas

Dr Boissarie St.

# Certification of miracles

The Catholic Church follows a strict protocol for formalizing miracle healings. Lourdes is a good example of how this process unfolds, from the statement of the person who has been cured to the proclamation of the miracle.

## Lambertini's exclusion criteria

Prospero Lambertini (1675–1758), who later became Pope Benedict XIV, defined the seven criteria to be met by any miracle cure, and these are still valid today:
• The disease must be severe, with an unfavorable prognosis.
• The reality of the disease and its diagnosis should be certain and accurate.
• The disease must be only organic or arising from injuries.
• The cure cannot come from a particular treatment.
• The cure must be sudden and instantaneous.
• The resumption of normal duties must be complete and without convalescence.
• There must not be a remission, but a permanent cure.

Furthermore, physicians currently analyzing miracle cures exclude some diseases in which it is difficult to prove that there has been divine intervention—as in some cancers, which have a high percentage of natural healing, and mental illnesses.

**1 The declaration**
The Medical Bureau receives medical reports of people cured by "divine intervention." Their history is studied to determine whether the recovery is complete and objective or just the impression of the patient.

**2 The context**
Information is collected about where the healing took place and under what circumstances. The faith of the cured party, his or her capacity for suggestion, and through the intercession of whom healing has occurred are analyzed.

**Dr. Patrick Theillier**
Head of the Office of Medical findings of Lourdes between 1998 and 2009, and a doctor since 1964, Theillier is author of several books on Lourdes. According to him, miraculous cures have declined because God now acts through physicians.

## A twenty-first century cure

On March 27, 2011, the Bishop of Angers, France, Emmanuel Delmas, made public the latest unlikely cure to have occurred in Lourdes. The patient was Serge François, a French worker who since 1990 had suffered from a herniated foraminal disk aggravated by postoperative complications, which, in addition to partially paralyzing his left leg, forced him to take morphine constantly. He was a regular visitor to the shrine, and during one of his pilgrimages in 2002, after he had left the sanctuary, Serge felt a sudden sharp pain in his leg, which disappeared after a while. A week later, he regained mobility and stopped feeling any pain in the leg. Today, he leads a completely normal life.

## Fewer miracles

In 1988, at a medical symposium on healing miracles, Lourdes physicians said that medical advances made it increasingly difficult to certify miracles. Hence, the 1983 reform: four miracles are no longer needed for the canonization of the martyrs; only two. Before the council of Vatican II, more than 100 were required.

## What is the LIMA?

Lourdes International Medical Association. Comprised of 12,000 physicians from 75 countries, it seeks the views of specialists in cases of people who are healed, before submitting the dossiers to the Medical Committee.

**3 Medical verification**
The Lourdes Medical Committee reports unique cures at its annual meeting, and one of its members questions and examines the person who has been healed. The opinion of specialists is sought, and new tests performed.

**5 Certification**
After medical and psychiatric evaluation, the International Medical Committee, as an advisory body, establishes a full assurance that the cure is exceptional, taking scientific advances into consideration.

**6 Proclamation**
The bishop of the diocese of the cured person, together with the diocesan commission, canonically recognizes the miracle. If it is a miraculous healing established by the process of canonization, the Pope signs the decree of the miracle.

**4 Ecclesiastical verification**
A commission headed by the bishop of the diocese to which the cured person belongs again analyzes how he or she experienced this healing physically, mentally and spiritually. If approved, the cured person is then allowed to make their cure public.

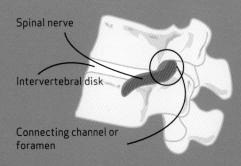

**HEALTHY VERTEBRA**

Spinal nerve

Intervertebral disk

Connecting channel or foramen

**Foraminal stenosis**
Is a narrowing of the channels, or foramen, by which the spinal nerves leave the spinal column. It causes intense pain in the limb associated with the nerve in question.

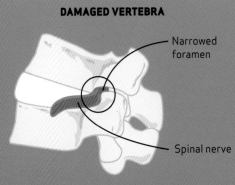

**DAMAGED VERTEBRA**

Narrowed foramen

Spinal nerve

**Original concept** Joan Ricart.
**Editorial coordination** Vicente Ponce.
**Design** Susana Ribot, Clara Miralles.
**Editing** Emilio López, Joan Soriano, Stuart Franklin.
**Authors** Jesús Ballaz, David Caminada, Albert Cañagueral, Eva
Melús, Francisco Javier Martínez, Federico Puigdevall , Ricard Regàs.
**Graphic editing** Alberto Hernández.
**Layout** María Beltrán, Carla Cobas.
**Computer graphics** Sol90 Images.
**Translation** Tradym.
**Pictures** Corbis Images; Getty Images; Science Photo Library;
National Geographic Stock; Age Fotostock; Topfoto; Other Images;
Cordon Press; Corbis; ACI; Granger; Alamy; Stéphane Compoint; Scala
Archives; The trustees of the British Museum; Metropolitan Museum
of New York Archives.